Adaptable Architecture

Adaptable Architecture provides thought-provoking insights into how we can prolong the useful life of buildings by designing them to be more adaptable, creating a more sustainable built environment. The book provides a theoretical foundation counterpointed by the experiences and ideas of those involved in the design and appropriation of buildings. It explains many approaches to designing for change, with lessons from history and over 30 case studies, which stretch our thinking beyond the conventional notions of adaptability. The authors explore many contingencies that make this a complex design phenomenon, by considering the purpose, design and business case of buildings as well as the physical product.

Full of summaries, diagrams, reference charts, tables and images of exemplar solutions for use as conversational tools or working aids, this book is for any professional or student who wants to research, question, imagine, illustrate and – ultimately – design for adaptation.

The authors conclude that a gap exists between what architecture wants to be (finished and static) and what it is (continually shifting in form and purpose). We should therefore see buildings as unfinished – imperfect forms in a state of flux – to meet the changing functional, technological and aesthetic demands of society.

Robert Schmidt III is an architect and academic. He is Senior Lecturer in Architecture at Loughborough University, UK, a visiting researcher at Chongqing University, China, and the founder of Idapu, a design and research practice. His recent work has focused on urban transformation strategies, architectural education and practice models.

Simon Austin is Professor of Structural Engineering at Loughborough University, UK. His research interests include 3D printing, concrete materials and structures, building systems, workplace design and design management. He co-founded Adept Management, an international consultancy specializing in design and engineering management.

Adaptable Architecture
Theory and practice

Robert Schmidt III and Simon Austin

Routledge
Taylor & Francis Group

LONDON AND NEW YORK

First published 2016
by Routledge
2 Park Square, Milton Park, Abingdon, Oxon OX14 4RN

and by Routledge
711 Third Avenue, New York, NY 10017

Routledge is an imprint of the Taylor & Francis Group, an informa business

British Library Cataloguing-in-Publication Data
A catalogue record for this book is available from the British Library

Library of Congress Cataloging-in-Publication Data
Names: Schmidt, Robert, III, 1977- author. | Austin, S. A. (Simon A.), author. Title: Adaptable architecture : theory and practice / Robert Schmidt III and Simon Austin. Description: New York : Routledge, 2016. | Includes bibliographical references and index.
Identifiers: LCCN 2015036560| ISBN 9780415522571 (hardback) |
ISBN 9780415522588 (pb) | ISBN 9781315722931 (ebook)
Subjects: LCSH: Architecture--Human factors. | Buildings--Utilization. | Architectural practice--Social aspects. | Sustainable architecture. | BISAC: ARCHITECTURE / General. | ARCHITECTURE / Professional Practice. | ARCHITECTURE / Sustainability & Green Design.
Classification: LCC NA2542.4 .S365 2016 | DDC 720/.47--dc23 LC record available at http://lccn.loc.gov/2015036560

ISBN: 978-0-415-52257-1 (hbk)
ISBN: 978-0-415-52258-8 (pbk)
ISBN: 978-1-315-72293-1 (ebk)

Typeset in Avenir
by Servis Filmsetting Ltd, Stockport, Cheshire

Printed and bound in India by Replika Press Pvt. Ltd.

To our invariably encouraging wives and children who provide the love and humour needed throughout our journey – Barbara, Sara, Lizzie, Greg, Bella and Emma.

And to the fortuitous circumstances seven years ago that would bring the two of us together.

Contents

List of figures

List of Tables

Preface

Adaptability is an aspiration that is very commonly requested in design briefs but rarely given proper attention during design. Such duplicity is often rooted in poor communication and definition of intent combined with an inability to value the benefits. We thus became interested in the role that adapting existing buildings can play in achieving a more sustainable built environment and in particular the potential facilitation of this by designing buildings that are more adaptable to change. *Adaptable Architecture* is the culmination of a five-year journey exploring the concept through research funded by the UK's Engineering and Physical Sciences Research Council and undertaken by a multidisciplinary team at Loughborough University supported by a host of practitioners.

Books on adaptable structures usually showcase bespoke, innovative case studies with little explanation of how they were appropriated; in other words, was the building modified as intended and if so did it produce the desired benefits? Moreover, texts on adapted buildings are often limited to conversions of use, thus marginalising other types of change that buildings have to endure. Our narrative is from a broader standpoint, seeking to establish a theoretical base from previous work and our own studies, counterpoised by the experiences and ideas of practitioners. Hence the subtitle of the book, intended as a resource for practitioners, academics and students who want to think, research, question, imagine, illustrate – and ultimately design for – adaptation of the built environment.

We explore many approaches to embodying a capacity to accommodate change, with anecdotes from history and more recent case studies. This stretches our thinking beyond the conventional notions that are considered in most projects. By considering client purpose, design practice, the physical product and the business case we reveal the contingent conditions that make adaptability a complex design phenomenon.

The book is in five parts including an introduction and conclusion. Part II contains a short history of adaptable architecture that identifies eight strands traced across contemporary design approaches. Part III presents a theoretical framework of concepts and models that emerged from, and shaped our journey into, adaptability, the models in particular forming a visual narrative that can help to define, communicate, create and evaluate adaptability. The case studies in Part IV cover a spectrum of design solutions from the everyday to the extreme, demonstrating adaptability in action and linked where appropriate to the theory.

The narrative from Chapter 5 onwards includes quotes from practitioners in the margin to illustrate industry perceptions of adaptability. These were obtained during face-to-face interviews with over 80 senior professionals

> *Personality and uniqueness of place are created in the interaction between people and architecture, not by architecture itself.*
>
> Lars Lerup (1977)

– including architects, engineers, developers, planners and contractors – that took place primarily in the UK between 2009 and 2011. The majority of interviewees were either a founder of the practice or an established director or partner; the quotations thus provide unique insights into the subject matter of the book, where their experience allowed them to speak confidently about their practice approach and the projects in which they played a leading role.

Information and resources contained in the book are supplemented by a website (www.adaptablefutures.com) that contains additional case studies, publications, visualisations and films.

Architecture *is* unfinished

It became evident that our findings question preconceptions of architecture – what it is and how it sits in a broader social context. We believe a chasm remains between a perception of what architecture wants to be (in isolation as a finished and static sculpted work) and the reality of what architecture is (continually shifting in form and purpose to accommodate changing needs). Architecture is situated in the messy, evolving everyday – architects and clients are merely two of many stakeholder voices that define and experience the built environment that frames our daily lives. But two of architecture's defining terms – space (building) and event (use) – have become synonymous, establishing buildings as permanent objects in their communities. Paradoxically, society's disposition to change creates a temporal disjunction between space and event that often renders contemporary buildings obsolete, and in increasingly shorter periods of time.

By questioning how buildings accommodate change, this dislocation of space and event requires architecture to be a receiver and agent of change, as Tschumi (1996) points out: 'Not to include the uncertainties of use, action, and movement in the definition of architecture meant that architecture's ability to be a factor of social change was simply denied.'

Thus we should see buildings not as finished, stationary works but imperfect objects whose forms are in flux, evolving to fit functional, technological and aesthetic transformations in society. The strong narrative that emerged from our explorations is one of context – a complex entanglement of specificity and generality. Every detail in a project is the result of this interplay giving shape to the spaces and buildings we experience.

Acknowledgements

Our gratitude is deep and widespread as the book is the culmination of a substantial research exploration, which would not have begun without the financial support of the Engineering and Physical Sciences Research Council in the UK. The funding brought together a group of multidisciplinary academics at Loughborough University and many kind, supportive practitioners that grew in number as our exploration opened new, sometimes unexpected, doors. The book knits together the conversations, contributions, feedback and participation of colleagues, fellow academics, designers (including many architects), constructors, clients, photographers, editors and friends. We are grateful to you all, especially our colleagues from the Adaptable Futures project – Alistair Gibb, Andy Dainty, Jim Saker, Christine Pasquire, Almudena Fulster, Toru Eguchi, Anupa Manewa, Graham Kelly and Rachael Grinnell.

A particular thank you is owed to those who generously allowed the research to extend beyond the theoretical by giving access to project documents, meetings and their practices, as well as participation in workshops, surveys and interviews. The book simply could not have been written without their help. These include but are not limited to James Felstead (CGL Architects), Graham Morrison (Allies & Morrison), Paul Scott (Make Architects), Soren Nielsen (Vandkunsten), Charles Holland (FAT), David Rowley (Nightingale Architects), Vincent Lacovera (AOC), Christophe Egret (Studio Egret West), Chris Gregory (TEC Architecture), Julian Marsh (Marsh:Grochowski), Paul Warner (3D Reid), Tom Ridley Thompson (SCAPE), Will Schofield (GHA), Alison Brooks (ABA), Nick Ebbs (Blueprint), Cany Ash (Ash Sakula Architects) and Steve Thomson (Haworth Tompkins architects). We also thank the photographers who have helped us to illustrate adaptability in action, on generous terms.

We reserve a special mention for James Pinder whose reading, writing and revising parts of the book were invaluable, especially at a time that coincided with becoming a father to his daughter Edie; this apparently takes a lot of time – welcome to the club James!

Part I

INTRODUCTION

Chapter 1

Motivating observations

Every building is adaptable – but to what end and at what cost? Such seemingly straightforward considerations weigh in any value judgement of whether to adapt or not. The new millennium has seen renewed interest in the adaptability of our built environment, motivated by a number of factors, not least the desire to 'future proof' buildings against social, economic and technological change. This attention has spanned planning, architecture, real estate, facilities management and engineering, and a variety of sectors, including housing, offices and healthcare. Leaman *et al*. (1998) reflects our own experiences, suggesting that adaptability is 'now commonplace in the vocabulary of briefing, building design and building management'. But the very obviousness of the aspiration, and attractiveness of the flexibility implied, has also resulted in it being frequently sought, but much misunderstood (Carthey *et al*., 2011). We are also minded of another slippery concept, value – of which Abraham Maslow said 'My belief is that the concept of value will soon be obsolete. It includes too much, means too many diverse things and has too long a history' – since we are in some sense investigating the 'value' of adaptability (Maslow, 1962).

Our aim is to bring some much needed clarity to the subject by providing a more nuanced insight into what constitutes adaptability in our built environment and the factors that give rise to different levels of adaptability in buildings. In doing so, we seek to look beyond what we have termed the 'black box' of adaptability – the stereotypical design characteristics, such as generous floor-to-floor heights, movable walls and open plan spaces, that are usually associated with adaptability in buildings. This narrow viewpoint takes account of a limited selection of physical solutions at the expense of not considering the actual user needs and invoking a broader range of tailored solutions. Although such design characteristics are important, they are only a small part of a complex picture; adaptability in our built environment is also contingent upon a wide range of other physical and social factors, which we seek to foreground (Figure 1.1).

There are three interrelated themes running through this book (Figure 1.2): the first is about meaning – *what* adaptability means to different stakeholders in disparate contexts and at varying points in time; the second is the factors that lead to different levels of adaptability in the built environment – the reasons *why* buildings are designed and built to be more or less adaptable; and the third is the characteristics that make buildings more or less adaptable, including the strategies and tactics for *how* to design and build for adaptability. Ultimately it is difficult to divorce the 'what', 'why' and 'how' of adaptability from each other – the themes inevitably overlap. For instance,

[T]he problem is temporary thus the solution must be as well.

Hertzberger (2005)

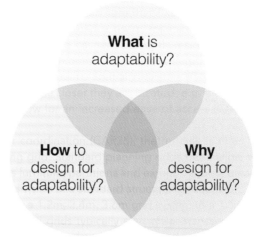

outside (physical variables)	stereotype (black box)	outside (social variables)
Storage space	Movable walls	Procurement process
Materials	Open spans	Regulations
Window size	Taller floor height	Market condition
Fire strategy	Access points	Local appreciation
Construction Method	Service strategies	Ownership model
Building form	Hightech components	Designer skills

▶ Figure 1.1
Looking beyond the 'black box' of adaptability

What is adaptability?

How to design for adaptability?

Why design for adaptability?

▶ Figure 1.2
The three interrelated themes that underpin this book

Any project that makes a serious attempt to address these three questions is already ahead of the pack.

one's notion of what adaptability means will inevitably influence whether or not it is deemed necessary in a particular context and how it could be realised in design terms. But we like to try to keep things simple (at least for now!) by introducing these three basic considerations separately.

1.1 Unravelling the 'what'

As we explore in Part II, the idea of adaptability in buildings is not new and has spanned many centuries and cultures. But this also means that adaptability is a fluid concept. Friedman (2002b) suggests that 'Misconceptions about adaptability are the outcome of the term's many definitions and interpretations' and this was certainly evident in our research in the construction industry. We found that its stakeholders use a diverse range of terminology when talking about adaptability – it meant different things to different people, with instances of shared meaning reflecting conventions, practices and priorities within particular sectors or projects, rather than within professional disciplines. In other words, notions of adaptability tend to be heavily influenced by context, an issue revisited in Part III.

Such differences in terminology are not just a matter of academic interest; developing a clear understanding of what adaptability means in practice

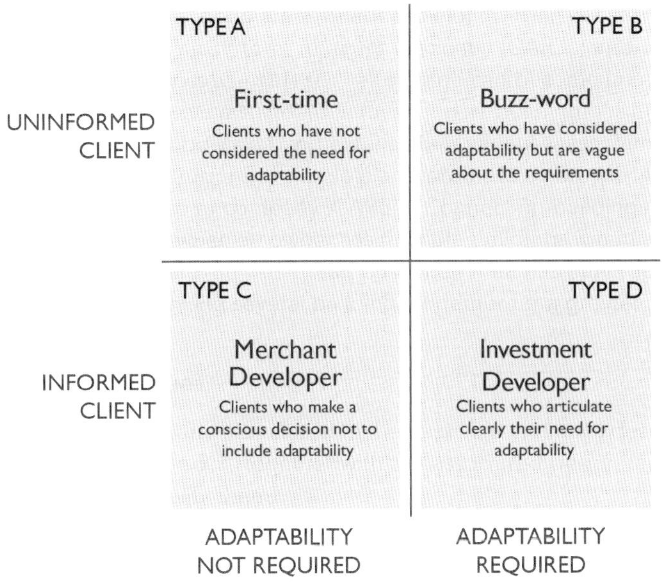

◀ Figure 1.3
Types of clients and their
understanding of adaptability

	TYPE A First-time Clients who have not considered the need for adaptability	TYPE B Buzz-word Clients who have considered adaptability but are vague about the requirements
UNINFORMED CLIENT		
INFORMED CLIENT	TYPE C Merchant Developer Clients who make a conscious decision not to include adaptability	TYPE D Investment Developer Clients who articulate clearly their need for adaptability
	ADAPTABILITY NOT REQUIRED	ADAPTABILITY REQUIRED

is particularly important in the briefing process, when clients communicate their intentions and objectives to designers. Decisions taken during briefing can have costly implications later in the building life cycle – during design, construction and operation – so it is critical that clients and designers speak the same language regarding adaptability. As illustrated in Figure 1.3, some clients do make informed decisions – these are usually experienced or repeat-order clients who have previously managed or procured buildings. However, others are less informed – adaptability is either something that they have not even considered or something that they have thought about but do not really understand (and furthermore may not yet realise this).

One of our objectives in this book is to provide designers and other practitioners with the knowledge and tools to raise clients' awareness of adaptability and helping to clarify their needs. In the first section of Part III (Chapters 4–7), we explain what adaptability means in practice and the different types that can be implemented in the built environment. The idea being that this will lead to the implementation of more appropriate design solutions – not only recognising opportunities for designing in adaptability but also avoiding unnecessary solutions that increase cost but are rarely implemented. These thinking tools also help keep adaptability on the agenda, reducing the likelihood that adaptability is inadvertently designed out of a building.

1.2 Clarifying the 'why'

The argument in favour of more adaptable buildings is based on the premise that they will be easier to change in the future, which in turn may give rise to other benefits, such as reducing the costs of adaptation, lessening disruption to building users and making the building easier to let or sell (Table 1.1).

A sustainable building is not one that must last forever, but one that can easily adapt to change.
Graham (2005)

Table 1.1 Motives and obstacles to developing adaptable buildings

Motives	Obstacles
Easier to make changes	Perceived additional costs
Cheaper to make changes	Short-term business models
Easier to sell a building	Lack of price signals
Fewer vacancies/rental voids	Valuation practices
Less disruption to building users	Discounting of future costs
Reduction in material waste	Compromises first use
Protect the built asset	Disconnect between funder/beneficiary
Good design/planning	Other design considerations are more important
Uncertainty about the future	Lack of life cycle costing
Long-term ownership	Difficult to prove benefits
Previous experiences	No legal obligation

Adaptability can be viewed as a means to decrease the amount of new construction (reduce), (re)activate underused or vacant building stock (reuse) and enhance disassembly/deconstruction of components (reuse, recycle) – prolonging the useful life of buildings (sustainability).

Decisions about adaptability are, at their heart, whole-of-life value judgements.

Buildings that cannot be adapted cost-effectively may not be fit for purpose and eventually fall out of use or are demolished. Adaptability can therefore be seen as a means to extending the life of our built environment, an important issue at a time when sustainability in buildings has become largely synonymous with the goal of reducing carbon emissions from buildings in use. The notion that the most sustainable building is the one already in existence has grown in currency in recent years and is underpinned by a growing awareness of the energy embodied in buildings during their construction.

The case might therefore seem axiomatic – why would you *not* design for adaptability, given the benefits it can bring? While all of the stakeholders in our study found adaptability to be desirable, it also revealed a number of obstacles (Table 1.1). Cost is usually the main obstacle, the argument being that adaptable solutions cost more than their non-adaptable alternatives. This is an argument that we want to challenge during the course of this book, because not all adaptable design tactics give rise to a cost premium – indeed, in some cases the opposite is the case. However, the focus on initial build costs also overlooks, or discounts, the downstream benefits of adaptability, some of which may manifest themselves in financial terms, while others may be more intangible or unquantifiable (but nonetheless significant). Our tendency to discount future costs and benefits when making intertemporal choices is hard wired into us and inherently undermines our ability to value outcomes in the (more distant) future. This is a significant barrier in that the majority of adaptability's benefits depend on future conditions. This book can provide you with concepts and tools to make informed decisions and provide a better appreciation of who can benefit from adaptability, when and in what way.

Other barriers, such as short-term development models, funding practices, and valuation methods, reflect the structure and procedures of the construction and real estate industries. These contingent factors and others are explored in Chapter 10 in an effort to clarify the why. Our intent is not to put forward solutions to these systemic obstacles, but to encourage you to model, and hence better understand, their influence when making decisions about adaptability in your projects.

1.3 Expanding the 'how'

One of our other objectives is to encourage you to think beyond the stereotypical design characteristics commonly associated with adaptability in buildings – what we described earlier as the black box of adaptability. As we explain in Chapter 8, our research identified 60 building characteristics that can enable adaptability in buildings, the majority of which fall outside the black box. However, designing and constructing for adaptability is not simply a case of working from a menu of off-the-shelf design characteristics – it also involves challenging the ways in which we think about buildings.

First, buildings are not static, monolithic objects, but a series of *layers*, which change at different rates (Chapter 6). For instance, a building's services are usually changed more frequently than its structure or fabric. This way of thinking about buildings and change can also be applied at different levels of the building's systems, for instance in relation to specific elements and components. Seeing buildings, and their constituent parts, in this way gives rise to the notion that adaptability can be facilitated by reducing the interdependencies between parts of buildings that have different rates of change. The book gives examples where dependencies have (and have not) been considered, and introduces a tool that can reveal such dependencies during the design process (Dependency Structure Matrix; Chapters 6–7).

Another critical consideration is to *challenge conventions* about how buildings should be designed, constructed and used. During the course of our research we encountered situations where project stakeholders devised innovative adaptability solutions, many of which challenged existing industry practices. As illustrated throughout Part IV, some of these designs were relatively sophisticated, while others were much simpler but nevertheless effective; for instance, a medical practice using magnetic door signs to stop rooms from being monopolised by particular users. The importance of challenging conventions underlines the fact that there is no one-size-fits all approach to adaptability in buildings.

In addition, we provide a set of design resources (Chapter 11) that can bolster your renewed way of thinking and supplement your current practices. The resources focus on engaging key concepts and the building over time, across stakeholders and throughout varying contexts. Some are quite conventional, such as critical parameters. For example, floor-to-ceiling heights and floor-loading capacities, which have long been seen as the holy grail of adaptability but have sometimes led to the adoption of counter-productive or wasteful design practices, such as the over-specification of mechanical and electrical services. We argue for a more nuanced consideration of such factors and the role they play in creating adaptability. In particular, we contend that such parameters need to be seen as the means not ends and therefore encourage awareness of the type(s) of change you are trying to enable in your projects and the most effective way of bringing it about.

A building is no longer a single object, but a combination of systems, each system with its own design process, production process and lifetime.

Leupen (2005)

While the book is set out to provide a flow of ideas, arguments and examples, it is also intended to be a text that you can dip into, and work backwards by finding an interesting case study that takes you back to the underlying principles. A visual compendium of the concepts and models that are presented as part of our theory of adaptability is provided at the start of Part III (p. 41). The theoretical elements are referenced throughout the case studies in an effort to exemplify their implementation.

Part II

A HISTORY OF ADAPTABILITY

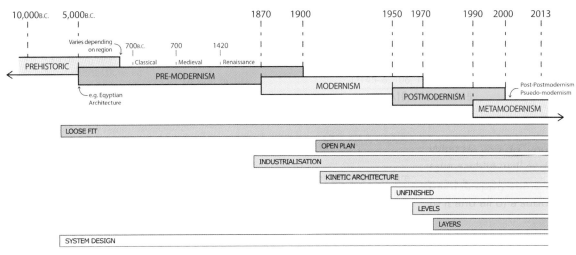

▲ Figure II.1
The eight strands of thought related to adaptability plotted relative to a general point in time from which they emerged

Chapter 2

Historical overview

2.1 Prehistoric and pre-modernism

Figure 2.1 exemplifies the primeval form of architecture as the primitive hut, which can be decomposed into two components – branches (support, structure) and leaves (protection, skin). Quatremere de Quincy (1788) classifies an additional two archetypes: cave (hunters, Egyptian) and tent (shepherds, Chinese) – see Figure 2.2. Fletcher (1946) notes that all three archetypes are a

Prehistoric shelters were 'functional responses to local climate, the availability of materials and temporal requirements, nomadic, seasonal or settled'.

Horning (2009)

▲ Figure 2.1
Laugier (1755) Primitive Hut

◄ Figure 2.2
Viollet-le-Duc (2010) first hut

single space where a variety of activities take place (eating, sleeping, entertaining, 'work'), while Leupen (2006) adds the distinction that the hut and tent are essentially the same, composed of two separable elements: structure and skin whereas, the cave is monolithic.

Thus, a simple description from which we can derive a basic form of architecture would be decomposable into two discretely functioning elements (i.e. modular design – structure and skin), spatially a 'large' single space used for a variety of activities (i.e. multifunctional space) and a result of local conditions and needs (i.e. generic archetype). As early civilisations began to grow, architecture began to develop into different building types, e.g. temples, market halls, amphitheatres and multi-cellular dwellings. While the differentiation of functions created unique building forms, construction elements remained relatively simple, repetitive and discrete. During this early period, building functions remained static over many generations, i.e. the stabilised needs often matched the longevity of the physical object.

Chinese wood-framing systems (Figure 2.3) were constructed with standardised modules, systems of dimensions defined by government regulations. These formed the foundation of the Japanese house philosophy of measurement – the distance between column centres known as *ken* (90cm $\times$ 180cm) – making it easy to change and extend. Both the widths and depths of all spaces are multiples of this standard unit and frame the remaining components – timber structure, doors and furniture – including the tatami mats which communicate the size of a space (e.g. 6 tatami). The traditional home contains no load-bearing walls, enabling easy changes to the post and beam structure and lightweight movable partitions (*fusuma*) as shown in Figure 2.4.

Traditional Japanese rooms bore no functional labels, rather as multifunctional spaces or *wa-shitsu* meaning a largely empty stage deriving its identity from its temporary occupants. Japanese culture thus understood buildings to

The traditional Japanese home provides an opportune framework to accommodate changing conditions – mixing physical, spatial and operational tactics

▼ Figure 2.3
Depiction of Chinese home (Viollet-le-Duc, 2010)

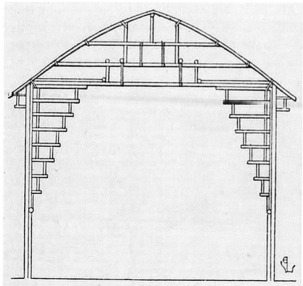
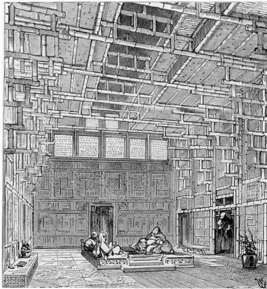

▲ Figure 2.4
Traditional Japanese home
Courtesy Toru Eguchi

be ephemeral, empowering a mentality to construct buildings that could be changed easily through the use of lightweight materials and 'non-permanent' physical connections.

European vernacular Renaissance architecture of the late seventeenth to early nineteenth centuries provides good examples of buildings that have stood the test of time. English terrace homes, Italian Renaissance *palazzi* (Figure 2.5) and Dutch canal homes, have a spatial generosity often dominated by a single dominant space surrounded by subdivided support spaces that changed over time. Their generous dimensions, redundancy and well-proportioned spaces unintentionally created a spatial ambiguousness, allowing them to adapt well to whatever function or activity necessary – e.g. offices, apartments, hotels, medical clinics. Despite partial integration of structure and skin, 'industrial' mills and warehouses during the latter part of this period boasted large and unobstructed spaces as a result of low-cost framed cast iron and timber structures.

The vernacular process, according to Brand (1994) and Sennett (2008), was simple, direct and evolved out of a shared experience between owner and builder, unlike today's complicated multi-stakeholder process. This chimes with Maccreanor (1998) who noted that flexible housing is often the result of *ordinariness* – through the use of robust and timeless techniques. In this manner, the accommodation of change grows out of the direct communication of needs as part of a gradual evolution of building materials and techniques. This is in sharp

What makes the old canal-houses so livable is that you can work, relax or sleep in every room.

Hertzberger (2005)

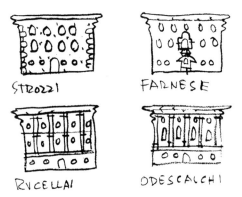

▶ Figure 2.5
Venturi and Scott Brown's (2004) Italian Renaissance *palazzi* subsequently converted to apartments, museums and other uses

contrast to the number of materials and techniques of today that rarely allow for the same level of maturity. Breaking this evolutionary lineage, the experience stored within these traditions is lost. Thus for Brand (1994) evolutionary forms will always adapt better than visionary solutions – as they are based on trial and error, embodying an understanding of culture, climate and conventions.

Vernacular architecture (pre-modernism) represents two of the three building types that Schneider and Till (2007) recognise as having accommodated change well: nineteenth-century industrial buildings and Victorian terraced housing (the third being 1960s office buildings). They highlight that, 'all three are direct in their construction and generic in their spaces; they tolerate change whilst still retaining identity – modest and work in the background'. The ordinariness of these typologies promotes a generic order from which a range of uses can be accommodated.

In American culture one can find a similar lineage for buildings built during the nineteenth century (Figure 2.6). Moudon's (1986) extensive study of a San Francisco neighbourhood attributed successful adaptations of the 'Victorian Box' as a combination of spatial configurations (e.g. identical size of each room – position rather than size attributed to the room's function) and construction techniques (e.g. balloon framing that placed the bearing walls on the

Better to look at the pattern books of identical terraces that successfully created our cities in the 19th century and rethink them for the 21st century, than to pursue the architectural utopia where every building looks different but in its high cost and inflexibility turns out to be exactly the same.

Lifschutz (2003)

▶ Figure 2.6
Venturi and Scott Brown's (2004) depiction of generic building forms that have accommodated a range of functions over time (the basilica, the loft building and the *palazzo*)

Table 2.1 Summary of positive pre-modern characteristics

Western pre-modern	Eastern pre-modern
Ordinary	
Based on experience (gradual evolution)	
Multifunctional space(s)	
Simple, direct, repetitive construction	
Durable, robust materials	Lightweight materials
Identical room sizes	Non-permanent connections
Spatial generosity	Storage space
Structural redundancy	Standard modules
Well-proportioned spaces	Dimensional coordination
'Character', Permanence	Ephemeral mentality

long side). Hence, we can see that pre-modern buildings (no matter the geography) benefited from simple, mature construction techniques and spaces that can be typified as polyvalent – used in a variety of ways with minimal physical changes.

Table 2.1 captures the positive characteristics of Western and Eastern prehistoric and pre-modern architecture. The obvious counterargument is that today's buildings provide a vast visual, physical and spatial variety that reflect distinct uses, occupiers and cultures that must respond to quicker and larger shifts in demand not common during this time period.

2.2 Modernism

The idea of adaptability or flexibility, while being discernable in historic examples, only became explicit in the modernist movement at the turn of the twentieth century (Figure II.1). The Industrial Revolution of the mid-nineteenth century was the main catalyst, generating an increased pace of social change along with new building materials, types of buildings and spatial standards that together gave rise to new urban conditions and the demand for buildings to accommodate change. Its principles evolved internationally through the work of influential architects such as Le Corbusier, Frank Lloyd Wright, Alvar Aalto, Mies van de Rohe and later on Louis Kahn and James Stirling. Jencks (1973) identifies six overlapping 'traditions' or 'attractor basins' offering different psychological and cultural positions – Figure 2.7. He is quick to suggest the idealist tradition as the dominant lineage that most closely fits the stereotype of a singular modernism, but suggests two interrelated ideologies that cut across most of the traditions – the idea of artistic freedom and autonomy (self-conscious, idealist and intuitive) and the idea of social equality (activist, unselfconscious, logical and idealist). The differentiations that Jencks offers are visible in the following chapter in relationship to our eight strands. But for now we present the more mainstream, common position of modernism of the idealist and logical traditions based loosely around a set of social ideals – humanitarian liberalism, reformist pluralism and a vague social utopianism.

Neither their precedent, nor the past, nor contemporary practice could inform architecture … it [modernism] would unlock the door to a shining future in which all buildings would be radically different from the past, or the war-torn present.

Habraken (1998)

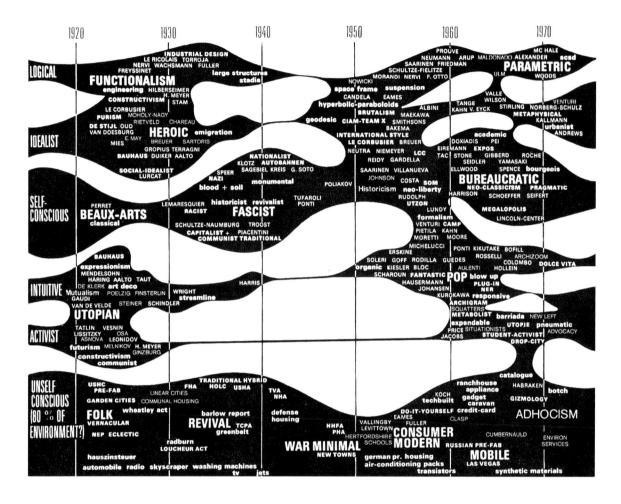

1920, 1930, 1940, 1950, 1960, 1970

▲ Figure 2.7

Modernism's evolutionary 'tree'

Jencks (1973); courtesy Galerie Patrick Seguin, Paris

Modernist architecture can be characterised as simple, cubic forms with a desire to express 'truth' by exposing structure and mechanical systems. This stylistic approach was embraced with the aspiration that architecture should express contemporary technology through the use of new materials and new ways of building. The progression of framed construction relieved walls of their load-bearing function, allowing for the development of the free plan (separating space plan elements and structure) and the use of lightweight cladding systems (separating the exterior skin from the structure). This progressive approach led to several projects utilising industrialised and modular construction techniques to improve and speed up the construction process.

It was modernism's pledge for abstract symbolism that gave way to the idea of 'pure form' and the tenet, 'form follows function'. This meant the architect could easily define the form of a building based on its use or as Jencks (1973) succinctly states, 'what the building wants to be'. This approach led to the decompartmentalisation of functions in pursuit of spatial efficiencies, which according to Hertzberger (2005) created over-specified solutions in mono-functional rooms, buildings and neighbourhoods. It is with this functionalist mentality that architecture cut away many of its overlapping areas by measuring itself through an itemised programme. Pawley (2007) argues this 'sought to correct conditions for use rather than usefulness itself' and thus created a demand for flexibility because the efficiently defined spaces were not usable in the (other) ways necessary. As Rybczynski (2001) sees it, modern buildings do not age well, in contrast to their predecessors, and 'lose their potency if they are not gleaming and machinelike'.

The concept of functional segregation is exacerbated by modernism's principle of universality in experience and symbolism which for Rabeneck *et al.* (1973) is clearly based on 'an artificial understanding of occupants' behaviours'. This fits well with Schneider and Till's (2007) modernist portrayal that the user is merely another design element that would, 'perform the same function again and again with no possibility of changing or combining any of the functions, not to mention doing things differently'. This reveals one of modernism's biggest failures, given the diversity of the world in which we live, and connects with Watkin's (2000) revelation that many better solutions sit within traditional architecture – suggesting a need to reconnect architecture with its pre-modernist history.

For Habraken (1998), modernism's principles removed the idea of separation between stakeholders and physical form. The ideology placed full control of the environment to the architect (top-down design control) and applied the principles to all scales from urban to furniture design (e.g. modernist thinking gave rise to mono-functional planning zones) or as Leupen (2006) put into words, 'a coarse single-level product'. This has produced architecture unable to adapt well to change over time. Modernism's desire to 'over'-utilise contemporary technology failed to understand user needs at the expense of technological fetishes or as Rabeneck *et al.* put it, 'This inventive "popular mechanics" approach is all too often an alibi for actually thinking about how people live or might want to live.'

Architecture (adaptability) is removed from the everyday and becomes a specialised solution.

But it's not all one-way traffic and Table 2.2 summarises some positive and negative aspects of the modernist movement in relation to adaptability. However, many of the negative aspects identified here remain today as a dominating perspective, suggesting a lack of evolution towards situating architecture in its real context.

Table 2.2 Summary of Modernism characteristics

Positive	Negative
Simple, cubic form	Efficient form (abstract symbolism)
Minimum distinction between inside and outside	Functional decomposition (mono-functional spaces)
Industrialised, modular construction	Neglect of context
Exposed detailing	Style over substance (performance)
Framed construction (functional separation)	Universality (objectify user)
'Natural' materials	Antihistoricism Expression of technology Single-level product

Chapter 3

Strands of designing for adaptability

We have identified eight strands of thought in the literature that are mapped on a timeline (Figure 3.1) and identify links between influential projects, approaches and individuals. They offer an evolution, a blurring and coalescing of ideas, starting with primitive forms of construction to modern-day approaches that are placed in three categories: *spatial* (loose fit, open plan), *physical bits* (industralisation, kinetic architecture, unfinished) and *building configuration* (levels, layers, systems design). There are clear overlaps, but the strands are structured in this way to present important distinctions. The themes oversimplify the complex interplay of projects and movements described below, but it is hoped that they provide an orientation through which a discussion can take place.

▶ Figure 3.1 (OPPOSITE PAGE)
Historic mapping of design strands

3.1 Spatial

Loose fit

The loose-fit strand pre-dates modernism's rise and is an essential characteristic of a pre-modern building's capacity to accommodate change – it is the functionalist or, as Lerup (1977) describes, behaviourist approach to architecture that creates the glove of architecture fashioned to fit the particular behaviour (function) at hand. In 1972 Alex Gordon, the then RIBA President, initiated a probe into long-life, loose-fit, low-energy buildings. It was his belief that these three characteristics would define a more sustainable built environment. The thinking can be linked to the multifunctionality of prehistoric shelters and traditional architecture which were more about providing ample 'generic' space for activities rather than prescribing spatial standards for specific functionalities.

Hertzberger (2005) suggests a loose-fit approach seeks the largest common spatial denominator. Venturi and Scott Brown (2004) switch the architectural adage of 'form follows function' to 'form accommodates functions' to be more appropriate to a dynamic world, offering a mitten analogy that provides wiggle space.

A loose-fit approach allows for greater user choice, minimising the predetermination of how the space will be used – the simple ambiguity of the space provides a safeguard measure. Generous dimensions and ambiguity accommodate adaptations to other uses. The issue then is the cost associated with space (and regulations). Structural costs and overall building height restrictions

Make your spaces big enough man, that you can walk around them freely, and not just in one predetermined direction! Or are you all that sure of how they will be used? We don't know at all whether people will do with them what we expect them to. Functions are not so clear or so constant; they change faster than the building.

Mies van der Rohe, quoted in Schulze (1985)

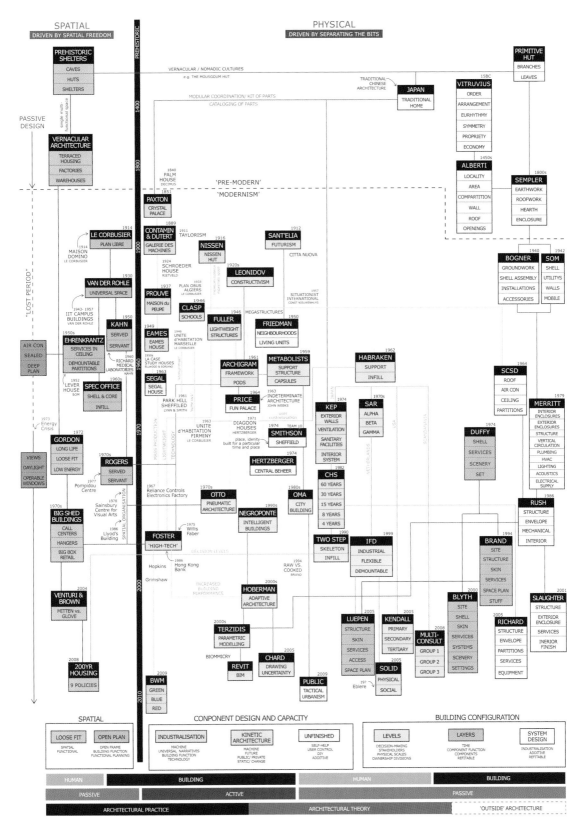

mean developers often try to pack in as many floors within a predetermined height. Horizontally, many developments still rely on a programme with rigid industry standards that are based on spatial efficiency to minimise costs and allow for a tight programme to often squeeze onto a given site.

Open plan

In 1914 Le Corbusier designed Maison Domino (Figure 3.2), a two-floor concrete structure (slabs, columns and stairs) plus partitioning. *Plan libre* would allow the user (and architect) ultimate flexibility in defining the living space(s) through a complete separation of structure and other elements. No longer required to perform as structural elements, walls could go anywhere based on functional requirements or spatial concepts. The project also recognised the potential to separate skilled (structure) and unskilled (partitions, cabinets) labour. The concept became a central tenet for all leading modernists, including Mies van der Rohe who pushed the concept to one of 'Universal Space' as a ubiquitous interior that benefited from an even distribution of servicing and minimum structural elements. Here we can see the merger of two spatial concepts – open plan and loose fit.

Louis Kahn built upon Mies's concept by proposing the separation of servant spaces from served spaces as a way to reduce obstructions in the latter, famously applied to the Richard Medical Laboratories at UPENN (Figure 3.3) where circulation and service ducts (brick towers) were located on the periphery of the laboratories. The Pompidou Centre is another example with a clear span of 75m, expressed services and exterior circulation, where everything was designed to be movable.

The principles of open plan became commonplace in the latter half of the twentieth century, impacting upon the office environment in the 1940s leading

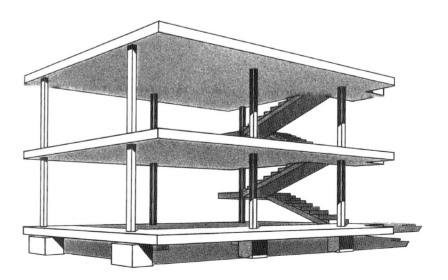

► Figure 3.2
Le Corbusier's Maison Domino
(plan libre)

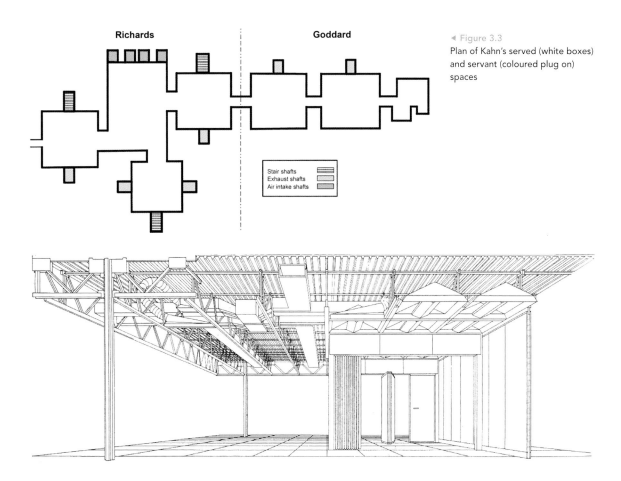

Figure 3.3
Plan of Kahn's served (white boxes) and servant (coloured plug on) spaces

Stair shafts
Exhaust shafts
Air intake shafts

Richards   Goddard

to steel-framed, deep-planned buildings serviced by mechanical air-conditioning. Ehrenkrantz and Wachsmann subsequently developed building systems that housed all the services within the ceiling space and subdivided the lightweight frame construction with demountable partitions (Weston, 2011) – Figure 3.4. Today, the approach has become synonymous with speculative office development and often part of a 'shell and core' construction approach that separates the generic infrastructural support (phase I) from the 'fit-out' to suit a particular occupant (phase II). Speculative development ties the *open plan* strand to the building configuration concept of *levels* discussed later on (section 3.3).

▲ Figure 3.4
Ehrenkrantz (1989) service design for SCSD schools in California

Spatial summary

The two spatial strands (loose fit and open plan) exist harmoniously as the former promotes a generous scale of space and the latter the removal of 'permanent' objects in space. Both align well with a pre-modernist disposition of spatial treatment, as will be illustrated, and link occasionally to physical strands as well. Table 3.1 summarises positive and negative characteristics.

CHAPTER 3 Strands of designing for adaptability   21

Table 3.1 Summary of characteristics for spatial strands

Positive	Negative
Loose spatial dimensions (oversize space)	Increased capital costs
Minimal permanent obstructions	Against planning objectives
Non-load-bearing partitions (functional separation)	Deep plan
Ubiquitous (universal) space	Reliant on mechanical system
Servant/served space (spatial zones)	Higher service demands
Standardised components and locations	Additional maintenance
Simple construction/plan	Economic, not human focused
User customisation (phased construction)	Artificial lighting
Functional freedom	Potential wasteful redundancy

Passive design considerations were picked up again in the 1970s and have re-emerged as an important consideration today.

3.2 Physical bits (component design and capacity)

Industrialised architecture

One of modernism's desires was the expression of modern technology and hence for many, industrialised architecture offered faster construction, a coordinated repeatable system (often in modules) and 'open' components across projects. An early example is Paxton's Crystal Palace (Figure 3.5) erected quickly in London, before being disassembled and rebuilt on the outskirts in Lambeth. The design utilised an iron frame with intermediate timber columns infilled with standardised wooden cladding units and glass panes – the modular unit was fixed by the size of glass panes.

The movable bits of such buildings aimed to accommodate multiple activities within a single space – often to smaller space standards. Thus, this approach to adaptability can be characterised as attempting to do *more with less*. Jean Prouvé was a strong advocate of linking architecture to its methods of production and the transfer of manufacturing technologies to architecture. His industrialised, standardised components (often aluminium) were often movable or demountable providing the user with the freedom of choice. Maison du Peuple de Clichy is an example of an open rectangular volume (service elements at the corners) utilising a prefabricated curtain wall and metal frame. Figure 3.6 shows Prouvé's 8 × 8m demountable house built in 1945 as a post-war housing solution as a lone room that can be packed on a single truck and constructed in a day by three people.

Component efficiency was also a driver behind much of Buckminster Fuller's designs including his geodesic dome structures and Wichita House based upon aircraft cargo components that were assembled in 16 days in the cold of winter (Baldwin, 1997). Other post-war industrialised systems respond to a shortage of facilities, such as the Consortium of Local Authorities Special Programme (CLASP) – a simple yet elegant system of lightweight standardised

components on a 2.5m grid. The buildings were 'designed' and constructed quickly throughout parts of England, but the structural and often spatial efficiency made them more difficult to adapt.

Big sheds appeared throughout the 1960s in the USA and 1970s in Europe. These large, free-standing, one-storey structures, initially for retail, are the 'ultimate' flexible buildings that can be fitted out to suit a variety of requirements. A lack of architectural input made them very cheap and perhaps a better model for adaptability than the (outdated) modernist version. However, as Christensen (2008) suggests, they have an ephemeral quality in their construction and longevity, although communities continually find ways to reconnect their needs to these abandoned boxes adapting them into homes, museums, community centres, churches and public offices.

The 'High-tech' movement in architecture, also referred to as Productivism, coalesces many of the previous generation's practical and theoretical approaches to adaptability – Mies's universal space, Kahn's served and servant spatial organisation, Prouvé's industralisation, Fuller's technology transfer and the Metabolists' incomplete form (discussed in the next section). They took Le Corbusier's metaphor 'the house is a machine for living in' and turned it into a literal aesthetic – developing a well-articulated metal box (a simple industrial

▲ Figure 3.5
Interior sketch of the Crystal Palace

A large, free-standing, one-storey warehouse building with one main room, ranging from 20,000 to 280,000 ft² used initially for retail purposes.

Christensen (2008)

shed) – thus, form is not a result of the functions they house nor the surrounding context in which they sit (Davies, 1988). The Reliance Controls Electronics Factory (1967) designed by Rogers and Foster is often cited as the first High-tech building, displaying its founding characteristics well with a simple rectangular open floor plan, exposed structure, dry, off-the-shelf components and an extendable undifferentiated plan – Figure 3.7. Thus, the object itself is highly crafted, usually of components that have been standardised for a particular project, exposed structure and services and utilising dry joints. Space is kept

as homogeneous as possible allowing any type of function to occur which is often aided by the versatility provided by certain (movable/configurable) components.

In relationship to the strand of 'unfinished design', 'space is an abstract entity that is devoid of specific qualities until it is inhabited and adapted by its users' (Davies, 1988). Thus High-tech buildings embraced the concept of 'incomplete' or 'open-ended' forms, enabling the building to grow or shrink as needed, e.g. Centre Pompidou – portions of the upper floors are used as roof terraces but can be filled in to create additional interior space. The use of dry joints extends the flexibility allowing vertical elements (doors, windows, walls) to be changed. Here we can start to see ties with the third group of approaches, building configuration (section 3.3), as well as enabling access and separation of building subsystems.

Kinetic architecture

While kinetic architecture's modern roots are split between the utopian visions of Sant'Elia's futurism and Leonidov's constructivism and expressionism, its conceptual roots lie in the portable structures of prehistoric times. Kinetic architecture encapsulates the ability to change its shape and location – from the scale of a component to the entire building – in response to changing conditions. The strand grows from the creative desire for unlimited architectural freedom in pursuit of a new (and better) architecture that moves away from the concept of architecture as a singular monolithic object in time.

Megastructure architecture aimed to remove the static theory of functionalism and embrace social change by enabling organic growth through society's evolving demands (Sharp, 2005). Jencks (1973), however, argues that megastructures aimed to *plan with* rather than *plan for* the future (multiple realities rather than just one) enabling a level of indeterminacy and empowerment to the user that would allow any activity to take place under a single roof. Architecture took on a performative role where pluralism and quickness of reaction would allow any activity to take place under a single roof.

Archigram, a group of young British architects, summarised their philosophy as 'an active architecture attempting to sharpen to the maximum its power of response and ability to respond to as many reasonable potentials as possible' (Jencks, 1973). For Fumihiko Maki of the Japanese Metabolist group, a *megastructure* was distinguished as, 'modular units [with a short lifespan] that attached to a longer-life structural framework' (Lin, 2010). Here we can see architecture as an expendable product for the first time embodying the shrinking lives of functions, yet the large infrastructural framework builds towards a longer life cycle as well.

Projects were often presented as 'a city on top of or within the existing city' as a method to add density to urban conditions. Projects like Huth and Domenig's *Ragnitz* integrated transportation lines and other infrastructural services as a secondary system to the customisable living units. A Dutch example is Friedman's *Spatial City* which proposed one city on top of another, an 'artificial topography' (3D directional grid on elevated shafts), in which layered levels would allow for

[The high-tech movement's] characteristic materials are metal and glass, that it purports to adhere to a strict code of honesty of expression, that it usually embodies ideas about industrial production, that it uses industries other than the building industry as sources both of technology and of imagery, and that it puts a high priority on flexibility of use.

Davies (1988)

Once the principle of general demountability has been established, the building becomes not a single artefact, which will one day wear out or outlive its usefulness, but a collection of artefacts of different types and with different life expectancies.

Davies (1988)

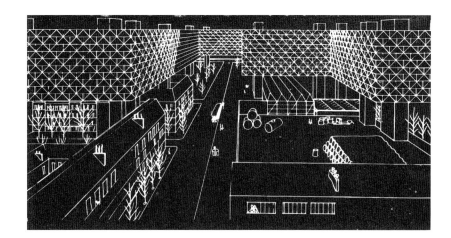

► Figure 3.8
Friedman's Spatial City
Courtesy Yona Friedman

[B]uildings on a massive scale, heroic structures to which smaller pods, capsules and partitions could be added or taken away: quietly relocated according to daily or hourly spatial demand.

Alison *et al.* (2006)

different uses to be contained within the same site (Figure 3.8). The mobile, temporary and lightweight structure was made up of trihedral elements based on a 6m × 6m module that would accommodate a variety of uses based on three principles: touch the ground over a minimum area, be capable of being dismantled and moved and be alterable as required by the individual occupant.

For the Japanese, Metabolism re-established links to traditional construction concepts such as prefabrication, modularity, circular growth and renewal. Kurokawa's Takara Beautillion (Figure 3.9) was assembled and disassembled in six days at the 1970 Osaka Expo and was composed of two elements – a framework of six-pointed crosses (steel tubes bent to a common radius) and

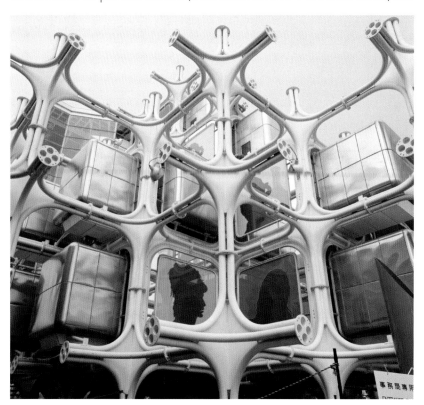

► Figure 3.9
Kurokawa's Takara Beautillion for the 1970 Osaka Expo
Courtesy Tomio Ohashi

mini-showroom capsules that plugged into the framework. The pavilion displayed the end joints of the framework that would allow additional framework units or capsules to be added when needed.

An interesting evolution of the megastructure concept was Archigram's 'Control and Choice' which utilised a small number of 'permanent' pylons that allowed for smaller, more flexible components to be plugged in rather than volumetric spatial units (capsule) – wall, skin, services and roof can now be changed as individual conditions (Jencks, 1973). This component-based application ties well with the layer strand (see section 3.3).

The growth in materials in the late 1960s led architects to experiment with inflatable and tensile structures, reflective of the industrialised trend (e.g. Prouvé and Fuller) to use minimum, lightweight, inexpensive, portable materials – in an 'instant' one could create exciting shapes.

Their origins lie with William Lanchester who patented a design for a field hospital in 1917 referred to as 'a large tent with no poles' that applied the principles of air-supported construction (Dent, 1972). Ant farm (1971) published *Inflatocookbook* – a DIY manual for inflatable architecture, while the French Utopie Group (Figure 3.10) proposed 'a transient, mobile architecture totally made from pneumatic, inflatable products – walls, floors, partitions, furniture, event the mechanical equipment was inflatable' (Jencks, 1973). Today they are used for temporary (and movable) structures such as tennis domes, fairground pavilions; noteworthy examples include Sir Norman Foster's *Computer Technology Ltd* (1971), Frei Otto's *Inflatable Pavilion* for the Rotterdam Expo (1958) and Nicholas Grimshaw's *Eden Project* (2001).

Components and systems that could respond to user or environmental conditions emerged at the end of the twentieth century. So-called intelligent buildings include building, space and business management, where building management or automation systems provide the hardware and software to

They can be low-pressure, enclose a large span of space with a slightly higher internal air pressure, while high-pressure structures apply the same principles to air beams.

Kronenburg (2007)

▼ Figure 3.10
French Utopie Group's Inflatable House, 1967
Courtesy Jean-Paul Jungmann

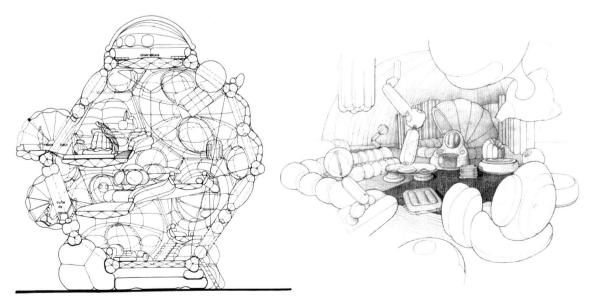

control mechanical and electrical systems within certain ranges and/or on various time schedules (e.g. ventilation, lighting, security). The systems allow buildings to adapt automatically to prevailing user needs and environmental conditions and have become commonplace in buildings – turning lights on and off, locking and unlocking doors and adjusting cooling and heating conditions.

The concept of intelligent building components, which often act in the background, has grown to include a wider range of components and functions generating more *adaptive* or *responsive* structures, allowing real-time changes based on a variety of environmental and human interactions. For Spuybroek (2005) this is 'true' adaptability engaged in the emergence of the event itself rather than a passive indeterminate response offered by other concepts such as universal space or industralisation. A functional example are the pillars in the courtyard of the Mosque of Medina which open up during prayer to provide shade for pilgrims (Figure 3.11). The trend is increasingly biomorphic, imitating nature's complex network of 'components' with constant feedback mechanisms.

'Unfinished' design

▼ Figure 3.11
Open pillars at the Mosque of
Medina provide shade

'Unfinished' design empowers the user to appropriate space to their needs, evident in several Dutch approaches such as Friedman's *Spatial City* and Habraken's *Levels*, but architects like Herman Hertzberger are concerned with user appropriation, not separation of ownership. For Lerup (1977) the concept

is rooted in interaction, not reaction, between humans and architecture; the user becomes an active element of the architecture and hence the physical components are just one of the elements that come to life – creating an openness, unpredictability and unfinishedness.

One of the most successful examples of this approach is the Central Beheer in Apeldoorn designed by Hertzberger where occupants spontaneously brought their belongings to appropriate the space. He is, however, clear that this is not about simply making empty spaces (a half-finished building), but about a balance between the scale and the relationship of spaces, allowing the user and the building to manifest a relationship. Hill (2006) likens this approach to software design in which the designer must enable adaptation to take place by allowing the object to 'learn' and the users to 'teach', creating a two-way interaction that takes place during use. In this way, the building form can remain essentially the same, but take on different uses by forming new relationships (different interpretations) with users giving the architecture its specificity in time and location.

However, too much freedom can be just as bad as too little and Hertzberger (2005) accepts a level of rigidity (a permanent base) from which the building can form an identity and increase opportunities for change – 'bridging the gap between formal order and daily life'. This point is important for Lerup (1977) as he stresses a clear distinction between Habraken's levels which view the 'scaffolding' as an opportunity for flexibility and how he (and Hertzberger) view it as a way to construct limits by anchoring activity in a specific place and time. Cedric Price's Fun Palace (Figure 3.12) also focused on a simple open structure rather than an enclosed monument capable of quick responses to the user's desires.

In a similar light, Alison and Peter Smithson were committed to creating a sense of place as a reaction to the Modernist ideal of universality. Their effort to create an architecture of change was based on human associations, they

It is the fundamental unfinishedness of the building, the greyness, the naked concrete, and the many other imposed (but also concealed) free-choice possibilities, that are meant to stimulate the occupants to add their own color, so that everyone's choice, and thereby his standpoint, is brought to the surface.

Herman Hertzberger, quoted in Mellor (1974)

Architecture should not be of neutrality, but one that is suggestive of as many propositions as possible without imposing any one specifically.

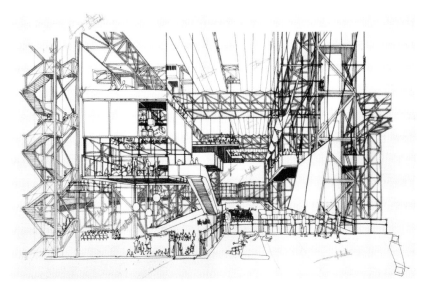

◀ Figure 3.12
Price's Fun Palace
Courtesy Cedric Price fonds Collection Centre Canadien d'Architecture/Canadian Centre for Architecture, Montréal

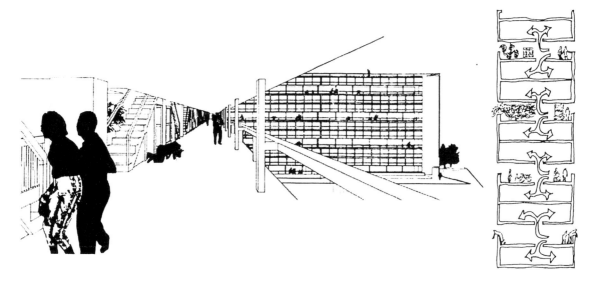

▲ Figure 3.13
Smithson's Golden Lane
Competition
Courtesy Smithson Family Collection

were committed to the interaction between community and architecture and often focused on the liveliness of circulation paths (Figure 3.13) as interactive interchanges – e.g. a 'deck' not a 'corridor'.

Hertzberger's Diagoon houses (Figure 3.14) provide another example where the basic frame allows the user to determine the number of rooms (how to divide the space) and functional uses (where they live and sleep). All the spaces are of generally the same dimensions and have equal access to the service core.

Extending this strand further we can progress into the expressive DIY movement that began with unskilled labour (painting, decorating) and subsequently has encompassed all areas of construction (Jencks, 1973). Walter Segal (1963) designed one of the more notorious 'self-build' prototypes that takes

▼ Figure 3.14
Hertzberger's Diagoon house
Courtesy Herman Hertzberger (left) and
Jörn Schiemann (right)

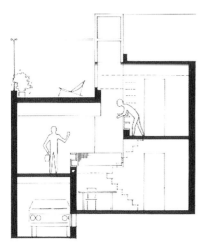

advantage of standard, uncut elements to produce a demountable timber frame and panelled system (Figure 3.15).

By making the user an active participant, this strand fundamentally readdresses the relationship and role between designer and user. Hertzberger relates architecture to a musical instrument free to adhere to the user's interpretation. Brand (1994) suggests that this type of approach surrenders a level of control on behalf of the designer by delaying certain design decisions to the eventual users – for Brand this is done by developing a building finished to varying degrees, 'some areas of the building should be "cooked" [highly finished and flashy] and some areas left "raw" [unfinished but usable]'.

Component design and capacity summary

This design theme has evolved from a tenet of technology through the development of industrialised components, to modern-day adaptive and parametric elements (Table 3.2). Critics of accommodating change via moving components often disapprove of the predetermination of how a building can change. The argument against technical primacy is also expressed as implicit control over the user. For Rabeneck *et al.* (1973) this approach is more about an

▲ Figure 3.15
Segal's self-build home
Courtesy Chris Moxette

One of the things which we are searching for is a form of architecture which … is not perfect and finite upon completion … like some music and poetry which can actually be changed by the users, an architecture of improvisation.

Rogers (1991)

Adaptability is a result of the user–building relationship

Table 3.2 Summary of characteristics for physical bits approaches

Positive	Negative
Standardised components and locations	Tight fit approach (do more with less)
Simple construction/plan	Lack of character (architectural quality)
Off-site construction	Lack of durability (cheapness of materials)
Configurable stuff (multiple states)	Isolated context
Modularity	Singular approach
Loose spatial dimensions (oversize space)	Vague design
Component separation (long/short life)	Lack of human-centric consideration
User customisation (user–building relationship)	Functional integration
Responsive to environment	Limits choices (predetermined)
Spatial quality/planning	

'architectonic' fascination than genuine adaptability or user empowerment. But one must stop to ask, within a spectrum of adaptability, are (say) three options not better than one (particularly if the user is not interested in engaging with the building)? Thus, while embedding the change capacity in physical components has limitations, it does provide a degree of adaptability that could otherwise be lost. However, the degree of freedom cannot be separated from the larger question of value. This moves the discussion from simply considering the physical bits to a wider range of contingent factors. As Gelis (2000) points out, while solutions such as demountable walls, raised floor systems, acoustical ceilings and furniture systems can all augment adaptability, they can also lead to a large amount of 'wasteful redundancy' if deployed without a proper overall scheme.

3.3 Building configuration

The three strands of building configuration are concerned with categorising elements of the building as levels, layers or subsystems to enable a better understanding of the building. Stratification of components into a classification system can help to reveal the effects of change on a building over time.

Levels

Support/Infill (SI) was developed as a reaction to the housing boom in the 1960s to empower the user. SAR (Stichting Architecten Research) was founded in 1965 by John Habrakan to promote SI concepts to industry and developed rules and guidelines supported by the government, including grid and coordination systems (Kendall and Teicher, 2000). SI equates levels of individuals' control with environmental levels in design and use to get at how 'things work' – clarifying physical boundaries (disentangling buildings) and social roles (unbundling decision-making) – Table 3.3.

The result is a process and architecture more attuned to the user's needs (consumer-oriented product), providing them with a variety of choice (mass

Table 3.3 Open building's 'two-fisted' approach

Social	Physical
User	Infill (fit-out)
Designer	Support (base building)
Society	Urban tissue (surrounding fabric)

customisation), while enabling future change in an otherwise collective environment. Level separation is made possible physically through attention to interfaces between components and spatial (modular) coordination and a conscious effort to think about the foreseeable life of the materials and systems and their relationships. The higher-level framework establishes principles of ordering or rules for the lower level (sequence of construction). Kendall (2009) characterises the two building levels: *supports* – longer-term use, public or common service-related design, heavy construction, long-term investment, equivalent to real estate (site) and long-term mortgage financing; *infill* – shorter-term use, user-related design, lightweight components, short-term investment, equivalent to durable consumer goods and short-term financing. User choices may include the size and subdivision of space, finishes, equipment and façade elements. Some examples of design tactics supporting SI thinking are open frame structure, intermediate zone for services, and façade infill system.

In 1984 SI morphed into OBOM (Open Building Simulation Model) and remains alive today as the Open Building (OB) movement, a CIB workgroup (CIB104). In a broader sense, OB has embraced the industrialisation of construction and other such approaches (e.g. design for manufacture, disassembly and reuse) that enhance level separation. The OB concept has evolved as the foundation for several distinct applications in the Netherlands, Japan and other countries (e.g. the INO Hospital in Switzerland).

IFD (Industrial Flexible and Demountable) is a Dutch government construction initiative from 1999 that offered financial subsidies to companies developing projects that embrace the three naming principles in response to a demand-led market for process and product flexibility (Geraedts, 2011). Industrialisation, enhances both types with prefabricated components/subsystems, better integration of the supply team and minimum work on site. The demountable characteristic focuses on reducing waste with components that are easily removed and relocated allowing the building to be scaled or moved.

Geraedts and Cuperus (2011) examined 5 of the 34 residential projects constructed over the eight years of the IFD programme where users were given spatial options at the beginning and provided a way to extend their homes (e.g. additional strip foundations – Figure 3.16); many used lightweight (demountable) partitions that allowed for spatial reconfiguration (flexibility), accessible services (e.g. raised flooring) and demountable façade panels (one project included a demountable timber structure). While positive, Geraedts and Cuperus point out that many IFD projects suffered from immaturity of technology, the conventional structure of the building process (e.g. coordination between stakeholders) and a lack of a target customer group. In many cases

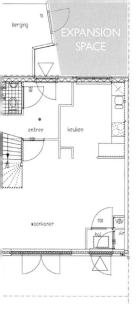

▲ Figure 3.16
Kersentium, an IFD residential project, which was expanded in red
Courtesy Rob Geraedts

users implemented a number of the design tactics deployed; on the other hand, a lack of information existed about the tactics used, landlord restrictions, noise problems and an absence of temporary solutions.

A second Dutch evolutionary strand of SI called Solid addresses two qualities: accommodation capacity (physical elements, individual) and preciousness (emotional value, society). The social half of the equation, preciousness, is focused on collective values, establishing a relationship with the larger community through the building's image and public spaces establishing a cultural durability i.e. 'support'. The 'private' half (infill) is the accommodation capacity that aims to allow the user the physical capacity to constantly adapt the building to different programmatic needs.

In the late 1960s Japanese housing policies moved from quantity to quality, implementing since then several SI applications to enable a more adaptable living environment. The Kodan Experimental Housing Project system (1973) categorised the building as a structural frame with four subcategories of components – exterior, interior, kitchen and bath, including interface details between each category to facilitate the industrialisation and use of 'open' components. The houses were sold from a menu to give the homeowner some choice.

The next evolution, Century housing system (CHS), began in 1980 and divided the building elements into five categories based on estimated component life expectancy (Table 3.4 and Figure 3.17). Component groups consist

Table 3.4 CHS's component categories

Component examples	Lifespan category	Average
light bulbs, packing	3–6	4
hot water heater, home appliances, piping, wiring	6–12	8
movable partitions, built-in furniture	12–25	15
exterior door and windows, roof	25–50	30
foundation, main columns and beams	50–100	60

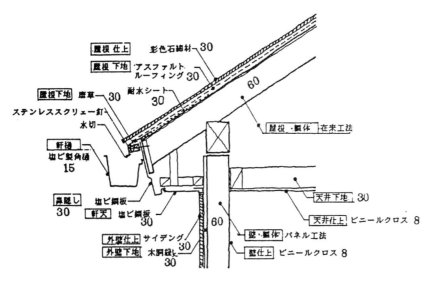

屋根 仕上　彩色石綿材　30
屋根 下地　アスファルト
　　　　　ルーフィング 30
屋根下地　唐草　30　耐水シート 30
ステンレススクリュー釘
水切
軒樋　塩ビ製角樋 15
鼻隠し 30　塩ビ鋼板
軒天　塩ビ鋼板 30
外壁仕上　サイデング 30
外壁下地　木胴縁 30
60
60
屋根・軀体　在来工法
壁・軀体　パネル工法
壁仕上　ビニールクロス 8
天井下地 30
天井仕上　ビニールクロス 8

◄ Figure 3.17
CHS drawing labels components
and their intended lifespan
Courtesy Yositka Utida

of the components, the connections outside the group and the embodied work needed to design, produce, construct and maintain the group's functionality. The central philosophy was that buildings need to be designed so that parts with long lifespans are not damaged when parts with short lifespans are replaced. However, the system proved too complex and 'rules' which were highly administrative destroyed the economic incentive (Utida, 1983).

The third evolution in 1990 is SI – Skeleton Infill which supplies buildings in two steps: first 'S' (skeleton) signifies the long-lasting part and social property and second 'I' (Infill/fit-out) represents the short-lasting private property. The NEXT 21 project by Osaka Gas (Figure 3.18) is a continual experiment documenting the efficiency (time, cost and material conservation) of changes endured (e.g. movement/addition of walls and rooms).

▼ Figure 3.18
Next 21
Courtesy Seiichi Fukao

The 18 customised 140m² residential units use standard and non-standard components allowing for individualised variety, but are highly coordinated in terms of component composition, performance, integration and location. Modular coordination is established through a rulebook to ensure cohesion between the individual units and the neighbourhood allowing adaptations to take place fluidly without the original designers. The generous floor-to-floor heights (lower level 4.2m, upper floors 3.6m) allow for a quality of openness, but also provide sufficient space to run all services, increased storage space and space for mezzanine and Japanese-style sunken floors 'kotatsu'.

The Japanese government still uses SI in their policies helping the concept gain widespread dissemination. In 2006, the Basic Plan for Housing (National Plan) indicated a transition to a stock-based housing policy promoting a '200-year Housing' initiative for extending the useful life of new housing (Minami, 2010). For the Japanese, an experience-based progression has added clarity, simplifications, priorities and knowledge about how buildings change through life, developing a matured and tested understanding.

Layers

[S]hells that last up to 50 years, services that last 15 years before they must be replaced, scenery which, these days, has a duration of five years or even less.

Duffy (1990)

The layers concept acknowledges that building elements have different lifespans that should be constructed distinctly. The term was coined by Frank Duffy who argued that buildings should not be measured in material terms, but in terms of time. Duffy's focus is on the office sector and includes the term 'sets' to characterise the everyday changes that occur with furniture and equipment. Duffy stresses this reconceptualisation of the 'building' changes how we understand initial and recurrent costs (Figure 3.19). Brand (1994) expanded Duffy's concept by seeing them as a set of 'shearing' layers that change at different rates – the more layers are connected, the greater difficulty and cost of adaptation, suggesting the design will be governed by slow changing components, e.g. structure restrains skin; skin restrains services (Figure 3.20).

▶ Figure 3.19
Cumulative capital costs over time
Duffy and Henney (1989)

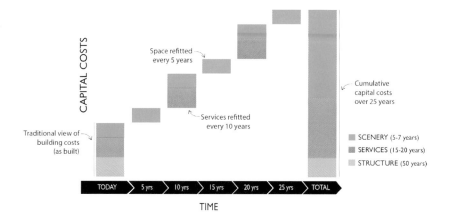

STUFF	1 day - 1 month
SPACE PLAN	3 - 30 years
SERVICES	7 - 15 years
SKIN	20 years
STRUCTURE	30 - 300 years
SITE	Eternal

However, if change is frequent or costly, trends of more rapidly chang-ing components can influence slower ones, e.g. constant rearrangement of stuff may require the space plan to include a raised floor (Brand, 1994). The layers include site as the eternal entity, structure (columns, floor slabs), ser-vices (ductwork, piping), space plan (interior partitions, ceiling tiles) and stuff (furniture, fixtures). Blyth and Worthington (2001) added skin, site and systems to Duffy's model. While skin and site are synonymous with Brand's terminology, systems is new and gives awareness to the rise in information technology and the growing disparity in the rate of change between IT services and other services. This chimes well with Blakstad's (2001) assessment that services consist of several layers and are complicated by an array of components – centralised, building elements (plant) and local, user elements (diffusers) and systems – more stable elements (water) intermixed with more volatile elements (IT). Services are additionally complicated because they are often concealed and embedded in other layers for cost or space purposes. Indeed it is not just the architectural elements that define a layer but the function an assemblage of elements fulfils as a whole. The concept can also be extended to an urban scale, as suggested by Friedman (2002).

The appropriate number of layers, and their relation to each other, must be decided for each project, according to its complexity, uncertainty, expected changes in use, and how the building process is organised and managed.

Blakstad (2001)

Systems design

Throughout history, architects have attempted to distill architecture to a col-lection of basic elements from Vitruvius's order – arrangement, eurhythmy, symmetry, propriety and economy (Wotton, 1903) – to Alberti's – locality, area, compartition, wall, roof and openings (Alberti, 1988). Such decompositional thinking has been applied to a handful of applications – e.g. Walter Bogner's (1942) division of the home into groundwork, shell assembly (walls and roof), installation units (kitchen, bathroom) and accessories, with interchangeable parts (wall partitions, doors, windows, roof shades, porch) (Schneider and Till, 2007).

Christopher Alexander is often cited as the founding thinker of how a complex design problem can be systematically decomposed into smaller more

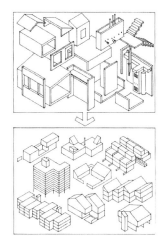

Ehrenkrantz's (1989) components
and building configurations

*The problem of
adaptability, therefore,
turns out to be more
complicated than at first
look, both as to just what
the objective is, how it
can be attained, and how
it relates to other human
ends.*

Lynch (1958)

manageable problems. Alexander's (1964) approach decomposed the object (urban house) into subsets (bundles) of parameters (components), analysed the subsets and (re)combined them to satisfy all the needs. He acknowledged the complexity of complex objects was not divisible as a tree but required a lattice-like form that creates exponentially more possibilities.

School Construction Systems Development (SCSD) in California was designed as a series of four subsystems – roof, air-conditioning, ceiling and partitions, allowing the partitions to be located anywhere on a 1.5m grid with controllable service locations. Production of the components became open in the construction of schools across the US and Canada. In addition, Ehrenkrantz designed a fibershell system for the US government as a kit-of-parts that could be configured to create a variety of buildings (Figure 3.21). Ehrenkrantz later went on to create a systems catalogue that specified the compatibility between different components and systems (Jencks, 1973).

Merritt (1979) defines nine subsystems: interior enclosures, exterior enclosures, structure, vertical circulation, plumbing, HVAC, lighting, acoustics and electrical supply. Merritt's subsystem classification spreads Brand's service layer across five subsystems (plumbing, HVAC, lighting, acoustics and electrical supply) although components are not tied to a particular subsystem. He concluded that for the majority of buildings, system analysis at the building level is too complicated given the high degree of interactions between building components and suggests optimisation is best suited at the subsystem level.

Rush (1986) argues designers think at the level of the building and not at the level of systems, thus integration is not considered carefully and therefore sought a visual way to conceive systems and their relationships. He identified four systems: *structure* (supports and stabilises), *envelope* (protects against climate and degradation), *mechanical* (controls heat, power, water, etc.) and *interior* (the inhabitable space) and was concerned with their level of integration and/or separation (modularity): *remote* (do not physically touch), *touching* (contact, but not permanent), *connected* (permanently attached), *meshed* (occupy the same space, more restrictive than connected), and *unified* (no longer distinct). His 'ball diagrams' (Figure 3.22), help to visualise the interdependence between the building elements and the systems.

In conclusion, systems design approaches design by defining sets of parameters and decomposing the building into subsets of components. Today, such thinking has evolved into parametric software with algorithms to control variables and create complex forms supported by advances in computer assisted design-to-fabricate methods. Building Information Modelling seeks to systematically code, organise, manage, update and track components from conception through use.

Building configuration summary

All three conceptual strands – levels, layers and systems design – attempt to balance change and stability by decomposing the building into discrete chunks (Table 3.5). The systems design strand focused explicitly on identifying distinct functions as a method for stratification, whereas layers blended

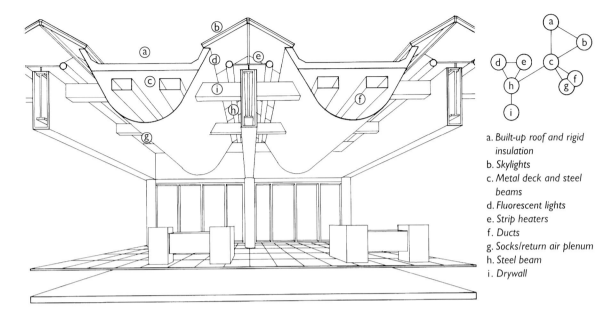

a. *Built-up roof and rigid insulation*
b. *Skylights*
c. *Metal deck and steel beams*
d. *Fluorescent lights*
e. *Strip heaters*
f. *Ducts*
g. *Socks/return air plenum*
h. *Steel beam*
i. *Drywall*

Table 3.5 Summary of characteristics for building configuration strands

Positive	Negative
Modularity (reversible)	Unconventional approach (inexperience)
Standardised components and locations	Immaturity of technology
Industrialisation/off-site construction	Component-focused
Hierarchy of components (lifespans)	Limits choices (predetermined)
Urban scale (context)	
Simple construction/plan	
User customisation (phased construction)	
Architectural quality (preciousness)	
Multiple ownership levels	

▲ Figure 3.22
Rush's (1986) 'ball diagram' to the right illustrates component relationships
Courtesy American Institute of Architects

functionality with a specific concern for differing component life cycles. The level concept attempts to balance the physical with the social – understanding that one cannot achieve adaptability without both.

Here decomposition is based primarily on separating levels of ownership to enable individual control. In this case, decomposition tends to be (a) fewer, of only two or three individual levels and (b) more abstract, interpretive labels. Despite Brand's (1994) acknowledgement of the importance of human appreciation, layers as a concept doesn't explicitly attempt to integrate the social, decision-making aspect of the built environment – something absent from systems design. The levels strand's integration of a social dimension is an important distinction and both layers and levels include the building context (urban tissue, site), whereas systems design focuses on decomposing the building removed from context.

The complexity of adaptability requires an alignment of physical and social forces at a particular moment in time – it is not something that one can simply design for and eventually retrieve on a rainy day – a false idealism that accompanies adaptability.

Part III

A THEORY OF ADAPTABILITY

DESIGN STRATEGIES & BUILDING CHARACTERISTICS

PHYSICAL	
DSI: MODULARITY	
CARI	Reversible
CAR2	Movable stuff
CAR3	Component accessibility
CAR4	Functional separation
DS2: DESIGN 'IN' TIME	
CAR5	Service zones
CAR6	Configurable stuff
CAR7	Multi-functional components
CAR8	Not precious
CAR9	'Extra' components
DS3: LONG LIFE	
CAR10	Durability
CAR11	Mature component
CAR12	Efficient services
CAR13	Good craftmenship
CAR14	Overdesign capacity
CAR15	Readily available materials
DS4: SIMPLICITY & LEGIBILITY	
CAR16	Standardised components
CAR17	Standard component locations
CAR18	Off-site construction
CAR19	Simple construction method

SPATIAL	
DS5: LOOSE FIT	
CAR20	Open space
CAR21	Support space
CAR22	Oversize space
DS6: SPATIAL PLANNING	
CAR23	Typology pattern
CAR24	Joinable/divisble space
CAR25	Modular coordination
CAR26	Connect buildings
CAR27	Standard room size(s)
CAR28	Spatial variety
CAR29	Spatial ambiguity
CAR30	Spatial zones
CAR31	Spatial proximity
CAR32	Simple plan
CAR33	Standard grid
CAR34	Simple form
DS7: PASSIVE TECHNIQUES	
CAR35	Multiple ventilation strategies
CAR36	Shallow plan depth
CAR37	Passive climate control
CAR38	Building orientation
CAR39	Good daylighting
DS8: UNFINISHED DESIGN	
CAR40	Space to grow into
CAR41	Phased
CAR42	User customisation
DS9: MAXIMISE BUILDING USE	
CAR43	Multi-functional spaces
CAR44	Use differentiation
CAR45	Mixed demographics
CAR46	Multiple/mixed tenure
CAR47	Shared ownership
CAR48	Isolatable
CAR49	Multiple access points
DS9: INCREASE INTERACTIVITY	
CAR50	Physical linkage
CAR51	Visual linkage

SCALES	
DS11: AESTHETICS	
CAR52	Attitude & character
CAR53	Spatial quality
CAR54	Building image
CAR55	Quirkiness
CAR56	Time interwoven
DS12: MULTIPLE SCALES	
CAR57	Good location
CAR58	Contextual
CAR59	Circulation (neighbourhood scale)
CAR60	A communal place

ADAPTABILITY TYPES

AT1	Adjustable
AT2	Versatile
AT3	Refitable
AT4	Convertible
AT5	Scalable
AT6	Movable

DESIGN RESOURCES

DR1	Design guidelines
DR2	Critical parameters
DR3	Scenario planning
DR4	Films
DR5	'Active' drawings
DR6	Benefit mapping
DR7	Evaluation tools
DR8	Organogram
DR9	Project precedents
DR10	Parti diagram
DR11	Workshop
DR12	Website

BUILDING LAYERS

L1	Social
L2	Space
L3	Stuff
L4	Space plan
LS	Services
L6	Skin
L7	Structure
L8	Site
L9	Surroundings

▲ Figure III.1
Lexicon for theoretical elements
(Continued)

CONTEXTUAL CONTINGENCIES

STAKEHOLDERS		PHASES	
CON1	Client mindset	CON11	Fragmented process
CON2	Architect mindset	CON12	Brief(ing)
CON3	End-users	CON13	Procurement route
CON4	Other stakeholders	CON14	Good management
CON5	Culture	CON15	Occupation
RULES		ECONOMICS	
CON6	Building regulations	CON16	Business models
CON7	Taxation	CON17	Valuation practices
CON8	Heritage protection	CON18	Market forces
CON9	Planning regulations	CON19	Funding methods
CON10	Industry standards	CON20	Risk

MODELS

M1	Design perspectives	M11	Benefit mapping
M2	Time and context	M12	Critical decision
M3	Harmonising approaches	M13	Funding method
M4	Building layers	M14	Linking
M5	DSM	M15	Framecycle
M6	Adaptability types	M16	Sources
M7	DfA	M17	Design process
M8	Fragmentation	M18	Causal links
M9	Building specification	M19	Cost certainty
M10	Value equations	M20	Pathways

▲ Figure III.1 (Continued)

▼ Figure III.2
Model toolkit

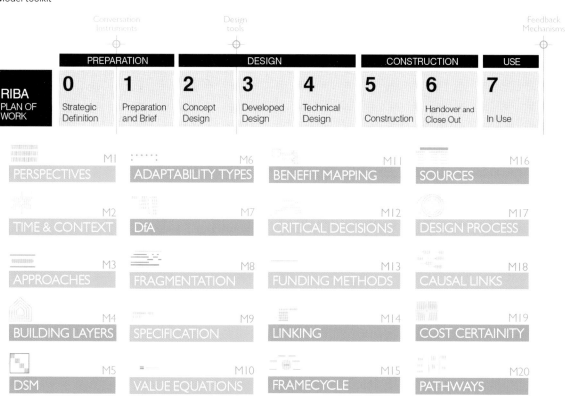

Chapter 4

Developing the concept

We contend that the process of designing buildings continues to be mired in the largely implicit and uncontested goal of the completed building as a finished product for a particular purpose, user and location. This book challenges this deep-rooted 'first-use' perspective and explores an alternative narrative in which this is just the starting condition; to live sustainably places an obligation on all those involved in the built environment to maximise each building's life, providing a setting for the changing needs of the community.

4.1 Defining the word

The etymology of the word *adapt* can be traced to early fourteenth-century Latin, *aptus*, meaning 'suited, fitted', through *adaptare* meaning 'to join' and Middle French as *adapter*, to its English roots in 1610 to mean 'to fit something for some purpose' (Harper, 2001). Current definitions have changed subtly, for example 'to make suitable to requirements or conditions; adjust or modify fittingly' (Random House, 2010). Adaptability then is concerned with the capacity to adjust or be adjusted to suit new situations. You might assume a simple and straightforward application of such a definition in the literature, but find dozens of interpretations, reflecting the very plasticity the concept seeks to describe (Figure 4.1). The same situation occurs in the built environment; for example Olsson and Hansen (2010) found that stakeholders 'either used different terminology or the same terminology with different meanings. Each of the projects tended to develop its own terminology.'

The architect who believes that his work is done as soon as the building is finished must be made to look as ridiculous as the scientist who believes that his experiment is complete as soon as he has assembled the apparatus.

Sir Andrew Derbyshire (2004)

▼ Figure 4.1

'Adaptability' has many meanings

60 practitioners were asked to write words they associate with adaptability. The larger the word signifies the more practitioners who wrote it

We found five overarching interpretations within the construction literature:

1 *Adaptive architecture* or responsive structures, is led by designers' fascination with the building's capacity to mutate with changing conditions through dynamic façades or transformable structures. These tend to be one-off, high-end solutions that respond to environmental changes in real time through sensors and actuators creating a varied response in performance.
2 *Adaptive reuse* finds new uses for underutilised or vacant buildings. Initially driven by market shifts and changes in social perceptions and desires, it is now a key tactic for area regeneration and sustainability, prolonging the operational lives of buildings. Adaptive reuse is commonly associated with converting office buildings to residential and industrial buildings to commercial or residential use.
3 *Accessibility for all* or inclusive design, is particularly strong in designing homes or buildings to accommodate a diverse range of users and their changing capabilities throughout life. In the UK, this is frequently driven by government policy such as Lifetime Homes, whereas an Australian standard (AS 4299, 1995) defines adaptability as 'a move away from designing special accommodation for different community groups with different needs'.
4 *Increased user control* (user customisation) is generally accomplished through physically separating parts of the building according to decision levels between stakeholders (e.g. owners and users – see Habraken, 1998). This has become commonplace with speculative office development (e.g. shell and core construction) and a client-driven practicality to accommodate changing work conditions that allow for spatial reconfigurations at minimal disruption and cost.
5 *Climate adaptation* represents the most recent appropriation of adaptability to understand how buildings can adapt to significant changes with their surrounding environment, including the capacity to reduce their burden on the environment by lowering energy consumption. This typically involves the integration of new technologies within new and existing buildings and the rebirth of passive design techniques.

Such characterisations are not mutually exclusive; they collectively suggest an overarching leitmotif for adaptability of *performance-based design* of which we can identify four underlying characteristics:

1 *The capacity for change* is either physically responsive or a passive accommodation to an internal or external change. Some offer a more descriptive distinction of the type of change as low frequency and high magnitude. The object of the change might be structure, space or environment, but the most often cited is differing use or function.
2 *Fitness for purpose* describes the match between the building and its users. Staying 'fit' emphasises the human–building relationship and managing the constant performance slippage between the supply of space and the demand for it.

3 *Value* can be summarised as maximising productive use, to fit both the use and the stakeholders' desires, at a minimum cost. Hence minimising the effort (time and cost) of change is a defining facet of adaptability.

4 *Time* is described in two ways: to indicate the speed of change (e.g. quick transformations) and through-life changes (such as future changes or extension of use). Thus, maximising the building's life, components or materials is a key feature.

The book takes the following definition of adaptability as a synthesis of the underlying characteristics: *the capacity of a building to accommodate effectively the evolving demands of its context, thus maximising its value through life*. We believe this provides a clear, robust view of adaptability that aligns with the five interpretations described above within the realm of performance-based design – maintaining functionality (maximising efficiency, minimising costs) with change over time. But one note of caution – adaptability as described in this book is primarily concerned with benefits arising from the use of buildings (that is experienced by the owners and occupiers), whereas some also refer to the beneficial effects on the supply side, during design and construction.

It is perhaps worth mentioning that many writers refer to adaptability and flexibility interchangeably, often in abstract contexts (Carthey *et al.*, 2011). Those that offer a distinction are often inconsistent across sources. For instance, some view flexibility as being about short-term changes to buildings, for example to a building's internal layout, and adaptability about more significant long-term changes, such as change of use (Leaman and Bordass, 2004). On the other hand Groak (1992) saw adaptability in terms of accommodating different social uses and flexibility being about accommodating different physical arrangements. However, we feel that such distinctions merely add to the misunderstanding of the subject and later offer six types of adaptability as a way of coping with the range of underlying motivations.

Correlation of the definition to the four characteristics: 'evolving' refers to 'change', 'demands of context' refers to 'remaining fit for purpose', 'value' = 'value' and 'life' = 'time'.

4.2 Time

Design can be conceived as the interplay of function, space and components. A snapshot of this *motion* is related to the client's immediate goals – the 'first use' which can isolate the building in a single moment in time. But in Figure 4.2 time is a fourth perspective that *moves* architecture from a static product (noun) to a dynamic process (verb) – illustrating how the three perspectives might evolve over time (independently, sequentially or in parallel).

Time can be linear (short-term/long-term) or cyclical (for example day/night, seasons or weekday/weekend) and will reflect the balance of political, economic, social, technological, environmental and legal factors of the moment (Figure 4.3). Our perception of time is also evolving – the convention of the eight-hour workday for example and more recently our hyper-connectivity through digital communication.

In his seminal work *How Buildings Learn* Stewart Brand (1994) argued that his intent was, 'to examine buildings as a whole – not just a whole in space, but whole in time'. For Brand – and Duffy (1990) – it is critical to conceptualise

Time is the essence of the real design problem.
Brand (1994)

► Figure 4.2
Design perspectives model (M1)
illustrating varying rates of change

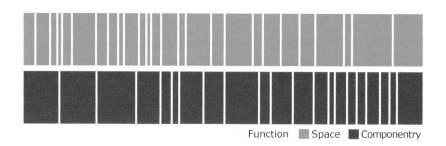

Function ■ Space ■ Componentry

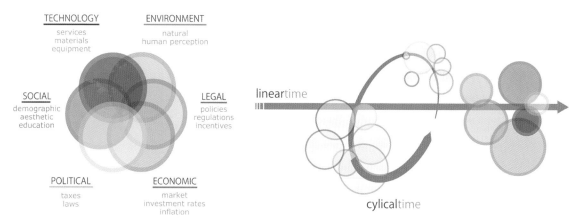

▲ Figure 4.3
Time and context model (M2)

the building not in material terms (concrete, glass, etc.), but as units of time. The architect's work is just the beginning, establishing a framework for a long, slow-moving process. Architecture has been likened to a slow piece of music with its many changes as its melody (Hollis, 2009). Design quality is thus emergent. Takenaka (2005) offers the analogy of a tree in which its shape grows pleasingly with time – where 'true' sustainability rests in how a building develops in time, not what it looks like at completion. For Mostafavi and Leatherbarrow (1993) the conscious inclusion of time, 'brings the virtual future of a building into dialogue with its actual present, as both are entangled in its past'. Hence, each design decision is composed of a particular longevity that can take on different forms when considered from a time-based, rather than form-based perspective – as Brand (1994) suggests, 'architects must "mature" from artists of space to artists of time'.

However, our track record isn't good as for many, great architecture embodies timelessness. Leupen (2006) quotes Mies's expression of the eternal laws of architecture – order, space and proportion – suggesting compositional qualities that endure generations rather than qualities of time (durability, changeability). Lawson (2005) suggests three ways designers tend to deal with time – procrastinate (deal with it later), non-committal design (design is bland, anonymous) and throw-away design (present-only) – none of which respond to time with any long-term comprehension. Till (2009) suggests that even designers who accept time, tend to simply create barriers against it or try to order it into a sequence of frozen instants – such strategies consider the aging of a building, but do nothing to address the uncertainty time presents. Architecture must be placed within time, and designing for adaptability involves the acceptance of time as a fundamental design variable, in both its predictable and unpredictable forms.

4.3 Unpacking change: recognising the demand

Change is a constant and one of the most powerful drivers in design. However, all changes are not the same; some are 'sharp and striking' (radical), while most are incremental (Baldwin and Clark, 2000). Thus, the nature (routine, non-routine), frequency (low, high) and magnitude (small, large) of changes will differ. Some will be internal to a building (within control), while others will be external (outside of control). Some are more visible than others, while many are poorly monitored. Changes are often complicated because they rarely occur in isolation; they often propagate, making the management of change more difficult (Eckert *et al.*, 2004). There is a consensus that the pace of change is increasing (Douglas, 2006) – some argue 'exponentially' (Blyth and Worthington, 2001), 'frantically' (Fernandez, 2003) – which has led to a growing uncertainty about the future.

There has been a tendency to categorise types of change in the built environment. For example, Slaughter (2001) defines three types that can occur over the life of the building – *function* (change in building use), *capacity* (change in building performance) and *flow* (environmental or user changes); while Gann and Barlow (1996) differentiate between *service factors* (physical issues) and *value factors* (financial issues). Langston *et al.* (2008) explain six types of obsolescence (a resulting condition of the inability to accommodate change) that cover most of the changes listed in the literature: physical, economic, functional, technological, social and legal obsolescence. Table 4.1 summarises the literature under these categories.

The change process is often one in which social shifts (causes) often require a physical reaction (effect), which result in a mismatch between demand (user desires) and supply (building capabilities). However, not all changes require a physical response, as some can be accommodated organisationally, individually or within the latent capacity of the building. The inclusion of time and the unravelling of change begins to envision a building not as a static object in space but as part of a dynamic interplay between form (building) and context (users and environment).

4.4 A building: what is it?

Buildings will be viewed differently by each stakeholder as they can be: an end product for the design team; an asset for an organisation; a formal manifestation of a style for an architectural critic or historian; or a symbol of culture and

These works of perfection don't exist in reality – they have undergone conditions of change: weather, war, age, built upon, used, pieces moved, hidden. Out of one another, inside one another.

Hollis (2009)

The problem is temporary thus the solution must be as well.

Hertzberger (2005)

Table 4.1 Change drivers accumulated from the literature

Physical	Economic	Functional
Weathering	Market fluctuations (real estate values)	Ownership/user needs
Wear and tear	Budget shifts	Organisational expansion/shrinkage
Vandalism	Ownership/use least cost alternative	Type of work (ways of working)
Incompatibility factors (chemical)	Reduction in lease lengths	Quality of workplace (employee comfort)
	Global competition	Flexible employment arrangements
Technological	**Social**	**Legal**
Information technologies	Fashion (aesthetics)	General legislation
Construction methods	Demographics (life expectancy)	Building ordinances (safety regulations)
Material performance	Lifestyle – mobility, density (urbanisation)	Construction standards
Product life cycles	Social agendas, trends	Government grant incentives
Transport facilities	Skills (sophistication of user)	Planning
		Environmental controls

heritage for society. The multiplicity of stakeholders is complicated through time as responsibility and knowledge is often split among those involved. Buildings are undoubtedly highly complex products – a unique combination of requirements and resources that endure design, construction and operational complexities. Leatherbarrow (2008) describes two ways to envision a building, one as 'nothing but a system of components', the other as a 'system of representations outlined in composition and experienced in perception'. The latter expresses the inclusion of time as the formation of user experiences, reinforcing the shift in how we conceptualise buildings from a static to a dynamic perspective. Ballantyne (2002) makes a similar differentiation in defining the difference between buildings and architecture, 'Buildings are solid objects, there is no doubt about that, but they are never in themselves architecture. Architecture is dependent on the observer's culture, and the ideas that are brought to bear on the building … architecture is in the mind of the beholder.'

Within this conceptual space, buildings (architecture) can be seen more as a continual process, a series of events that is continually redefined through its inhabitation, or use – 'society in built form' (Lerup, 1977). However, as Till (2009) explains, today's conventions still define buildings based on functions, through room labels with prescribed dimensions (i.e. space standards) that accommodate an arrangement of furniture. Thus, despite the rejection of modernism's 'form follows function' dogma – architecture continues to be defined in response to a brief, defining each space for a particular subfunction or activity. The problem lies in the inherent confrontation between space and use, reflecting our inability to define what a library, school or park is supposed to be; Tschumi (1996) goes on to propose there is no cause and effect relationship between the two terms – evidenced through the way the functions of buildings have changed over time – while others suggest a widened gap rather than a complete disassociation (see Hertzberger, 2005 or Rabeneck et al., 1973).

Venturi and Scott Brown (2004) and Leupen (2005) suggest revised concepts in an attempt to loosen our disposition for functionalist labels: temporary (flexible) vs. permanent (fixed), polyvalence, semi-permanence, changeability, symbolic and communicative functions – 'a time-based architecture must assume functions to be largely unpredictable except in the most general of terms' (Leupen, 2005). Nevertheless, certain building types are more susceptible to change than others – for example dynamic (offices, healthcare, schools) versus stable (museum, government) – and Brand (1994) makes the point that adaptation is generally easier in 'low-road' buildings, while it can be more difficult in 'high-road', long-lasting buildings with a sustained purpose.

4.5 Context: situating the building

Alexander (1964) viewed design as the combination of an object's form (the solution) and context (the problem) – the objective then is to assure a 'good fit'. Julta (1993) stresses the poor form–context relationship that exists with many buildings as a result of being designed as works of art that have only cosmetically attempted to deal with their surroundings – a condition that has been exacerbated by modernism's inside-out approach that viewed context as a passive background. It has not always been like this, as Collins and Collins (1965) highlight the European Renaissance principle of how buildings and outside spaces were designed together as a single element. Many of the types of change we have described can be understood as initiating from the form's contextual forces that interact with the physical building – political, historical, economic, cultural, etc. In this symbiotic relationship, the contingencies are exacerbated because they rarely operate under conditions having the same boundaries in space, time or meaning. As Bryson (1997) explains, the built environment at any point in time is the evolutionary result of an accumulation of circumstances and decisions made by assorted individuals at different moments.

Despite industry's fixation on the static object, there has been a shift in the literature suggesting that a building should be understood as a dynamic equilibrium created through a network of relational conditions via the transient *agency* of elements in time. This intellectual shift has been explained through the interplay of *behaviours* as Tsukamoto and Kaijima (2010) describe a design world composed of three types of elements – human beings (daily, repetitive acts), natural elements (basic laws of physics) and buildings (a unique sentient creature). Elements within these typologies are of different physical and temporal scales that generate different rhythms (behavioural characteristics and cycles). Tsukamoto and Kaijima's (2010) work is an attempt to synthesise these rhythms or contextual forces into a harmonious architecture. Harrison (1992) singles out information technology as a distinct element that affects the dynamic relationship between the human (organisation) and building.

Leatherbarrow's (2008) desire to define a building purely by its performance (what it does) isolates it from human experience (use) and perceptions (aesthetics). But he goes on to define building performance as a result of contextual

There is no architecture without everyday life, movement and action.

Tschumi (1996)

The best buildings are precisely of their time. They reflect the values, virtues and vices of their time.

Rybczynski (2001)

that a building may possess, but is not intrinsically bound – e.g. through its materiality, image or formal specificity. For example, despite having a particular form and unique image, the building can provide a 'loose-fit' open plan underneath.

The loose-fit camp represents the mainstream approach by providing spatial redundancy. It embodies a broader interpretation of how a building may be used – as one architect put it 'we are always trying to make a "loose-fit" between the programme and the architecture'. The core rationale is the dynamic demand posed by the constantly changing world that buildings inhabit. This is a reaction to the modernist tenet (or indeed that of architecture more generally) of architecture's static nature. Supporters argue that you must accept the notion of fluid change and attempt to design with this in mind. It's about being under-specific, designing things to be capable of doing several things, or things that you don't know about. However, even within the loose-fit group, there was an acknowledged danger of the flip side – designing a solution that is 'too loose' and unable to accommodate the immediate needs of the user.

On the other hand, tight-fit is a reaction to the generic blandness that modernism revealed, or as one architect elegantly contended, 'there's something very nice about a tailor-made suit that only fits me'. This camp argues that adaptability does not require spatial redundancy or imply that the results are inherently inflexible. The promoters of a 'tight-fit' approach felt in reality buildings get adapted for other qualities inherent in 'good' architecture irrespective of whether or not the building embodies 'loose-fit' spatial qualities – i.e. 'good architecture' trumps 'spatial redundancy'. Society tends to keep things that they like and are done well; i.e. design a good building for today that is capable of being knocked around and it will go beyond any single use.

Despite designing only for immediate needs, defenders of this approach remain critical of the brief in an effort to ensure a proper fit between the client's immediate needs and the design. Some explained the inclusion of a loose-fit approach can be the result of 'second-guessing' or a 'cop-out' on the client's part. This position was articulated by the need to work through what the client actually needed as opposed to utilising a generic descriptor to accommodate not actually thinking about how they want to use the building. The attempt here is not to hone in on a single pathway (no adaptability), but to start to eliminate the improbable (infinitely adaptable). Thus, adaptability like most things operates best under appropriate conditions. This position is cautious of 'the Meisen view of universal space'. However, the idea of 'second-guessing' in and of itself is not always a wasteful act, particularly if there is experience that may dictate otherwise.

The majority of designers acknowledge the need to incorporate aspects of both extremes, and the starting point may reflect the type of client. Some believe it is the role of the architect to determine which parts should be highly specific and which are better served as more generic. The level of specificity does not inherently make a space more or less adaptable; it may, however, affect how change can be accommodated. An argument can be made that a loose-fit approach allows the architecture to work less and requires the users

If you make it too loose-fit, then anything goes and it means that the organisation has got no way of structuring their change and their expansion.

Adaptability can be very specific, but it is still adaptability. It is trying to take them [the client] with you and make sure they understand the limits of what they can do and that those limits are appropriate really.

Once you get into that and work out what they actually want to do, it is actually nothing to do with movable walls. It is just that they haven't quite decided what sized classes they're going to teach.

to adapt more (see human-centric approach below) – i.e. less constraints at the space plan level gives the user more freedom to adapt the space at the stuff level (furniture, fit-out). In contrast, a tight-fit approach requires the building to be more accommodating to the user (building-centric) as there are only so many spatial interpretations a user may deploy. This dichotomy between building and user underlies the argument that the building is not the only thing capable of adapting.

5.2 Strategic focus: technology-driven vs. planning-driven

An alternative scepticism for several architects arose with the use of technology as a means to promote adaptability, which was often associated with the High-tech movement. This was viewed more broadly as aestheticising flexibility through componentry rather than implementation of it in reality. This solution type was perceived to be accompanied with a high price tag and often complicated by the bespoke nature of the solution. The manifestation of adaptability in this case was felt to be driven by commercial interests, a way of mitigating risk in fear of obsolescence – if it is adaptable, then I can charge a premium as it is not just one thing, but three. This pessimistic perspective was not shared by all, in the sense that those options do provide value to the client as a legitimate form of risk mitigation. However, the affirmation of adaptability being reduced to an aesthetic was justified through precedents (e.g. Sainsbury Visual Arts Centre; Lloyd's Building) that showcased 'a lack of evidence of its implementation as intended' and 'the rhetoric exceeding the reality'.

The technology-driven approach was also thought to limit adaptability because the solution was restricted to a set number of predetermined conditions. The predetermination of the solution was linked to a modernist notion of adaptability by limiting the solution to a very specific type of lifestyle, scale or work pattern – adaptability through 'physical movement, changing partitions, grids with connections in them'. Suspicion towards these types of solutions was combated with simple, subtle aspects that don't often get talked about, 'the fact that the rooms are well planned and generous and the materials will last well'. Despite certain tactics adding costs, much can be resolved through good planning. For example, the ability to sub-let a floor or divide a floor is the result of simple architectural planning (e.g. multiple access to core). Cost is often determined by whether the adaptability is inherent or whether the adaptability is equivalent to redundancy – the latter of which will almost always add costs.

The simplified planning approach regarding adaptability was characterised as purely making sensible decisions rather than a quantifiable amount of redundancy – understanding how people may use a space and plan for that. Adaptability in this world-view is about catering to an occupational process rather than a built product, 'the whole project has been about process and methodology rather than physical outputs and it has actually helped them as an arts organisation to understand more about what they're doing and how they work with space'.

You could have more Lloyd's building because it has the bolt hole for where you put the next escalator but is that really that adaptable to have a bit more of the same thing.

If you look at some of the buildings that are most adaptable they are like the terraced house that has proved to be an infinitely adaptable form of building. It is not a technology or an innovation driven approach to adaptability but it may be to do with the size and the shape and how it fits into context.

5.3 Object of adaptability: building-centric vs. human-centric

The idea that the building must adapt is as limiting as expecting the occupants to be adaptable. A pertinent example is a client who had built their building designed to be highly adaptable with standardised, modular components, movable partitions, etc. (CAR2&16). At the same time, they occupied an older building where everything was fixed including brick and block partitions. The former was much more expensive to manage because it could be adapted, and they exploited this with regular changes. In contrast they just moved people around in the older building and the occupants had to adapt to deal with its limitations. Whether one led to better business productivity or not is unknown, but the contrasting solutions led to very different approaches for accommodating change within the same organisation.

But this is an extreme case: most believe that the organisation and the building must change together – that it cannot be one extreme or the other. This relates to understanding organisational need rather than pre-subscribing physical solutions – rethinking the organisation and how they do things rather than attempting to use a technology to resolve an issue. One can apply the building layer concept (Figure 6.1, M4) to the stakeholders (social layer) that can be subdivided into a series of layers, e.g. end users, owner and developer/investor, where each has a different role (function) and rate of change to be accommodated.

Generally if you're uncomfortable, you won't sit there in an uncomfortable state if you don't have to, you'll move or you'll change it yourself.

Chapter 6

Buildings as layers

6.1 Layer definitions

One of the clear findings in our research was the interest in seeing a building as a set of layers, whose interaction define in some way its resistance (or otherwise) to change. We have developed Brand's (1994) model for building decomposition (Figure 6.1), which envisions a building as a set of 'shearing' layers that change at different rates – the more the layers are connected, the greater the difficulty and cost of adaptation. His model has been expanded to cover a broader interpretation of the layer concept, adding two layers that are crucial when considering the building in time. These are called (continuing the alliteration) – *social* (humans in and around the building, e.g. users, owners, neighbourhood community) and *surroundings* (larger physical context in which the building sits, e.g. neighbouring buildings, public space). These two modifications are a clear reflection that buildings (and their constituting parts) cannot be thought of in isolation to their surrounding context and that users along with their social perceptions and agendas 'shear' against the building layers.

The additional layers (social, surroundings) can be subdivided into sublayers, e.g. Figure 6.1 decomposes the surrounding layer with seven 'surrounding' bubbles (e.g. natural elements and transportation links). We have avoided explicit labelling of each layer's lifespan as this depends on the components chosen for a particular typology and contextual conditions. The model instead suggests the relative rates of change through the proximity of arrows for each layer – thus space plan 'arrows' are much closer (faster) than those for structure.

6.2 Influence of change on the layers

In our review there were some clear messages about the susceptibility of each layer to changes either planned or implemented in the case study buildings that documented 290 adaptable design solutions. Of these, 200 related to a single building layer (69 per cent), 67 solutions were associated with two building layers (23 per cent) and 23 stretched across three or four layers (8 per cent) – i.e. a majority of adaptable solutions pertained to a single layer with 92 per cent of the solutions linked to either one or two building layers.

Table 6.1 illustrates the prevalence of each layer among the 290 solutions with each numerical column (1–4) indicating the number of solutions for each layer that were independent (1) or linked to multiple layers (2, 3 or 4 respectively). A relationship between layers here represents a dependency – spatial,

building layers nominal categorisations that describe the building at a given scale that allow for the stratification (decomposition) of the building as a way of gaining further insight into how it will change over time.

social humans in and around the building that interact with and play a role in the life of the building.

stuff components/objects that reside inside the space users inhabit.

space plan components that enclose the spaces users inhabit.

services components that supply and transport physical flows – energy, water, communications, elevators.

structure components which support the primary transferring of vertical loads and horizontal bracing.

Social layers could include – individual, work group, department, branch and organisation.

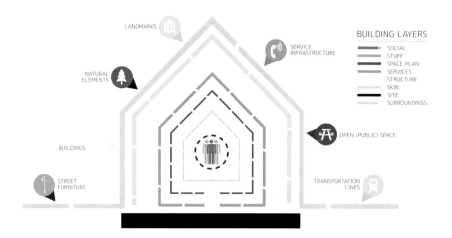

LANDMARKS

SERVICE
INFRASTRUCTURE

NATURAL
ELEMENTS

BUILDINGS

OPEN (PUBLIC) SPACE

STREET
FURNITURE

TRANSPORTATION
LINKS

BUILDING LAYERS

SOCIAL
STUFF
SPACE PLAN
SERVICES
STRUCTURE
SKIN
SITE
SURROUNDINGS

Table 6.1 Decomposition of the 290 solutions relative to the building layers

Layer	1	2	3	4	Total	Total % (290)
social	8	10	4	—	22	8
space	24	8	2	—	34	12
stuff	31	15	4	—	50	17
space plan	61	36	14	2	113	39
services	8	13	16	2	39	13
skin	36	18	9	2	65	22
structure	13	18	8	2	41	14
site	11	11	4	—	26	9
surroundings	8	5	2	—	15	5

site the legal boundary in which the building sits.

surroundings the larger physical context in which a building sits, outside of its specific lot boundaries, comprising both human-made objects and natural geographic conditions.

The propensity for the solution to affect only a single layer should be higher given that only adaptable design solutions were captured from the case studies (opposed to all solutions).

structural and/or service (see section 6.3). This means that the interdependency may be physical (touching) or conceptual in design terms. Thus, the particular solution implemented and the change desired will determine whether or not the interdependency between layers will be affected – i.e. the solution may have a built-in tolerance to absorb propagation across components or layers.

Space plan clearly emerged as the most prevalent layer relating to almost 40 per cent of the 290 adaptable solutions – followed by the skin layer at 22 per cent. The surroundings (5 per cent), social (8 per cent) and site (9 per cent) layers were the least designed for with the remaining layers relatively evenly distributed among the solutions (space, stuff, services and structure). Unsurprisingly, the stuff and space layers were found to be the most independent (approximately two-thirds of their solutions) with the services layer being the most dependent (only one in five solutions were independent). The prevalence of the services layer increased with solutions that were contingent to multiple layers – this is concerning given the independence of the services layer was consistently discussed as the layer that can make the biggest difference in terms of cost savings. The independence of a number of other layers including the space plan and skin emerged close to 50 per cent.

Table 6.2 visualises the distribution of relationships between layers where the grey diagonal illustrates a single building layer. The colour of the remaining cells represent the type of relationship(s) or not that were found between the two layers – e.g. dark blue cells exemplify relationships that were revealed in multiple incidences that spanned 2, 3 and 4 layer solutions. The surroundings layer materialised as having the fewest links to other layers. Space plan and services layers were linked to all other layers – however, many of the services layer links occurred in fewer cases. Additionally, the table identifies relationships that surfaced repeatedly among the solutions – this is visualised with an x in the relevant cells. Looking across Tables 6.1 and 6.2, arguably a subset of interdependent building layers emerges – space plan, services, skin and structure (coloured dark blue in Table 6.2).

Table 6.2 Distribution of relationships between building layers

	Social	Space	Stuff	Space Plan	Services	Skin	Structure	Site	Surroundings
social									
space									
stuff									
space plan			X						
services				X					
skin				X					
structure				X		X			
site									
surroundings								X	

	no relationship
	Isolated layer
	2 layers
	2 and 3 layers
	3 layers
	1,2,3 and 4 layers
x	strong link

The space plan layer is the most dominantly designed for and linked layer.

A number of strategies became evident to reduce the effects of change:

1   Keeping as many elements as possible outside the structural layer created an immutable infrastructure around which change can occur – e.g. the use of a framed solution separates the function of structure (columns and beams), space plan (internal partitions) and skin (exterior façade), while a load-bearing solution combines two or more layers.
2   The separation between the shortest (stuff and space plan) and longest (structure) lifespan components is often proposed as a way of enabling a user to reconfigure their space.
3   Movable solutions are primarily of the stuff and space plan layers purposefully separated from other space plan elements and the service layer.

Table 6.3 provides examples of such strategies organised by building layer.

Table 6.3 Example design tactics for building layers

Building layer	Design parameter	Tactic examples
Space	room	standardisation, big-volume and clusters
Stuff	furniture systems	standardised, modular, movable
Space plan	partition walls	sliding, demountable, non-load-bearing, glass
	flooring	raised floor systems, carpet tiles
	organisational solutions	planning grids for electrical outlets, lighting and partitions
Services	access	exposed, gridded systems, removable panels, clear zones
	capacity	20% surplus
	zoning	user and area control
Skin	façade	demountable, standardised
Structure	wide spans	6–10.8m
	high storey height	4–7.5m
	increased load capacity	oversized foundations, floor loadings
	prefabricated members	trussed rafters, cross-laminated timber

6.3 Understanding dependency: DSM explained

Our research revealed DSM to be one of the most powerful tools available to reveal the complex interdependencies between building systems that are the bane of adaptation. A dependency structure matrix (DSM) is a square N × N cell matrix that maps the relationships between elements within a single domain. DSMs are powerful devices that capture the dependency state of a system, each pair being either independent (blank cell), dependent (X depends upon Y) or interdependent (X depends on Y and Y depends upon X). They not only present an excellent graphical picture but can also be manipulated to identify optimal patterns and disentanglement strategies. DSMs are either *static* (e.g. of a product or organisation) or *time-based* (of activity). Browning (2001) presents an excellent overview.

Static DSMs are analysed by clustering, which involves rearranging elements into chunks or modules that have a high amount of interactions internally and low interactions externally – Figure 6.2. Another strategic manoeuvre is to isolate elements that have high interactions across several chunks as *bus* or *integrating components* (Sharman and Yassine, 2004).

Time-based DSMs represent a temporal flow (a process architecture) and are optimised through sequencing (Eppinger and Browning, 2012). *Sequencing*

▶ Figure 6.2
A DSM model (M5) composed of eight elements (A–G) before and after clustering

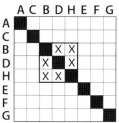

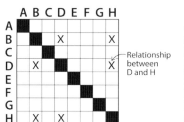Relationship between D and H

(also called *partitioning*) orders activities into a logical sequence identifying sequential, parallel, coupled and conditional relationships between tasks. This type is ideally suited to the planning and management of complex design processes including the Analytical Design Planning Technique – ADePT (Austin *et al.*, 2000).

Most DSMs are binary (either a dependency exists or doesn't) but some use numerical values, colour or other symbols that capture additional attributes of the system, to indicate the importance, strength or type of interaction. Identification of relationship types, while not always necessary for the analysis, helps gather and verify relationships between elements. A variety of relationship types exist, most of which evolve from Pimmler and Eppinger's (1994) four types: spatial (adjacency), energy (energy transfer), information (data or signal exchange) and material (material exchange). The work reported here builds upon the types proposed in the literature, but have been translated to accommodate building terminology and context. Three distinct types of flows are applied: (1) structural (e.g. gravitational, lateral), (2) spatial (e.g. adjacency, circulation), and (3) service (e.g. energy, water). Table 6.4 illustrates the types of dependencies classified under each type of flow and Figure 6.3 shows an example from a case study of a building that mapped the physical and spatial dependencies between building components in a static DSM.

Table 6.4 eBuilding relationship types

Primary class	Sub-class							
SE = Service	W = Water	E = Energy	A = Air	D = Data/Com.	GW = Grey/Black Water	SA = Sanitation		
SP = Spatial	CI = Circulation	D = Distance	AD = Adjacencies	L = Light	S = Sound	M = Material	PR = Proportions	V = Visual
ST = Structural	GF = Gravitational Forces		LF = Lateral Forces					

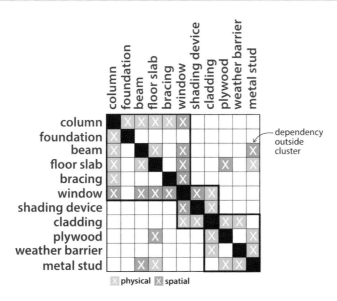

◄ Figure 6.3
Example of a clustered DSM based on dependency types

The method clearly relies on thorough validation of the dependencies, sometimes complicated by the different ways (and degrees to which) elements can depend on another. Once assembled, matrices can be manipulated manually or automatically using an algorithm. Manual clustering can be challenging in identifying appropriate cluster boundaries and the decision perhaps arbitrary. However, it does offer several benefits, bringing into play the system architect's tacit knowledge, but requires a logical process as well as expert knowledge. One helpful approach is to test preconceived modules by individually adjusting the boundaries with rules (see Schmidt III et al., 2011).

In addition to using clustering to optimize the product architecture, static DSMs can also be used to analyse the impact of change. The concept of following dependencies within a DSM to assess the impact of change is rooted in its process origins (see Steward, 1981). More recently, Eckert et al. (2004) applied the concept to a product DSM to classify components based on their behaviour during change events, quantifying the number of changes a component absorbed (dependencies in) against the number of changes propagated (dependencies out). The work also includes a probability or risk factor associated with each change by including a degree of likelihood the change would occur. The classification system has recently been applied to a retail project in the construction industry and proved helpful in addressing the cost magnitude of change (Grinnell et al., 2012). Both applications for a static DSM – clustering and impact analysis – are applied to the Cellophane House in sections 6.4 and 7.8 as technical examples.

6.4 Cellophane House, part I: clustering analysis

The building layers model (M4) was used in conjunction with the DSM tool to assess the adaptability of the Cellophane House (Figure 6.4). The analysis centred on identifying and isolating functional modules – i.e. how well do the building's components group into isolated layers? Functional modules and layers should not be confused as being the same, although the two concepts are used here harmoniously as organising (layers) and analytical method (modules) – hence a goal of the analysis is to see how the building's system aligns with and/or breaks the layers model.

The Cellophane House is an exemplar industrialised building that explicitly sought to reorganise the production and product conditions compared to conventional construction and therefore is well suited to a discussion of adaptability. It was designed by Kieran Timberlake Architects as the result of a competition held in 2007 by MoMA – Home Delivery: Fabricating the Modern Dwelling. The unique context of the competition encouraged a self-contained product reducing many of the complexities found in a conventional building. Key to the design concept were transparency, lightness and mass customisation of a standardised (structural) product platform through the use of standardised 'infill' products. The majority of the building was produced off-site as volumetric elements in New Jersey and came to New York on trucks. Being a full-scale prototype makes the *system architecture* relatively simple, while

▶ Figure 6.4 (OPPOSITE PAGE)
Cellophane House
Courtesy Peter Aaron/OTTO for Kieran Timberlake Associates

still being sophisticated from the point of view of an industrialised building – enabling a clear analysis and discussion.

Figure 6.5 shows the initial DSM structured in the five layers plus connection materials, graphically exposing the extent of interaction between the layers. With the exception of the structure layer, the remaining layers are sparsely defined. Inside the remaining layers are small groups of components (e.g. 12–14, 30–1 and 32–3). The addition of connection materials as *bus components* shows an important characteristic in that some carry dependencies across layers while others are sparse and limited to one layer.

Figure 6.6 illustrates a manually clustered matrix restricted to moving elements within the layers (with the exception of components identified as buses and the distribution of connection materials that were sparsely populated) revealing 10 clusters. Just six 'floating' dependencies exist now outside the refined clusters demonstrating how well the designers disentangled the building systems, a key objective of an exhibition building. In addition two components, wall partition (19) and flooring (23) *pin* clusters (6, 7 and 8) together within the space plan layer.

The next step used this DSM as a starting point to run a clustering algorithm in Loomeo, a powerful DSM clustering software. Ten clusters were identified tightly bound along the diagonal (Figure 6.7) placing at the top three integrating components plus those with no other dependencies. The exception is the cluster 'Services (ventilation)' that is *pinned* between bus components 'bolts & fasteners' (39) and 'structural frame' (4). The clusters are small and compact. Seven dependencies (2 asymmetrical) were highlighted outside the clusters. 'LED lights kitchen' (26) appears to *pin* clusters 9 and 10 (binding the space plan and stuff layers). This *pinning* (with 'kitchen appliances' (32)) appears to *hold away* 'kitchen cabinets' (33) from 'flooring' (23). Two questions were prompted by the analysis:

(a) Should the components at the top of the matrix be left independent or should they form a cluster(s)?
(b) With approximately half the floating dependencies, should wall partition (19) form an auxiliary bus to which multiple clusters are *pinned*?

The design of the Cellophane House included several IPDs (Integrated Project Deliveries) which are a multi-technological complex part produced as a separate product process and delivered as a 'finished' product to be installed on site – for a detailed breakdown, see Vibæk (2011).

Observations from the manual manipulation (Figure 6.6) and automated clustering (Figure 6.7) led to a final iteration of the DSM that attempted to: remove the floating dependencies; investigate the remaining clusters and component classifications in comparison to the IPDs; and lastly sequence the modules as an indication of their rate of change – *structure*, the longest lasting building layer, at the top left to the quickest *stuff* layer at the bottom right. The result of the three steps is presented in Figure 6.8. The relationship between 'flooring' (23) and 'stairs' (24) is the only floating dependency that remains (floater 1). This is due to the 'flooring' (23) being *pinned* between two clusters, cluster (10) stuff and cluster (9) space plan. An alternative solution would have the 'flooring' (23) as an auxiliary bus changing how the dependency is viewed. On the other hand, 'partition wall' (19) also has dependencies in three clusters, but is resolved to a certain extent by *pinning* 'flooring' (23) and 'LED lights kitchen'

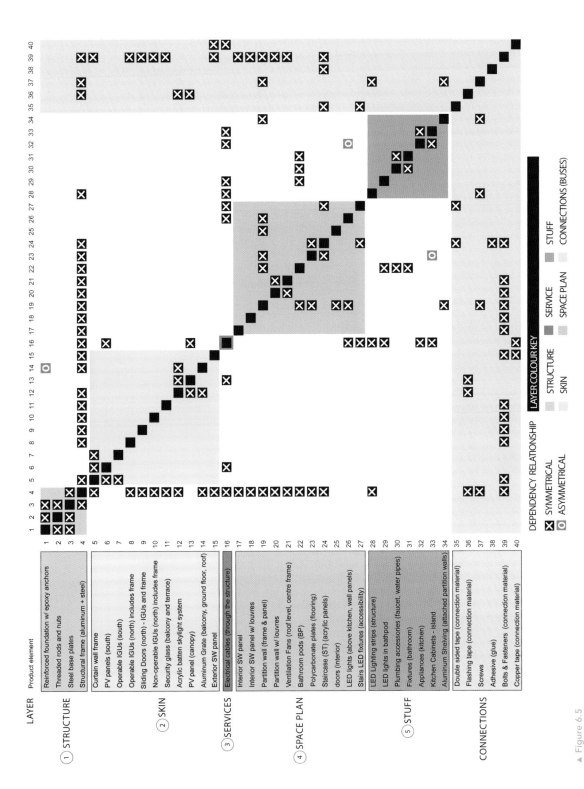

▲ Figure 6.5

Initial DSM in layer order reveals their interactions

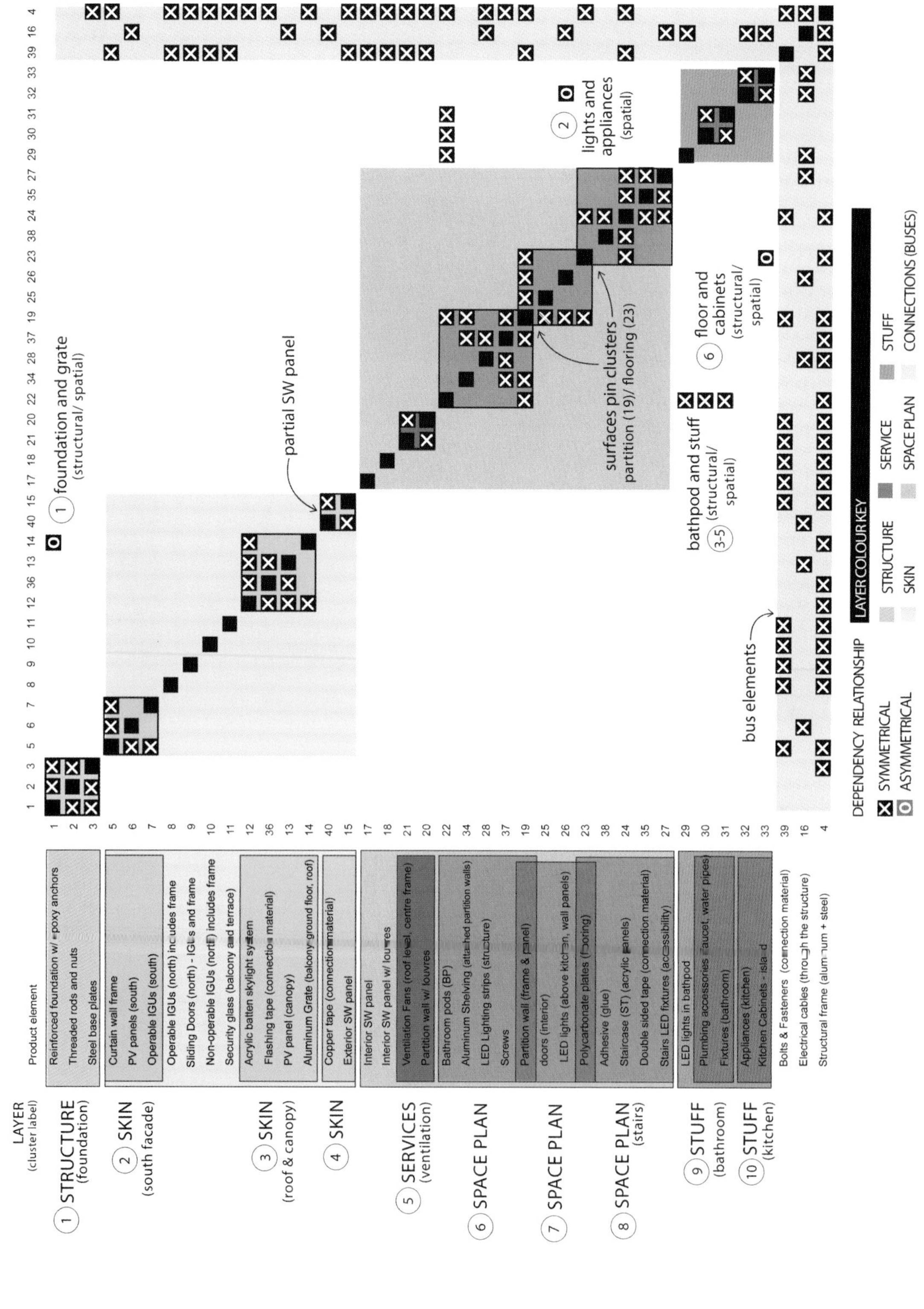

▲ Figure 6.6
Manually clustered DSM (within layers)

PART III A THEORY OF ADAPTABILITY

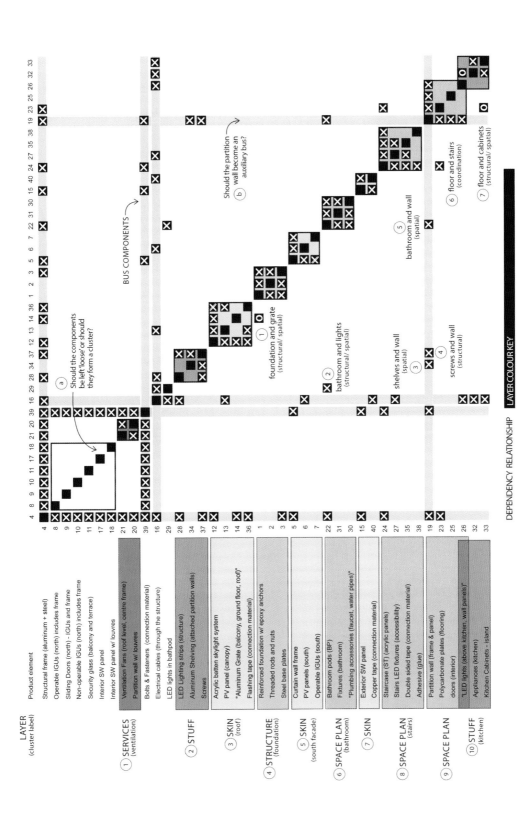

▲ Figure 6.7

Loomeo's automated clustered DSM

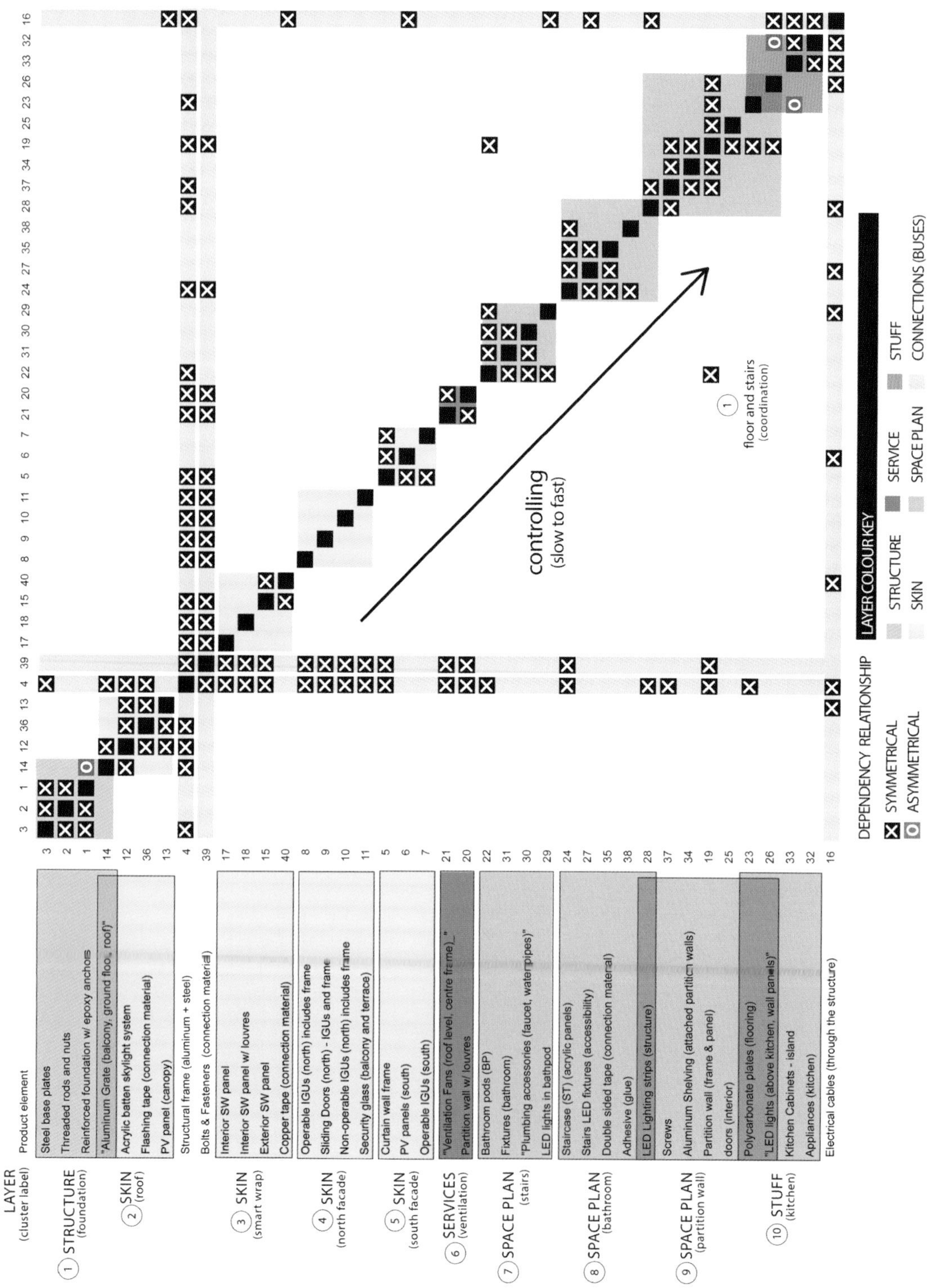

▲ Figure 6.8
Final clustered DSM

(26) to cluster (10) – creating an overlap between the three clusters. It is also worth mentioning that two overlaps in clusters are not due to a component being *pinned* between multiple clusters, but because the same component has two different applications in the system yet represented only once in the DSM ('aluminium grate' (14) and 'acrylic batten skylight' (12)). This reflects a representational issue, not a system one). Whereas in the previous case, 'flooring' (23) and 'LED lights kitchen' (26) are *pinned* between layers as a consequence of the design. This would be worth further investigation as it links change between elements of the highly changeable *stuff* layer with elements of the slower *space plan* layer. It is also problematic because the 'partition wall' (19) is *pinned* to another *space plan* cluster linking (8) 'Space plan (bathroom)' to the *stuff* layer.

The categorisation of components within layers can be to a certain extent subjective, but it's also important to note that the process can be enlightening by revealing new ways of seeing a building system. There were three instances where components were initially categorised in one layer and ended up in another. The 'interior SW panels' (17 and 18) were considered as part of the *space plan* layer since they formed the interior portion of the wall and were physically separate from the exterior SW panels which were considered part of the *skin* layer. In the end, the three components were clustered together – (3) Skin (smart wrap) – reflecting an IPD and nestled against the 'structural frame' (4) and 'bolts & fasteners' (39) buses. In this case, assembly or production logic lent itself as a more logical way of clustering them rather than leaving the components isolated (a potential limitation of a product DSM). A second pair of *space plan* elements – 'partition walls w/ louvres' (20) and 'ventilation fans' (21) – were clustered together and determined a service function – (6) Services (ventilation). Lastly, some swapping occurred between the *stuff* and *space plan* layers. Three elements (29–31) left the *stuff* layer to form the bathroom cluster bundling them with their integrating 'component bathroom pod' (22). Another approach would have been to leave the three components clustered together within the *stuff* layer and allow the bathroom pod to act as an auxiliary bus, given the likelihood of those components changing more frequently than the bathroom pod itself.

A last observation relates to bus components. The system was designed for elements to fix to the 'structural frame' (4), so it makes sense that this component is acting as an integrating element. 'Bolts & fasteners' (39) acting as a second bus component is a result of modelling the connection materials and the dependency between 'structural frame' (4) and attached components thus splits into two types (structural and spatial). The third bus component 'electrical cables' (16) are interwoven into the 'structural frame' (4) and can create serious propagation issues with any changes.

Overall, the system clustered well into discrete groups that were for the most part isolated within a single layer and integrated by three bus components (structural frame, bolts & fasteners and electrical cables). Previous clustering attempts of other building systems generally have significantly more dependencies between clusters (see Schmidt III *et al.*, 2009); whereas, a single 'floating' dependency within the same layer can be very favourable.

Chapter 7

A typology of adaptability

The notion of literal adaptability presents problems when it is translated from the realm of the ideal into that of the real.

Alan Colquhoun (1981)

adaptability type can be defined as a classification for a particular change objective that shares a subset of characteristics and tactics under the umbrella of adaptability

The concept of universal adaptability is a myth, it 'is both technically and economically unachievable' (Finch, 2009) and as Leaman and Bordass (2004) point out, 'The essence of adaptability is to invest in the outset in the things you are really going to need, and to leave to others the option of adding (or subtracting) things you are not sure about.' De Neufville *et al.* (2008) add that, 'flexibility is only valuable if it is exercised effectively (when the time is right) and efficiently (at acceptable cost and disruption)'. If throwing every possible solution for adaptability at a building can be a waste of time, money and resources – how do you determine what might be needed in the future?

One answer lies in thinking more specifically about the type(s) of change that might occur and about how they can be accommodated. In an effort to describe the changes envisaged, the literature often categorises types of adaptability – this can pertain to what changes (e.g. spatial layout, building volume or building use), the speed or magnitude of the change and whether or not physical alterations are needed. The difficulty lies in the inconsistency and interchangeability of language and lack of criteria. During our research we hypothesised a comprehensive set of adaptability types related to the *type* of change. Subsequent analysis of the literature largely confirmed them, with some adjustments, as illustrated in Figure 7.1. The purpose of the types is to make explicit the nature of adaptability that is desired – to improve on the imprecision in language as stakeholders often struggle to articulate their goals through the design process.

Despite a difference in labelling, changes in *use*, *physical layout* and *size* are found consistently throughout the literature. Some chose to subdivide a type, such as Priemus (1968) who makes a distinction between multifunctionality (use in different ways without physical changes) and polyvalence (use in different ways with physical changes. We chose to split layout into two categories that reflect two different, but very common, timescales; hence change of *task* (daily or weekly basis change of furniture, equipment or user) and change of *space* (a more holistic spatial reconfiguration).

We also found references that extend beyond spatial layout to include the capacity to change the building's components or *performance* (see Arge, 2005) – the concept includes the capacity to adapt to new technologies or enhance performance (refitable). Our *movable* category was unsurprisingly less common in the literature – despite its place in history dating back to pre-historic shelters. It is not a common requirement but held its place, as it has

ADJUSTABLE

plug 'n' play services

adjustable seat

movable equipment

CHANGE OF TASK

VERSATILE

glass partitions can be moved

open plan space

CHANGE OF SPACE

REFITABLE

reversible connections

accessible service zone

CHANGE OF PERFORMANCE

SCALABLE

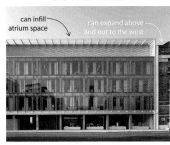

can infill atrium space

can expand above and out to the west

CHANGE OF SIZE

CONVERTIBLE

office or warehouse depending on the market

CHANGE OF USE

MOVABLE

can move depending on the weather

CHANGE OF LOCATION

established a market particularly for temporary solutions. Our work thus sets out six types of change, namely:

▲ Figure 7.1
Adaptability types illustrated

> *Adjustable* – change of task/user
> *Versatile* – change of space
> *Refitable* – change of performance
> *Convertible* – change of use
> *Scalable* – change of size
> *Movable* – change of location

We have found that such a concise but comprehensive vocabulary can assist briefing and clarify goal-setting. The six types of adaptability can be organised along a spatial–physical spectrum that coincides with the 3Rs of sustainability (Figure 7.2). The spatial types – versatile and convertible were found to be much more prevalent than physical types. In addition, spatial and physical types of adaptability behave differently – e.g. spatial types are spread throughout the building layers, while physical types are more concentrated in one or two building layers.

The reader may then ask how such capacities for change are built into a design. Our answer is each requires certain building characteristics (Chapter 9).

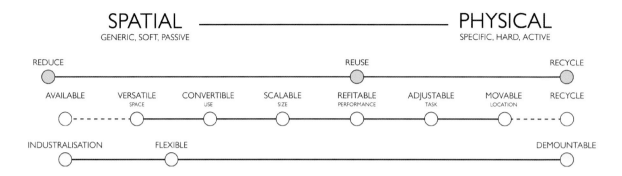

SPATIAL ——————————————————— PHYSICAL
GENERIC, SOFT, PASSIVE   SPECIFIC, HARD, ACTIVE

REDUCE   REUSE   RECYCLE

AVAILABLE   VERSATILE   CONVERTIBLE   SCALABLE   REFITABLE   ADJUSTABLE   MOVABLE   RECYCLE
                    SPACE   USE   SIZE   PERFORMANCE   TASK   LOCATION

INDUSTRALISATION   FLEXIBLE   DEMOUNTABLE

Each type is described below with reference to brief examples; many more are presented in the case studies section of the book (see Part IV).

7.1 AT1 – Adjustable

Designing a building to be adjustable involves ensuring that the 'stuff' inside the building, such as furniture, fixtures and equipment, can be reconfigured easily to accommodate changing tasks. The high frequency of changes may relate to occupants, environmental conditions or technology. Adjustable solutions provide a more efficient workplace and increased user comfort (e.g. the shape, configurability of furniture and fixtures). It may reduce the demand for new equipment for different tasks and increase the users' control over their environment such as light levels or furniture location.

Examples of adjustable design can be found in a number of sectors, but particularly where occupants engage in a variety of tasks in the same space, such as in education, healthcare or R&D. For example, Mossbourne Community Academy provided adjustable desks that conceal computers allowing them to be used for multiple purposes and the dining hall is stocked with collapsible furniture. In addition, the office sector is one in which adjustable design has become increasingly important in recent years, as changes in information technology and working practices have increased the versatility of our daily routines.

GlaxoSmithKline, a large pharmaceutical company, developed FlexiLab to help to respond to the expensive reorganisation of its laboratories which were limited by fixed configurations (Figure 7.3). The design allows the scientists to adjust their working units (fume cupboards, local exhaust ventilation systems, benching, etc.) to a variety of tasks within a compact area.

7.2 AT2 – Versatile

One of the most common adaptability types is versatility to change the spatial layout of a room. Such changes may be brought about by variations in activities, organisational structure/philosophy, ownership or occupant. An organisation can avoid costly refits and reduce disruptions with services, lighting and acoustics that can be easily configured. Spaces can be easily and cheaply

▲ Figure 7.3
Flexilab system
Courtesy GlaxoSmithKline

rearranged to address different activities (e.g. after-hours or special events), new work patterns (e.g. open plan, hot-desking), or a change in the number of users (e.g. permanent or temporary fluctuations). A number of the building's physical parameters can shape the versatility of a space including: the number and location of columns, the plan shape and depth, the overall area, the location of services and lighting, and the movability of walls, furniture, and fixtures. The changes primarily affect the '*stuff*', '*space plan*' and '*service*' layers.

The Sainsbury Centre for Visual Arts (SCVA) took advantage of a prefabricated steel lattice frame to provide a 35m span of uninterrupted open space by 135m in length. The versatility of the space is strengthened with the use of movable study rooms, partition screens, display cases and stands (Figure 7.4).

7.3 AT3 – Refitable

Refitable design strategies involve changing the performance of a building by altering its space, services or skin. These can occur with changes in law, regulations, environmental conditions, technologies or materials. This often requires access through, or the temporary displacement of, components in the *stuff* and *space plan* layers. The most common complication arises when the existing service system is entangled with other layers (e.g. *structure* or *skin*). An example of a refitable design strategy would be 'designing in' the potential to change a building's skin and services so that they can achieve improved levels of thermal performance in order to mitigate against the risk of obsolescence due to potential climate change, higher energy prices or new legislation.

Large, open interior space of SCVA
Courtesy Katherine Wall

Designers should therefore consider the different lifespans of components and how they will be replaced by considering construction and deconstruction processes. The way the building is detailed becomes extremely important – recesses or gaps enhance the refitability over butting or overlapping thus minimising the points of contact between systems.

The ability of building owners to easily refit and change the energy performance of their buildings is likely to become increasingly important in the future, particularly as energy-efficient buildings become more attractive to occupiers and start to command a premium over 'hard to treat' buildings. SCVA is a good example of a refitable cladding solution based upon a kit of parts with five types of panel: flat glazed, solid or grilled, and rounded solid or glazed (Figure 7.5). The scale and connection enabled a single person to quickly unfasten the six bolts and refit new panels – reducing the construction time and costs (Lambot, 1989).

7.4 AT4 – Convertible

Convertible, sometimes perceived as synonymous with adaptable, refers to a change in use prompted by alterations in the market, social demands, ownership or occupancy for instance. Many buildings are converted to accommodate new functions, even though such a change was never envisaged when it

was originally designed. Conversion is easier between similar structural typologies (short span, wide span or 'big box'), but can also happen across types with proper planning. Switches between types tend to work more frequently in one direction (e.g. offices to residential). The capacity for multiple conversions depends on the capacity and location of various physical elements (e.g. services, circulation, acoustics, floor loadings and fire design). Providing a higher than necessary (for first use) floor capacity is a simple tactic that can allow for increased loading later. Other critical parameters include storey height, structural grid, plan depth and total usable area. The conversion of offices to residential or hotel also requires consideration of the location and number of cores when first designed, as they will require more points of penetration (e.g. additional service risers).

Examples in the UK include Victorian mill buildings and 1960s office buildings that have been converted to residential use. One of the most famous examples of adapted buildings in London is the Tate Modern (power plant to museum). However, some buildings are specifically designed with change of function in mind. For instance, 3D Reid's Multispace concept was developed to enable building owners to alter the use in a development scheme to reflect evolving market conditions, without having to alter the building's shell and structure (Davison *et al.*, 2006). Another example of designing for convertibility is SEGRO's Energy Park in Vimercate near Milan (Figure 7.6), which was

designed to be fitted out either as an office, warehouse, laboratory or store. As an investor-developer with a long-term interest in the buildings that it develops, SEGRO sees adaptable design as a key part of its business strategy for responding to changing occupier demand for buildings.

7.5 AT5 – Scalable

Scalable relates to the building's capacity to change size – can you add or take away from the building horizontally or vertically? A company may change size frequently due to market conditions, budget shifts, or social conditions. The notion of designing buildings to be scalable is particularly appealing to organisations with financial constraints, plans for growth or contraction, or uncertain future space requirements. Different elements will play a role depending on whether you're adding vertically (e.g. additional load capacity for the slabs and foundation, type of roof structure, access plan and building height regulations) or horizontally (plot density, circulation/access points and service capacity). Adding on to a building can benefit from the use of simple shapes or modular components as well as local materials are most easily matched/replaced in the future.

For example, in the 1970s the National Health Service (NHS) introduced the Nucleus Hospital programme during a period of limited capital

▲ Figure 7.7
Extension (left) onto the existing building (right)
Courtesy Swanke Hayden Connell

spending, the idea being that small-scale hospitals could be built (with a standard template of 1,000m² blocks) to house a nucleus of departments that could then be expanded at a later date, as more capital funding became available (Francis *et al.*, 1999). The Civil and Building Engineering building at Loughborough University is another example of a structure that was designed to be scaled as part of a modular tartan grid master plan, but when demand for additional space a rose not all the provisions were utilised as envisioned. The irregular shape addition did not follow the original grid, but took advantage of several of the building's physical features: the square shape, structural redundancy and shape of the perimeter columns, lack of load-bearing walls, foundation pads, and the ease of removing the modular exterior wall/windows (Figure 7.7).

7.6 AT6 – Movable

Movable (change of location) is the least likely to occur of all the types but can be necessary under certain conditions and with particular building typologies. As changes in demographics, market and environment continue to increase pace, does designing every building to last a long time in a single location still make sense? Certain building typologies clearly lend themselves to transient conditions/events (e.g. concerts, festivals, theatre sets) demanding easy set-up and quick removal. Temporary enclosure of exterior space can provide additional space for an event or fluctuations in occupational capacity. Movable is tied heavily to the *refitable* type, the structural solution chosen, plot density (accessibility) and scale of components.

One of the most notable examples of a movable building is the British Antarctic Survey's Halley VI Research Station (Figure 7.8), which was designed with legs and skis so that it can be periodically moved inland as the ice sheet on which it sits slowly moves out to sea (Abley and Schwinge, 2006). However, while truly movable buildings are few and far between, it is not unusual for specific parts of buildings to be designed to be movable. For instance, the Igus factory in Cologne includes stand-alone office pods that can be moved around the factory's floor as business processes change.

7.7 Occurrence of the types

In our review of 290 design solutions from the case studies we found that 174 related to a single adaptability type (60 per cent), 107 solutions with two types (37 per cent) and just nine solutions (3 per cent) that stretched across three

▼ Figure 7.8
Movable module of the Haley VI project
Courtesy Hugh Broughton Architects

Table 7.1 Distribution of design solutions among adaptability types

	ADJUSTABLE	VERSATILE	REFITABLE	CONVERTIBLE	SCALABLE	MOVABLE
ADJUSTABLE (task)	27					
VERSATILE (space)	10	59				
REFITABLE (performance)	—	1	25			
CONVERTIBLE (use)	1	68	6	45		
SCALABLE (size)	—	6	6	7	18	
MOVABLE (location)	—	—	—	—	—	—

adaptability types. Table 7.1 shows the distribution of the solutions where the blue diagonal illustrates the solutions pertaining to a single type and the white cells those that related to two types.

Tables 7.2 and 7.3 give the percentages for two conditions – single adaptability type (7.2) and the relationships between pairs of types (7.3). The data reveals that versatile and convertible have a strong presence as the sole purpose of the adaptation, while adjustable, refitable and scalable form a second tier and movable did not occur. Versatile and convertible have a strong combined relationship as well with 63 per cent of the linked solutions and almost one in every four solutions overall. The table also indicates tendencies between other types albeit not as strong (e.g. adjustable and versatile) along with conditions between types that have almost no relationship, such as adjustable and scalable. The findings indicate spatial types have a significant relationship to each other while the physical types are more independent.

We found that most of the time the implementation of one adaptability type did not hinder another; however, some tensions can arise in combination. For example, the versatility of a space can be affected by how it is heated. Underfloor heating pipes allow more adjustability and versatility within a room, as it frees up wall space (display area and storage) by removing a fixed object (radiator). A problem arises, however, if the space plan is reconfigured (e.g.

Table 7.1 does not visualise the nine solutions that stretched across three adaptability types.

Table 7.2 Percentage of single type solutions

Single adaptability type	Percentage of solutions (174)
Adjustable (task)	16
Versatile (space)	34
Refitable (performance)	14
Convertible (use)	26
Scalable (size)	10
Movable (location)	0

Table 7.3 Relationship tendency between types

Relationship between two types	Percentage of solutions (107)
Adjustable and Versatile	10
Adjustable and Convertible	1
Versatile and Convertible	63
Versatile and Scalable	5
Versatile and Refitable	1
Refitable and Scalable	5
Refitable and Convertible	8
Convertible and Scalable	7

move a wall) as it will likely require a change in the layout of the pipes underneath, which are typically embedded in the screed (a service and structure interaction). This solution improves the performance initially at the expense of future change (versatility and refitability). A separate example is pumping cold water through a concrete slab to activate the thermal mass and allowing the slab to be thinner. The caveat is the caution required when attempting to drill holes in the slab for partitioning that can lead to costly repairs – thus it can be seen to limit future adaptability options with regards to penetration (space plan versatility); however, it can also be seen to enhance adaptability as grilles don't have to be moved around when a space is changed and half the ducts are no longer necessary (ventilation is still required).

7.8 Cellophane House, part II: impact analysis

In this analysis the adaptability types are applied as discrete scenarios to the Cellophane House project to examine change propagation by tracing component dependencies within the DSM constructed (see Chapter 6, section 6.3). An impact analysis was carried out on each of the scenarios as follows:

1 Identify component(s) which would be affected.
2 Trace the row of the component that is identified, highlighting the horizontal component's dependencies.
3 Assess each dependency regarding the effect the change of the horizontal component would have on the vertical component.
4 If the vertical component is physically affected it is highlighted and its row is assessed in a subsequent iteration (e.g. round 2).
5 Steps 2–4 are repeated until propagation ends.

A feasibility rating for each of the scenarios was then assigned by the DSM modeller based on the number of components affected via the propagation and the nature of those changes (e.g. amount of work and cost). A simple three-level scale was adopted identifying whether the scenario was feasible, somewhat feasible or not feasible. Separately, an assessment of the scenarios was carried out by a system expert (an architect with extensive knowledge of the building system), who rated the feasibility of the system to accommodate each scenario using the same scale based on his knowledge of the system.

Table 7.4 presents the results of the analysis. The feasibility level assigned to each scenario is captured in columns 3 and 4 – A (system expert) and B (DSM modeller). The numbers (1–3) reflect the feasibility level of the scenario – *feasible* (1), *somewhat feasible* (2) and *not feasible* (3). In addition, some of the scenarios were determined to be impossible to assess based on the information presented in the DSM and are labelled – *unclear* (x). Scenarios were deemed *unclear* for one of two reasons: the scenarios and the DSM were at a different granularity level or a new component was added in the scenario that was not included in the DSM. In both cases additional information was needed to carry out the analysis. The feasibility levels are accompanied in the adjacent columns with positive/negative rationales.

Table 7.4 Analysis for 30 change scenarios applied to Cellophane House

Type	Scenario	A	B	System expert (A)	DSM modeller (B)
Adjustable	Add additional furniture	1	1	(+) No problems	Flooring (23)
	Adjust lighting	1	3	(+) Capacity within fixtures (26–9)	(−) Electrical cables (16), (−) fixtures (26–9)
	Alter room temperature	2	2	(+) Natural ventilation, (−) poor air tightness	(+) Natural ventilation, (−) system limitations
Versatile	Add a new partition	2	2	(−) Component scale, (−) lack of space	(−) Flooring (23)
	Alter a partition	3	2	(−) Component scale, (−) relationship w/installations (22)	(−) Flooring (23)
	Alter bathroom pod	3	3	(−) Fixed position w/partition walls (19) and vertical shaft	(−) Partition walls (19), (−) assembly
	Alter structural frame	3	3	(−) Specific capacity of each member	(−) Number of dependencies
	Alter kitchen layout	2	2	(−) Component specificity	(−) Cables (16)
	Move staircase	3	3	(−) Structural composition	(−) Flooring (23), (−) assembly (24)
Refitable	Replace bathroom pod	2	3	(−) Volumetric assembly (22), (+) Structurally independent	(−) Partition walls (19), (−) volumetric assembly (22)
	Replace a partition	2	1	(−) Component scale, (−) lack of space	(+) Bolts (39)
	Add mechanical heating	2	3	(−) Poor air tightness	(−) Partition walls (19), (−) electrical cables (16),
	Replace flooring	1	1	(+) Simply lifted out	(+) Kitchen cabinets (33), appliances (32)
	Add ceiling	2	1	(+) Simple to install, (+) enhance acoustics	(+) Bolts (39)
	Replace façade panel	1	1	(+) Easy to disassemble and insert different solution	(+) Bolts (39), (+) copper tape (40)

(Continued)

Table 7.4 (Continued)

Type	Scenario	A	B	System expert (A)	DSM modeller (B)
	Replace panel material	2	x	Take panel off and change in factory	wrong granularity
	Add shading device	1	1	(+) Could be installed on exterior or integrated into panel	(+) Bolts (39)
	Replace ventilation fans	1	2	(+) Unbolt	(−) Partition wall (20)
	Add new lighting	1	3	(+) Redundancy in electrical cables (16)	(−) Electrical cables (16)
	Replace structural member	2	3	(−) Structural integrity	(−) Number of dependencies
	Enclose terrace for winter	2	x	(+) Lightweight solution	insufficient information
Scalable	*Enclose terrace complete*	3	x	(−) Insufficient load capacity	insufficient information
	Remove 3rd floor	2	x	(+) Partial disassembly	wrong granularity
	Add space horizontally	2	x	(−) Creates a deep plan	insufficient information
	Make lower floor an interior	3	x	(−) Insufficient foundation; (−) floor height	insufficient information
	Add structural member	1	2	(−) Depends on structural capacity	(−) Number of dependencies
	Split dwelling into two	3	x	(−) Circulation	insufficient information
Convertible	*Alter functional use*	1	2	(−) Acoustics, (−) thermal control, (−) lighting control	(+) Panels, (−) lighting, (−) bathroom pod, (−) kitchen cabinets
Movable	*Change locations*	1	1	(+) Good reusability of materials, (−) climate conditions	(+) Bolts (39)

Example scenario: add a new partition (versatile)

A single scenario is presented to illustrate the process. In this case, both agreed on the feasibility level – *somewhat feasible* (2), but offered different rationales for coming to the same decision. With regard to the DSM, review of the *partition wall's* row (round 01) indicated there were eight dependencies that should be considered (Figure 7.9). All but two, 'structural frame' (4) and 'flooring' (23), were dismissed, of which only the latter was deemed damaging due to the 'structural frame' (4) having enough redundancy. The flooring, however, would need to be removed to attach the partition to the frame. The 'flooring' (23) is simply laid on top of the 'structural frame' (4); however, review of the dependencies in its row (round 02) highlights a dependency with 'kitchen cabinets' (33) that may have to be moved to lift the flooring out. In such a case, propagation would continue, moving 'appliances' (32) and re-routing 'electrical cables' (16).

The propagation path for the scenario was given a score of 'somewhat feasible' (2), as there are no binding connections, and the change only requires the replacement or alteration of the flooring and potential movement of other components. However, the propagation path spans several layers (*space plan, structure, services* and *stuff*) breaking the layer separation model. The scenario was also deemed 'somewhat feasible' by the system expert, but highlighted

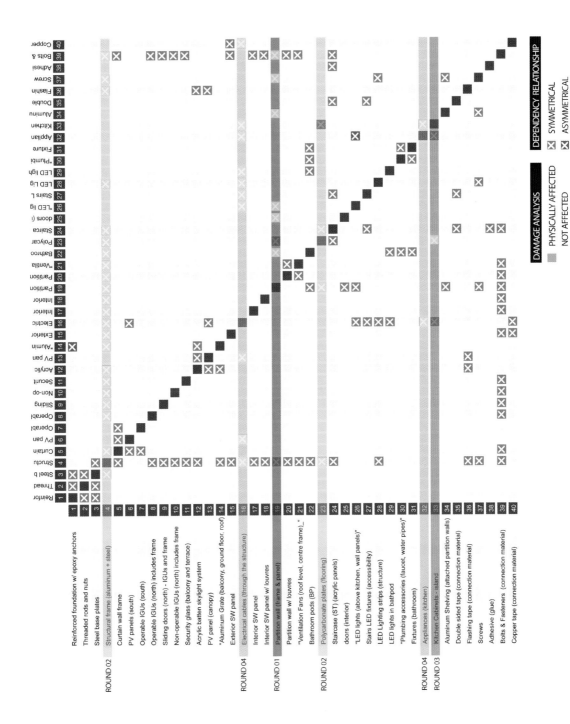

▲ Figure 7.9

Impact analysis for new partition wall

different difficulties: while the 'flooring' (23) is simply laid on top of the structure, they are large sheets that prompt issues with size and weight in a small house (a tension not obvious from the DSM).

Implications of analysis

Both the system expert (75 per cent) and the DSM modeller (65 per cent) identified a high percentage of scenarios as being either feasible (1) or somewhat feasible (2). With the majority of scenarios explored, propagation was restricted to a few components and only two or three rounds. This compares favourably with a previous study of a complex retail centre (Grinnell *et al.*, 2012) where as you would expect change propagated throughout more components and for several more rounds. Figure 7.10 is from the retail study and shows the number of components affected in each round of the four scenarios investigated.

Despite the relatively simple propagation in this 'sparse' example of Cellophane House, a comparison of the analyses of the DSMs and system expert approaches revealed that the DSM offered several insights beyond the intuition of the expert, in line with Alexander's (1964) assertion of the complexity afforded by today's design objects:

1 Access to the 'ventilation fan' (21) was not considered; however, was captured through the service dependency with the 'partition wall' (20).
2 Aware the 'flooring' (23) would have to be removed to add or move an 'interior partition' (19); however, did not initially acknowledge that the 'flooring' (23) would have to be replaced or cut because of its spatial relationship with the partition wall.
3 Did not consider the 'hidden' dependency of the 'electrical cables' (16) routed inside the 'kitchen cabinetry' (33) and 'structural frame' (4) as a potential issue.

DSMs can offer insights beyond the intuition of the designer.

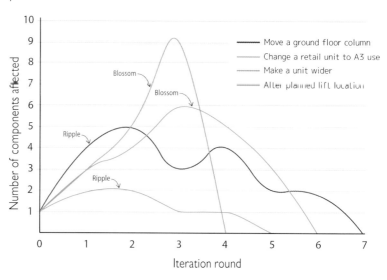

▶ Figure 7.10
Number of components affected and rounds
Grinnell *et al.* (2012)

4   Regarding replacement of the 'bathroom pod' (22), did not foresee the complications of having to move a 'partition' (19) and the impact of that propagation.

More generally the system expert's considerations beyond the direct dependencies (second round) were unreliable, highlighting the ability of a DSM to reveal propagation beyond what the individual can comprehend. On the other hand, the exercise also revealed aspects that the DSM could not cope with but the system expert was able to intuit:

1   Additional component information (e.g. structural capacity of members, tolerances, configurations) to assess some scenarios more accurately.
   • The scale of components in some cases had an added effect on their capacity to be altered or replaced (e.g. interior partitions).
   • Exact component locations (e.g. lighting locations on the structure).
2   Scenarios at a different granularity level than the DSM constructed (e.g. insertion of materials into panels, removal of a chunk and assembly of the bathroom pod).
   • Spatial characteristics of the system as a defined building (e.g. floor height, corridor width).
3   Policy restrictions.
   • The effect that change will have on the building's performance (e.g. increase acoustic, thermal performance).

The analysis of the change scenarios illustrated that the building could respond well to a majority of the adaptability types (*scalable* being an exception). It also revealed a handful of problems, e.g.:

1   Binding the electrical cables (16) with the structural frame (4) creates a significant problem in terms of layer separation and access for future change.
2   Volumetric solutions, such as the bathroom pod (22), can be difficult in regards to future change in terms of removal and installation.
3   While bolts and fasteners are a good solution for final disassembly, they require additional work (drilling new holes, replacement of bolts, and numerous connections) compared to other connection methods (e.g. plug 'n' play).

Conducting the two types of DSM analysis (impact and clustering; see Chapter 6, section 6.3) shed insight into the effectiveness of these methods as well as into the specific adaptability of an industrialised building. Germane to the analysis, major issues with the system architecture were evident in both forms of analysis. For example, the potential problems with the pinning of clusters 8, 9 and 10 within the clustering analysis were demonstrated through the impact analysis of such scenarios as 'add a new partition' and 'replace a bathroom pod'. This link is important as a validation for both techniques.

The impact analysis based on specific scenarios exemplified well the potential issues identified within the clustering analysis based on general principles of change.

Chapter 8

Design strategies, characteristics and tactics

In the first section of Part III we laid out our arguments for seeing a building as a set of layers that shear against each other (Chapter 6) in response to time and change (Chapter 4). We then proposed six motivational goals – adaptability types – that encompass the purpose(s) of any adaptation strategy (Chapter 7). These two concepts and their associated models (M4 and M5) form the cornerstones of our theory of adaptability. This chapter explains some of the more detailed constructs, including design strategies for adaptability, associated building characteristics and underlying design tactics. They form three core and interrelated elements when considering adaptability from the supply side. While this chapter introduces each one, they are concisely visualised at the start of this section (Figure III.1), defined and described in more detail in the following chapter and exemplified in the case studies presented in Chapters 14–16.

Design strategy is an overarching approach towards a way of doing things (methodology) that can be defined through a set of building characteristics (features, capabilities) and design tactics (methods, solutions).

8.1 Design strategies

A design strategy provides the designer with a way of thinking about the building and, in this context, adaptability. Thus, the design strategies are high-level labels for approaching adaptability and its design – but the design strategies presented here are not limited to designing for adaptability as adaptability exists as one of many interrelated design considerations.

The 12 design strategies can be thought of as a menu of options – each distinctively different yet some of the nested characteristics blur the higher-level distinction and could fit under multiple strategies. The strategies are grouped into four areas – Table 8.1.

Table 8.1 High-level decomposition of design strategies

Physical elements	Spatial aspects	Building character	Contextual
DS01: Modularity	DS05: Loose fit	DS11: Aesthetics	DS12: Multiple scales
DS02: Design 'in' time	DS06: Spatial planning		
DS03: Long life	DS07: Passive techniques		
DS04: Simplicity and Legibility	DS08: Unfinished design		
	DS09: Maximise building use		
	DS10: Increased activity		

The connectivity between design strategies is visualised in Table 8.2. A degree of connectivity between each of the strategies can be calculated according to the percentage of connections between each pair of strategies' characteristics – e.g. DS1 has four characteristics and DS2 has five characteristics which give 20 possible links (hence five connections is 25 per cent). The table shows the well-connected (X – 30 per cent or higher) and moderately connected strategies (O – between 20 per cent to 30 per cent). It can be seen that the loose-fit strategy (DS5) is linked to almost every other strategy – the exception being design 'in' time (DS2) which is the least connected strategy. The remaining strategies are related to two to six strategies. Regarding the *physical* (DS1–DS4; yellow) and *spatial* (DS5–DS10; blue) clusters, the spatial strategies were slightly more connected internally (67 per cent) and externally (36 per cent) than the physical ones (50 per cent and 31 per cent). The two building-scale strategies – *aesthetics* (DS11) and *multiple scales* (DS12) – linked only to spatial strategies.

Table 8.2 Connectivity between design strategies

	Design strategies	1	2	3	4	5	6	7	8	9	10	11	12
1	Modularity		O		X	X	O		O	O			
2	Design 'in' time	O								O			
3	Long life				O	O			O				
4	Simplicity and legibility	X		O		O	X		O				
5	Loose fit	X		O	O		X	X	X	X	X	O	O
6	Spatial planning	O			X	X			O	O	O		
7	Passive techniques					X					X		O
8	Unfinished design	O		O	O	X	O			O			
9	Maximise building use	O	O			X	O		O				X
10	Increase interactivity					X	O	X				X	O
11	Aesthetics					O					X		
12	Multiple scales					O		O		X	O		

8.2 Building characteristics

In describing their approach to adaptability many designers described to us the features – or as we will call them characteristics – of a building that they strived to include – e.g. the building is adaptable because of A, B and C. We identified 60 universal building characteristics in the 290 solutions from our case studies, of which 57 per cent related to a single characteristic with the rest linked to multiple characteristics. The revealed links between the 60 characteristics are visualised in Figure 8.1 with an X indicating a solution embedded the two characteristics.

The spread of connectivity among characteristics is summarised in Table 8.3, with the majority (66 per cent) having up to 11 connections (out of 59). The majority of the heaviest linked characteristics are spatial (multifunctional spaces 48 per cent, joinable/divisible 40 per cent), while many of the

Building characteristic is defined as a prominent feature pertaining to the building and/ or its constituting parts.

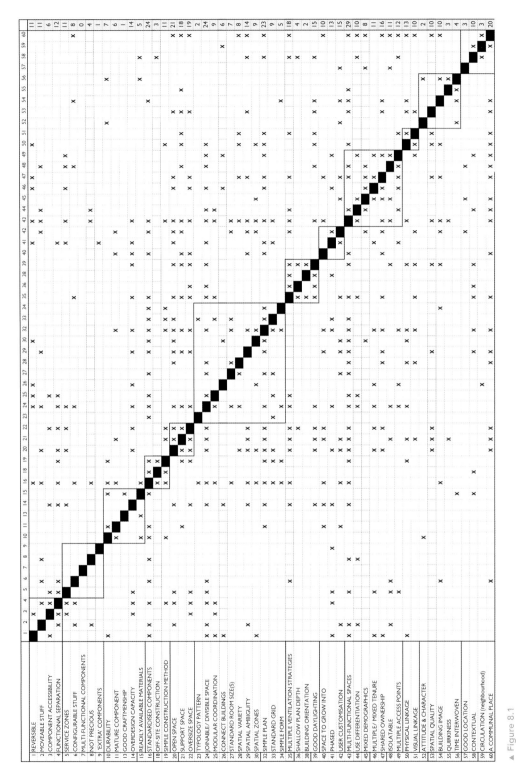

▲ Figure 8.1

Relationships between characteristics

Table 8.3 Spread of connectivity among characteristics

0% (no connectivity)	1	2%		no connections
1–9% (very low connectivity)	14	25%	66%	(1–11 connections)
10–19% (low connectivity)	23	41%		
20–9% (moderately connected)	9	16%		12–17 connections
30–9% (well connected)	6	11%		18–23 connections
40% or above (highly connected)	3	5%		24 or more connections

least connected were physical characteristics (multifunctional components 0 per cent; 'extra' components 2 per cent). This finding would support the inclination for spatial strategies and characteristics to be more dependent than their physical counterparts.

8.3 Design tactics

Our third and lowest level descriptors are design tactics. These represent a set of 135 specific technical solution types found across our case studies presented in Table 8.4. Some tactics were repeated under multiple characteristics. It was concluded that redundancy among the tactics between characteristics was inevitable given the entangled relationship between the characteristics themselves; however, further delineation could be made with the application of the design tactic at the specific solution level in relationship to the multiple characteristics served.

Design tactic is a specific method to achieve a goal/approach (strategy) – i.e. provides a way of doing.

Table 8.4 The 135 design tactics

#	Tactic Name	Related Characteristic(s)	#	Tactic Name	Related Characteristic(s)
DT1	Reversible connection	CAR1, CAR3, CAR6, CAR8, CAR19	DT15	Adjustable fixtures	CAR6
DT2	Intermediate component	CAR1	DT16	Primary/temporary functions	CAR7, CAR45, CAR49
DT3	Loose furniture	CAR2	DT17	Cheap materials	CAR8
DT4	Movable partitions	CAR2	DT18	Existing/temporary space	CAR8
DT5	Simple & minimum finishes	CAR3, CARI9	DT19	General surplus capacity	CAR9, CARI4
DT6	Access space	CAR3	DT20	Specific surplus capacity	CAR9, CARI4
DT7	Framed structure	CAR4	DT21	Weatherable materials	CAR10, CAR56
DT8	Spatial separation	CAR4	DT22	Low maintenance	CAR10
DT9	Layered exterior	CAR4	DT23	Knockable	CAR10
DT10	Wing control (chunk of building)	CAR5, CAR46, CAR48	DT24	Mature building technology	CAR11, CAR19
DT11	Floor control (horizontal slices)	CAR5, CAR46, CAR48	DT25	Practice-based	CAR11
DT12	Tenant control (spatially)	CAR5, CAR46, CAR48	DT26	Efficient devices (reduce heat gain)	CAR12

(Continued)

Table 8.4 (Continued)

#	Tactic Name	Related Characteristic(s)	#	Tactic Name	Related Characteristic(s)
DT13	Adjustable furniture	CAR6	DT27	Service monitoring	CAR12
DT14	Adjustable partition	CAR6, CAR24	DT28	Local source (water, energy)	CAR12
DT29	Hand made traits	CAR13,	DT67	Spatial adjacencies	CAR29
DT30	Industrialised solution	CAR13, CAR18	DT68	Spatial transitions	CM.29
DT31	Natural materials	CAR15	DT69	Vertical organisation of uses	CAR29
DT32	Local materials	CAR15, CAR58	DT70	Opens to outside (9b)	CAR29
DT33	Reclaimed materials	CAR15	DT71	Functional qualities	CAR30
DT34	Standard product	CAR15, CAR16	DT72	Fixed vs. flexible space	CAR30
DT35	Standardised solution	CAR16, CAR19	DT73	Central location	CAR31
DT36	Standard grid	CAR17	DT74	Close proximity	CAR31
DT37	Standard distance from	CAR17	DT75	Orthogonal shapes	CAR32
DT38	Prefabricated solution	CAR18	DT76	Multiple rectangles	CAR32
DT39	Box-shaped	CAR19	DT77	Rectangle	CAR32
DT40	Wide span	CAR20,	DT78	Planning grid	CAR33
DT41	Thin columns	CAR20	DT79	Structural grid	CAR33
DT42	Extra space (not in the brief)	CAR21	DT80	Box-shaped	CAR34
DT43	Storage space	CAR21	DT81	Vertical walls	CAR34
DT44	Exterior space	CAR21	DT82	Cross ventilation	CAR35
DT45	Wide circulation (10a)	CAR21, CAR22, CAR43, CAR50	DT83	Stack ventilation	CAR35
DT46	Additional circulation	CAR21, CAR50	DT84	Mechanical ventilation	CAR35
DT47	Undefined space	CAR21, CAR43, CAR47	DT85	Minimum distance	CAR36
DT48	Tall floor heights	CAR22	DT86	Control heat gain	CAR37
DT49	Enlarged ground floor	CAR22	DT87	Thermal mass	CAR37
DT50	Enlarged spatial area	CAR22	DT88	Natural cooung	CAR37
DT51	Universal image (familiar)	CAR23, CAR54	DT09	Maximilse natural ventilation	CAR38
DT52	Standard room sizes	CAR23	DT90	Reflect use patterns	CAR38
DT53	Standard room locations	CAR23	DT91	Maximise north/south exposure	CAR38
DT54	Standardised specificity (scale, equipment)	CAR23, CAR43	DT92	Indirect light (reilected transferred)	CAR39
DT55	Add/take down a wall	CAR24	DT93	Direct light (openings, permeable skin)	CAR39
DT56	Create/remove opening	CAR24, CAR26	DT94	Shallow plan depth	CAR39
DT57	Number/location of core	CAR24	DT95	Expand into roof	CAR40
DT58	Spatial coordination	CAR25	DT96	Expand onto roof	CAR40
DT59	Grid coordination	CAR25	DT97	Expand floor plate	CAR40

#	Tactic Name	Related Characteristic(s)	#	Tactic Name	Related Characteristic(s)
DT60	Create link	CAR26	DT98	Underground	CAR40
DT61	Market standard	CAR27	DT99	Neighbouring site	CAR40
DT62	User defined	CAR27	DT100	Existing site	CAR40
DT63	Informal/ formal (variety)	CMR28	DT101	Shell & core (trvo stage construction)	CAR41
DT64	Room sizes (variety)	CAR28, CAR46	DT102	Bare bones (genoric infrastrcuture)	CAR41
DT65	Interior/exterior (variety)	CAR28	DT103	Empty space (stuff level)	CAR42
DT66	Finishes/furnishings (variety)	CAR28, CAR43	DT104	Custom finishes	CAR42
DT105	Underused space	CAR43	DT121	Colour	CAR52
DT106	Open space	CAR43, CAR5I, CAR53	DT122	Art	CAR52
DT107	Use zones	CAR44	DT123	'Human' finishes	CAR53
DT108	Mixed uses (17a)	CAR44	DT124	Striking image (unique)	CAR54
DT109	Use differentiation	CAR45	DT125	Unresolved geometries	CAR55
DT110	Variety of contract types	CAR46	DT126	Nooks & crannies	CAR55
DT111	Common space	CAR47	DT127	Historic narrative (design concept)	CAR56
DT112	Hot-desking	CAR47	DT128	Transportation links	CAR57
DT113	Shared identity	CAR47	DT129	Supplementary uses	CAR57
DT114	Individual space(s)	CAR48	DT130	Topographic	CAR58
DT115	Multiple tenants	CAR49	DT131	Relational	CAR58
DT116	Secondary entrance	CAR49	DT132	Linked circulation points	CAR59
DT117	Direct links	CAR50	DT133	Direct access	CAR59
DT118	Prominent design feature	CAR50	DT134	Mixed demographics	CAR60
DT119	Views (outward looking)	CAR51	DT135	Social space	CAR60
DT120	Transparent materials	CAR51			

8.4 Relationship between strategies, characteristics and tactics

The structure of these three key concepts is illustrated in Figure 8.2, which is an extract of the full mapping. It can be seen that the building characteristics are clustered within a design strategy creating a nested (1:many) relationship, while the design tactics and building characteristics have a categorical relationship (many:many) – i.e. one characteristic relates to multiple tactics and vice versa. We have termed this the design for adaptability (DfA) model as it aligns nicely with the terminology of the 'design for x' community.

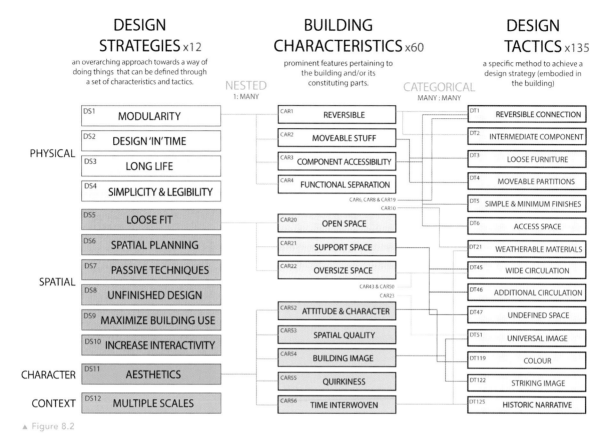

DESIGN STRATEGIES x12

an overarching approach towards a way of doing things that can be defined through a set of characteristics and tactics.

BUILDING CHARACTERISTICS x60

prominent features pertaining to the building and/or its constituting parts.

DESIGN TACTICS x135

a specific method to achieve a design strategy (embodied in the building)

NESTED
1: MANY

CATEGORICAL
MANY : MANY

PHYSICAL
- DS1 MODULARITY
- DS2 DESIGN 'IN' TIME
- DS3 LONG LIFE
- DS4 SIMPLICITY & LEGIBILITY

SPATIAL
- DS5 LOOSE FIT
- DS6 SPATIAL PLANNING
- DS7 PASSIVE TECHNIQUES
- DS8 UNFINISHED DESIGN
- DS9 MAXIMIZE BUILDING USE
- DS10 INCREASE INTERACTIVITY

CHARACTER
- DS11 AESTHETICS

CONTEXT
- DS12 MULTIPLE SCALES

Building Characteristics:
- CAR1 REVERSIBLE
- CAR2 MOVEABLE STUFF
- CAR3 COMPONENT ACCESSIBILITY
- CAR4 FUNCTIONAL SEPARATION
- CAR6, CAR8 & CAR19
- CAR10
- CAR20 OPEN SPACE
- CAR21 SUPPORT SPACE
- CAR22 OVERSIZE SPACE
- CAR43 & CAR50
- CAR23
- CAR52 ATTITUDE & CHARACTER
- CAR53 SPATIAL QUALITY
- CAR54 BUILDING IMAGE
- CAR55 QUIRKINESS
- CAR56 TIME INTERWOVEN

Design Tactics:
- DT1 REVERSIBLE CONNECTION
- DT2 INTERMEDIATE COMPONENT
- DT3 LOOSE FURNITURE
- DT4 MOVEABLE PARTITIONS
- DT5 SIMPLE & MINIMUM FINISHES
- DT6 ACCESS SPACE
- DT21 WEATHERABLE MATERIALS
- DT45 WIDE CIRCULATION
- DT46 ADDITIONAL CIRCULATION
- DT47 UNDEFINED SPACE
- DT51 UNIVERSAL IMAGE
- DT119 COLOUR
- DT122 STRIKING IMAGE
- DT125 HISTORIC NARRATIVE

▲ Figure 8.2

Model for DfA (M7) exemplifies relationship structure between key concepts

Chapter 9

Building characteristics in detail

In this chapter we consider the 60 building characteristics, the relationships between them and links to the building layers and adaptability types, two of the most important models in our theory of adaptability. Many of the characteristics will be familiar to designers, who will be particularly interested in how they play out in the context of adaptations as well as how they map to specific design strategies.

9.1 Descriptions

DS1 Modularity

The four building characteristics related to the modularity design strategy are outlined in Table 9.1, together with the associated design tactics and case studies that exemplify them.

This design strategy focuses on the way physical bits are defined as functional entities, assembled and the subsequent capacity for them to be separated later. Reversible examples (CAR1) spread across several layers. From the perspective of the *skin* layer, framed solutions enable panelised cladding systems, simply connected to or hung off the edge of a slab. For most projects, exposed fasteners allow easy access and the capability of changing the panels quickly (CAR3). A framed solution separates the function of *structure* (columns and beams), *space plan* (internal partitions) and *skin* (exterior

Table 9.1 Associated elements of DS1 Modularity

DS1 MODULARITY separation of the physical parts of the building into defined functional entities	**CAR1**	**Reversible**	capacity for the construction to be separated into its constituting parts (with minimum if any damage)
	CAR2	**Movable Stuff**	furniture, equipment or fixtures that can be moved throughout the building freely
	CAR3	**Component Accessibility**	components within the building are easily accessible; other components are not damaged in the process
	CAR4	**Functional Separation**	separation of functions into different constituting parts; 1:1 function to component relationship
	Design tactics		DT1–9
	Case studies		A4, A5, A14 and A15

façade), while a load-bearing solution would combine two or more layers (CAR4). In several case study projects the use of non-load-bearing partitions allowed internal walls to be adapted without disturbing the structure. Providing non-loading bearing partitions is often preferred for interior walls, being a satisfying middle ground between load-bearing partitions (highly restrictive) and demountable walls (high cost for infrequent use). While combining functionalities within a single component can reduce initial costs, the result may lead to unwanted knock-on dependencies and complications when a change is required. A bed pod solution is a good example of combining several conventionally separate (configurable) objects (CAR6) into a single solution that can enhance the versatility (AT2) of a space, but potentially hinder adaptability in terms of the adjustability (AT1) and/or refitability (AT3) depending on future needs.

Movable stuff solutions (CAR2) are primarily of the *stuff* and *space plan* layers purposefully separated from other *space plan* elements and the *services* layer. The size and weight of the object will influence users' ability (and likelihood) of moving an object. Examples of component accessibility (CAR3) often provide access to service elements via dropped ceilings or raised floors. Figure 9.1 illustrates two examples of enlarged service zones including one that wraps the building with an accessible 2m zone. Whilst accessibility is a key feature with regards to reversibility (CAR1), it does not always mean the solution is reversible. The main service distributions will often need to run above circulation routes and/or in centralised locations (e.g. service cores) to increase the accessibility. The capacity to separate service elements from other layers and provide proper access to them often requires ample floor-to-floor height. Accessibility to services is also important to facilitate a refit of energy sources, e.g. plug in CHP or Biomass.

DS2 Design 'in' time

The five building characteristics related to the design 'in' time design strategy are outlined in Table 9.2, together with the associated design tactics and case studies that exemplify them.

The design 'in' time strategy is concerned with the capability of physical parts to provide options for the users 'in' time. For example, at one point the lighting could be distributed uniformly through a space and at another focused on particular spots (CAR6). One common way services can be zoned (CAR5) is by floor, where each floor has dedicated on-floor plant that enable mechanical services to be retrofitted or removed according to a tenant's needs. This type of adaptability is augmented by a higher than conventional floor-to-floor height (CAR22).

Several configurable elements (CAR6) are common to conventional buildings that can be controlled through a Building Management System, e.g. lighting levels and room temperature. In some cases, the automated controls can be overridden locally by the user. While not configurable, other components can serve multiple purposes (CAR7) such as exposed structural members (e.g. concrete soffits can provide thermal mass). Operable windows (CAR6) are also

[CAR7] By using concrete, we can avoid surface finishes which reduces the amount of materials used, it improves indoor air quality, it reduces time on site, expenditure on initial fit-out, all sorts of things. It provides fire protection, acoustic protection, thermal mass, all sorts of things tied in with servicing.

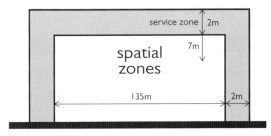
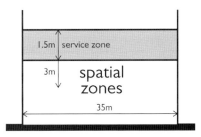

▲ Figure 9.1
Examples of occupiable service zones

Table 9.2 Associated elements of DS2 Design 'in' time

DS2 DESIGN 'IN' TIME capacity of the physical parts to provide options for the users ('in time')	CAR5	Service Zones	separate control/distribution of services among defined areas to allow for increased user control
	CAR6	Configurable Stuff	furniture; equipment, etc. which have multiple states
	CAR7	Multifunctional Components	does not move or change states but can serve multiple functions
	CAR8	Not Precious	often cheap, temporary solutions and can withstand a degree of knockability
	CAR9	'Extra' Components	provisional inclusion of components that go beyond the necessary means of the building to function
	Design tactics		DT1, 10–20
	Case studies		A1, A7, A13 and A14

multifunctional components as well as providing natural daylighting (CAR39), good views (CAR51), natural ventilation (CAR35) and passive climate control (CAR37).

While multifunctional components suggest objects having multiple functions (1:many), functional separation (CAR4) suggests a 1:1 relationship between function and object. The tension here can be alleviated through a finer grain of functions between primary, permanent functions such as *structure* or *skin* and temporary, additive functions such as a projection surface. Thus, multifunctional components suggest an additive function on top of a primary function as opposed to combining two primary functions that can severely restrict change.

The more obvious applications of not-precious solutions (CAR8) are temporary solutions that fulfil a need, often at cheaper cost. In other instances, the 'preciousness' of materials can have adverse effects on the user taking ownership of the space and appropriating it as they feel fit. A less precious material thus encourages occupants to use/change the space as needed, permitting the *space plan* to evolve. Standardised components (CAR16) that can be pulled 'off the shelf' (CAR15) encourage this.

The provision of extra components (CAR9) is most commonly applied to service elements to ease reconfiguration or expansion. A common practice is to provide ubiquitous electrical or IT services to an office despite only requiring a portion in the first instance.

[CAR10] The thing about a desk today with these new materials is that it is fantastic on day one and then on day two it is less good and as it gets older it gets worse and worse and worse, but if you had an old Victorian desk that was made of wood – it had a quality about it that as it got older it sort of told you something about its past. And I think that has to do with long lastingness as one form of adaptability.

DS3 Long life

The six building characteristics related to the long life design strategy are outlined in Table 9.3, together with the associated design tactics and case studies that exemplify them.

Buildings are often designed without explicit consideration of a design life that will vary greatly in perception between stakeholders. The lifespan is predicated on several non-physical factors – however, from a physical perspective certain characteristics enable a longer building life. For example, materials that can be knocked around or resist decay (CAR10) include brick, stone and concrete which have mass, reduce maintenance, have warmth to them, look good and provide a comfortable level of familiarity. Moreover, durable materials (CAR15) are associated with simple construction methods (CAR19) and can be linked to local industries and thus readily available for future changes – a clear case of sustainable construction.

Table 9.3 Associated elements of DS3 Long life

DS3 LONG LIFE consideration of the physical parts to last a long time	CAR10	Durability	capacity to last a long time; to be knocked around; to resist decay and weather well
	CAR11	Mature Component	a proven component or system that has evolved over time
	CAR12	Efficient Services	reduction in the use and amount of off-site energy or water required
	CAR13	Good Craftsmanship	allows for an increased standard of design and longevity
	CAR14	Overdesign Capacity	components designed beyond the designated capacity to allow for a change in conditions
	CAR15	Readily Available Materials	materials that are produced locally and naturally increasing future accessibility and replaceability
	Design tactics		DT19–34
	Case studies		A2, A8, A9 and A11

However, durable materials don't necessarily resist change. There is a hierarchy within the layer conceptualisation that implies durability plays a role particularly with the *structure* layer and more generally with longer lasting elements. A robust infrastructure can accommodate unpredictable changes when knocked about due to its resilience, enabling the surface layers to change as part of human nature.

Good craftsmanship (CAR13) implies a greater level of care by the use of good-quality, natural materials expressed through clean, articulate details. It is often the result of a high level of resolution through mature, local methods of working. Both hand-made and precision-machined parts can support a conscious component-based approach in an effort to produce a well-crafted, resolved object. The reuse of solutions allows lessons to be learned, reapplied and improvements made. Some designers deliberately seek to reuse (and improve) proven solutions between projects to demonstrate continual

[CAR11] You know, when you've had a few thousand built, there's a chance it'll have been got right … people don't expect to go in and buy a prototype car; they want to know that it's gone through all those stages and that it works.

improvement and high design quality (CAR11). Repeat clients or project types can aid this process.

Designing the structure to accommodate additional loads (or an extra floor) is a common example of overdesign (CAR14) as are service elements with excess capacity. Figure 9.2 illustrates how an addition to Loughborough University's Civil and Building Engineering building tied into the oversized columns of the original building. Indeed regulations and standards (CON7) can require additional capacities for future use, e.g. Lifetime Homes demands that ground floor spaces are sufficiently large enough for the turning radius of a wheelchair; the bathroom and bedroom need a removable panel for a hoist; and joists need to be trimmed for the addition of a lift. The inclusion of efficient services (CAR12) can also improve building longevity by reducing demand and operational costs. This may include the collection of water, production of energy on-site or the metering of services to educate users. Various technologies can reduce

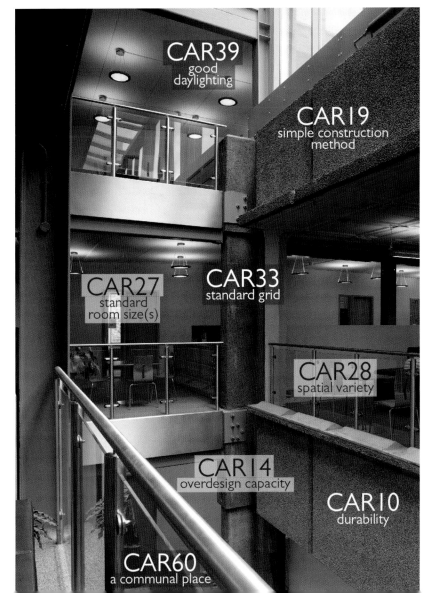

◄ Figure 9.2
Oversized columns (centre) with other CARs highlighted
Courtesy Swanke Hayden Connell

service demands including reducing heat gains with high specification lighting, high-efficiency glazing assemblies and solar control glazing.

DS4 Simplicity and legibility

The four building characteristics related to the simplicity and legibility design strategy are outlined in Table 9.4, together with the associated design tactics and case studies that exemplify them.

Many designers feel buildings have become too complicated resulting in higher costs to construct and maintain. The idea embodied in design strategy DS4 of providing a simple, straightforward building relates strongly to the repetitiveness of standardised components (CAR16), the legibility of off-site solutions (CAR18), promotion of a single, simple design concept (CON2) and ameliorating budget constraints (CON20). Simplicity and legibility is characterised by simple ideas, designing things out, straightforwardness and thinking about the way stuff goes together. For many, this embodies an implicit language of good detailing, e.g. clean and exposed joints.

Standardised components (CAR16) can improve quality through repetition, maximising interchangeability, minimising storage of spares, improving component replacement and increasing reusability. Common examples include core elements such as toilets and staircases. Most buildings include structural elements (columns, beams) of standard sizes and specifications. Many of the case studies make use of a standardised cladding system including standardised window openings and types. An affordable housing scheme, Almen+, uses a standardised window opening that can be 'filled' differently depending on the homeowner's desire (CAR42) – French balconies, ordinary windows, blinding panels, etc. (Figure 9.3).

Locating components in standard locations (CAR17) improves the building's legibility. Placing hidden service elements in standard locations is a good example of benefiting from simplicity. Fittings and fixtures are often standardised and located in standard grid locations, including partitioning, office furniture and modular storage. The cleanliness and precision offered by off-site construction (CAR18) is also considered to improve the legibility of how systems come together.

Traditional construction materials are not only regarded as durable (CAR10), but accompanied by more straightforward construction methods. Simple and

Table 9.4 Associated elements of DS4 Simplicity and legibility

DS4 SIMPLICITY and LEGIBILITY use of simplicity and legibility with regards to components and construction methods to enable change to occur more readily	CAR16	Standardised Components	standard off-the-shelf components and/or bulk use of a component designed for the building
	CAR17	Standard Component Locations	components are located in standard locations
	CAR18	Off-site Construction	a higher quality of construction through off-site assembly
	CAR19	Simple Construction Method	simple, legible structural system
	Design tactics		DT1, 5, 24, 30, 34–9
	Case studies		A2, A8, A11 and A15

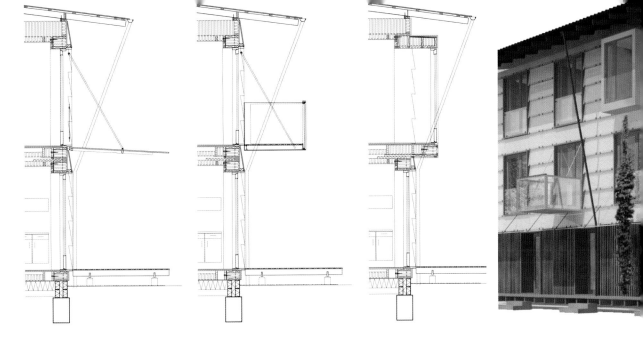

familiar solutions empower users to adapt a space and contractors believe this also promotes good craftsmanship (CAR13).

Exposed structures (CAR19) have become an accepted trend in buildings, removing the need for false ceilings, column/wall covers and additional floor materials. This is partially an aesthetic measure (CAR53) and partially to support passive climates (CAR37). Removing the need to conceal services also reduces the spatial constraint by improving the separability (CAR1) and accessibility (CAR3) of elements. Cost savings from simple construction can enable more costly tactics to be deployed such as wide circulation (CAR50), additional social space (CAR60) and taller floor-to-floor heights (CAR22).

DS5 Loose fit

The three building characteristics related to the loose-fit design strategy are outlined in Table 9.5, together with the associated design tactics and case studies that exemplify them.

This design strategy moves beyond modernism's efficient approach to spatial dimensions in an effort to establish a 'loose' relationship between programme and space. The provision of open space (CAR20) allows it to be divided in any way needed (CAR24). A common tactic is to remove permanent

We actually are always trying to make a, kind of, loose fit between the programme and the architecture. Designing buildings very specifically for one specific, kind of, use is like a, sort of, recipe for disaster.

Table 9.5 Associated elements of DS5 Loose fit

DS5 LOOSE FIT spatial considerations beyond a minimal standard or that defined by the brief	CAR20	Open Space	a large space that is relatively undisturbed with immovable obstacles (e.g. columns)
	CAR21	Support Space	spaces typically not defined in the brief, but are necessary for functional support
	CAR22	Oversize Space	space that is sized larger than the market standard or functional necessity in plan or section
	Design tactics		DT40–50
	Case studies		A2, A4, A7, A8 and A9

obstacles within the space in an effort to create a universal environment. Office plan versatility (AT2) at its simplest is a combination of open plan space and movable stuff (CAR2) – this can be aided by organisational structure, spatial proportions, service strategy, structural grid and cladding solution.

Open space can reflect a range of clear spans, e.g. in residential design from 4m to 8m (project A8 is 6.5m; project A11 is 7.6m) whereas office design typically ranges from 15m to 20m. A larger span usually means wider columns and deeper beams, both of which are weighed against cost and other spatial parameters. In addition, open spaces are often limited by fire regulations (CON7) that require special consideration regarding means of egress. In a constrained application, the delivery of an open space is not always homogeneous across floors. Often the top floor can have fewer restrictions than lower floors given reduced structural loads. Open plans also benefit from higher, double-height sections that enhance perceptions of openness and comfort.

Extra or unused spaces that are not commonly described in a brief (CON13) can provide opportunities for spatial adaptability. Circulation space is often considered to be an opportunity to provide something more than merely a movement route (CAR21). These are the spaces where the human interaction can be enhanced and room uses determined by how people meet, interact and communicate (CAR60). Storage is an example of a soft-use space – the strategic location of support space that can be easily relocated to allow for growth in a primary functional area. Exterior spaces are frequently the cheapest part of a building, often the most noticeable and memorable; however, they are often poorly exploited in terms of extending the building's functionality.

The most common deterrent to oversizing space (CAR22) is cost because adding additional floor-to-floor height or square metres to the plan undoubtedly increases the capital cost – Figure 9.4. Taller floor-to-ceiling heights provide the flexibility to add a false ceiling and/or a raised floor (CAR3), to run services separate from the structure (CAR4), improve cooling (limitations; CAR12) and increase the amount of natural light (CAR39) that can permeate the floor space. However, they are not only constrained by higher costs (CON20), but also by planning legislation (CON7) that can restrict the overall height of the building envelope, in which case a client will often want to fit as many floors within that envelope as possible. Similar to open plan, the size of space that is considered oversized is contingent to the use – high ceilings for residential can be above (2.9m) whereas offices is above (3.5m). Double-height spaces also provide the potential to grow internally with mezzanine levels (CAR40).

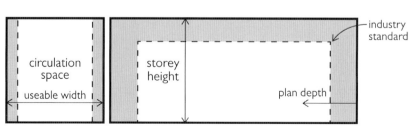

▶ Figure 9.4
Oversize space concept diagram

PART III A THEORY OF ADAPTABILITY

DS6 Spatial planning

The 12 building characteristics related to the spatial planning design strategy are outlined in Table 9.6, together with the associated design tactics and case studies that exemplify them.

Spatial planning is a common design strategy that gives occupants spatial options to use a building in different ways. Speculative development by its very nature is a typology pattern (CAR23) embodying trends and universal characteristics of a use that generally are characteristic for a specific period of time – some evolutions are cyclical while others are linear. The goal is to enhance the intended use by identifying patterns that work within existing buildings, allowing designs to develop based on evidence rather than intuition – the inverse can also be said about identifying problems and designing them out.

Rationalising room sizes (CAR27) into groups is a widespread tactic to improve room interchangeability on large-scale projects like hospitals. On the other hand, by providing a variety of spatial sizes (CAR28), rooms can support different activities by providing diverse environments: small/large; formal/informal; and interior/semi-enclosed/exterior. The key is to strike an appropriate mix of standardised rooms and variety. Open plan space (CAR20) is often provided in balance with cellular or enclosed spaces. Joinable/divisible

A good architect will actually be able to gift something that wasn't in the brief for nothing, simply because of the way they've organised the space.

Table 9.6 Associated elements of DS6 Spatial planning

	CAR23	Typology Pattern	designed to a typology or standardised use/spatial pattern
	CAR24	Joinable/Divisible Space	space that can be joined or divided to support multiple spatial configurations
	CAR25	Modular Coordination	spatial coordination between systems which have physical consequences
	CAR26	Connect Buildings	capacity to link together or separate buildings
	CAR27	Standard Room Size(s)	a series of rooms that are of all the same size
DS6 SPATIAL PLANNING spatial consideration for the way spaces are laid out; their boundaries, dimensions and relationships to one another	CAR28	Spatial Variety	a variety of sized rooms to cater to different uses and sizes of groups
	CAR29	Spatial Ambiguity	blurred boundaries between interior and/or exterior spatial uses through soft boundaries or proximity
	CAR30	Spatial Zones	spatial separation of different types of functional spaces into designated areas
	CAR31	Spatial Proximity	central location or close proximity of related elements
	CAR32	Simple Plan	a geometrically simple plan, deducible into a series of linear/rectangular shapes
	CAR33	Standard Grid	standardised dimensions with few anomalies
	CAR34	Simple Form	straight vertical and horizontal surfaces; few complicated forms such as curved or slanted
	Design tactics		DT14, 51–81
	Case studies		A3, A4, A6, A7, A14 and A15

[CAR30] *Our first move was to say ok, if we took the bathrooms and the kitchens out of the plan, stuck them on the outside of the tower block, you could actually suddenly have massive amounts more freedom with how the flats were planned.*

[CAR33] A client may only need a square footage which is smaller than the next grid module and they'll want to chop it off there. We try to explain to them that this additional square footage will cost very little in comparison and you'll get a more adaptable solution because you have a standardised module across the whole length of the building and not one odd bay on the end.

space (CAR24) relates strongly to open space, but its effectiveness depends on reasonable proportions, sensible depth and good natural light along with the solution's ease of transformation and user need. When dividing a single tenant space into one for multiple tenants the characteristic may be coupled with service, access and security divisibility (CAR48). The blurring of space (CAR29) can augment this approach by providing soft boundaries and proximity of spaces that create variety (Figure 9.5). This, however, can work against the sale-ability or the market value (CON21) by not providing clear labels, dimensions and spatial distinctions.

Spatial zones (CAR30) group similar types of spaces into a spatial cluster; 'served and servant' spaces fit nicely under this characteristic. The most common application is to group together fixed spaces often referred to as a core (vertical circulation, service risers, toilets) which allows the remainder of the space(s) to change as needed. With residential developments wet spaces (kitchen and bathroom) can be considered fixed spaces since they require connection to piping. Spatial proximity (CAR31) suggests elements are easier to change the closer they are located; e.g. the central positioning of an element can allow for an increased ease of access (CAR3) and multiplicity of directions.

With modular coordination (CAR25), the module is often a spatial dimension or a planning grid. Standard planning grids often align different physical elements such as furniture, partitions and exterior façade, being more effective when they are a division of a standard structural grid (CAR33). Typical planning modules vary from a 1.2m, 2.4m, 3.6m grid system to a 1.5m, 3m grid or 4.5m grid. Larger structural grids typically start off at standard modules, but often get pushed, pulled, chopped and twisted based on site, programme or formal desires. A standard grid can ease the provision of a standard room layout (CAR27) and a simple plan (CAR32).

A rectangular plan is often regarded as offering the most possibilities. For some architects, spatial quality (CAR53) is defined in section (the three-dimensionality of space) and the simplicity (organisation, legibility) of the plan is a starting point for adaptability through an efficient plan. A simple plan allows better control of the construction in three dimensions, whereas a complicated plan can create difficult junctions and details to resolve (CAR19). Some shapes do not provide ideal spaces to work with, particularly for sub-division (CAR24), e.g. wedge-shaped flats that fan out from a circular plan, a

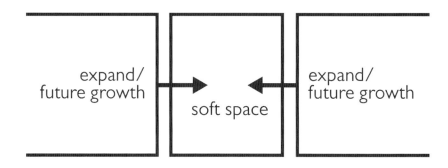

▶ Figure 9.5
'Soft' space concept diagram

drum-shaped plan and a boomerang-shaped building in response to its site boundaries. It can be difficult to fit furniture efficiently (CAR32) into triangular spaces and support spaces (CAR21) such as storage can become unusable.

Some projects also have a standard vertical grid. A building of simple form (CAR34) facilitates its subdivision and extension in various ways. Simple, universal forms (vertical extrusions of simple plans) promote a non-specific image free from a particular use or company (CAR54). Connecting buildings (CAR26) is often a consideration when an owner has multiple buildings within a particular site (e.g. business park, university campus) or an area has been developed with a strategic vision linking several buildings together for a greater purpose.

DS7 Passive techniques

The five building characteristics related to the passive techniques design strategy are outlined in Table 9.7, together with the associated design tactics and case studies that exemplify them.

The design strategy of passive techniques exploits a building's surroundings, removing the need for conventional mechanical systems, reinforcing simplicity as a good policy for adaptability. Despite each characteristic's ability to exist independently, the design tactics associated with this design strategy's characteristics are highly interwoven.

Multiple ventilation strategies (CAR35) increase occupant control (CAR6) and energy efficiency (CAR12) through naturally (wind-driven or stack) and mechanically ventilated systems. Systems can work together (mechanical system aids air chimneys) or in isolation. A shallow plan depth (CAR36) can support natural ventilation (CAR35) and daylight penetration (CAR39) minimising energy consumption. Shallow plans may not be ideal for all uses since they can limit floor plan configurations and may not make full use of the site. Many projects include an atrium space to bring light into the centre of the plan as well as roof lights to allow light to penetrate from above – see Figure 9.6 for a variety of tactics.

Building orientation (CAR38) takes advantage of the natural conditions of the site to maximise natural daylighting and solar gain along with reducing solar glare and overheating. Residential design in particular can take advantage of

[CAR32] If you look at any building that we've done you will find really simple squares, rectangles, you won't find wibbly-wobbly lines, but what you find in section is quite interesting, even very subtle things that make you feel drama about a space.

It's about reducing solar gain on different façades by having smaller openings where you need and larger openings where you're allowed … just being slightly smarter about how you put the building together and not designing in problems for yourself that you're going to have to design yourself out of.

Table 9.7 Associated elements of DS7 Passive techniques

DS7 PASSIVE TECHNIQUES the building's shape, materiality and orientation provide additional options for heating, cooling and ventilating the building	CAR35	Multiple Ventilation Strategies	capacity to be naturally or mechanically ventilated
	CAR36	Shallow Plan Depth	generally less than 15m in depth
	CAR37	Passive Climate Control	reduced need to mechanically control internal environment
	CAR38	Building Orientation	prevailing direction of the building takes advantage of natural conditions
	CAR39	Good Daylighting	capacity for the majority of the spaces to be daylit
	Design tactics		DT82–94
	Case studies		A2, A8, A11 and A14

▶ Figure 9.6
Tactic 'tree' for good daylighting

The look of a building tells the story. The south façade looks different to the north for quite obvious reasons.

the spatial location of activities that occur at different points of the day. While the use of technology to reduce service demand is considered efficient services (CAR12), passive climate control approaches (CAR37) are separated into roof overhangs, overhanging eaves, louvred solutions, night cooling, solar gain in the winter, stack effect, etc.

DS8 Unfinished design

The three building characteristics related to the unfinished design strategy are outlined in Table 9.8, together with the associated design tactics and case studies that exemplify them.

To leave space for somebody else to come after you to change it or add to it or take away and that you ought to allow the capacity for change in a way that your ego is undisturbed.

The design strategy unfinished design questions the relationship between where the designer stops and the user begins to find a solution that can be appropriated without unduly limiting spatial options. Space to grow into (CAR40) refers to tactics that extend the building outside of its initial boundaries. Vertical expansion is linked particularly to overdesign capacity (CAR14) given the structural provision (foundation, floor and load-bearing capacities) needs to accommodate additional floors or spaces above. Circulation plan and points of entry (CAR50) are also fundamental to a building's ability to grow and shrink on a site. The design for the Gateway Sixth Form College uses a shared circulation street (CAR43 and CAR47) to branch extendable fingers for each faculty (Figure 9.7).

There's an interesting relationship then between what is set and what you leave open because you can go too far in either direction, to either extreme.

The distinction between phased (CAR41), and user customisation (CAR42) – both of which take place within the existing boundaries of the building – lies in a space's readiness. User customisation (CAR42) is considered finished despite explicit opportunities for the occupants to appropriate the space, while phased (CAR41) is unusable and requires additional work (e.g. shell and core; fit-out distinction). User customisation can be provoked by material, spatial and solution choices providing the user a sense of ownership and identity with the building. The success of a project can hinge on the users' ability to customise the space and work in it when needed.

Table 9.8 Associated elements of DS8 Unfinished design

DS8 UNFINISHED DESIGN capacity to add to or 'complete' an aspect or layer of the building	CAR40	Space to Grow Into	provisions for additional space (non-existing) to be added horizontally or vertically
	CAR41	Phased	'unfinished' space that requires additional work to make it usable
	CAR42	User Customisation	usable 'finished' space that is designed to be decorated or appropriated by the user
	Design tactics		DT95–104
	Case studies		A3, A6, A10 and A12

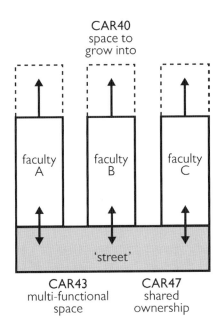

CAR40
space to
grow into

faculty
A

faculty
B

faculty
C

'street'

CAR43
multi-functional
space

CAR47
shared
ownership

◀ Figure 9.7
Expansion plan for each faculty

Speculative office development exemplifies the two choices: a space can be finished to a specification level (Grade A, B – a finished standard in industry) and a market value can be assigned to it; or a space can be left unfinished and require an additional phase of construction to finish the space. The former would be considered user customisation (CAR42) only requiring the addition of *stuff* (furniture, equipment); whereas, the latter would be considered phased (CAR41) requiring the user to hire a contractor to finish the space (*stuff, services* and *space plan*). Designing a speculative office space to a certain specification can be risky given the speed of organisational change today, although an uncertain market can be mitigated by the coupling of a generic infrastructure and a good location (CAR57).

The key to the project is to build a robust infrastructure which can accommodate a range of uses since the value is unknown whether it's offices, large flats, student housing, a bit of retail and so on, so the concept was to fit spaces out just to the minimum but in a good location with great access.

DS9 Maximise building use

The seven building characteristics related to the maximise building use design strategy are outlined in Table 9.9, together with the associated design tactics and case studies that exemplify them.

This design strategy aims to improve the efficiency in *how* and the overall time with *when* the building is being used. A multifunctional space (CAR43) can be characterised as a large open area (CAR20) with movable furniture (CAR2) that can accommodate a variety of activities, such as an atrium or courtyard space that serves as a large undefined space for events (CAR60). Several case studies involve the ground floor as a differentiated multifunctional space (CAR44) to enhance community engagement. A mixture of furniture can support a variety of activities. In addition, new technology can often add or remove physical and/or spatial dependencies nested inside a building as removing spatial dependencies allow room functions to change more easily.

One of the things I tried to do in this house is to de-specify space.

Table 9.9 Associated elements of DS9 Maximising building use

DS9 MAXIMISE BUILDING USE increase the timeframe in which the building is used throughout the day, week and year	CAR43	Multifunctional Spaces	space that can be used for multiple uses
	CAR44	Use Differentiation	inclusion of a mixture of uses
	CAR45	Mixed Demographics	services more than a single demographic
	CAR46	Multiple/Mixed Tenure	occupied by multiple tenants that may or may not operate under the same tenure agreement
	CAR47	Shared Ownership	space that is shared by multiple individuals or organisations
	CAR48	Isolatable	space or a wing that can function in separation from the rest of the building
	CAR49	Multiple Access Points	provision of multiple entry points that can serve different uses or users
	Design tactics		DT10–12, 16, 45, 47, 54, 64, 66, 105–16
	Case studies		A1, A5, A6, A7 and A10

I think the interesting thing is that actually adaptability is more about being able to change the names on the door.

Use differentiation (CAR44) is increasingly part of policy (CON10), mandating developments to contain a level of mixed use. This characteristic can intensify the use of the building (and the urban block more generally) minimising vacant periods and hence increasing the commercial viability of an expensive asset (CON21). In one study, the design team investigated how to bolt on a variety of facilities to stadiums to make them a daily destination (e.g. leisure centres and sports gyms). On the other hand, local policy forced a developer against their inclination to add residential units to an urban development that is located in a noisy area with poor air quality (CON10).

Buildings that are mixed use or open to the community after hours will generally attract mixed demographics (CAR45). The majority of commercial projects have some level of multi-tenancy (CAR46) or mixed use. Multiple and mixed tenure can complicate building systems particularly if the tenants stretch across different hours of the day or week requiring separate access and services. Implementation of the isolatable characteristic (CAR48) is typically a result of multiple characteristics such as service zones (CAR5), multiple access points (CAR49) and mixed demographics (CAR45). The success of multiple access points is improved by the appropriate physical linkage and security (separation) measures to join/divide spaces (CAR24) for different uses. With shared ownership (CAR47) there is often a reduction in the specificity to which a space may be defined. Allowing shared amenity services for building tenants creates overlap in ownership and better utilisation, such as shared meeting rooms, catering facilities and an entrance lobby. Multifunctional and shared ownership can, however, create tensions and requires a good management system (CON14). In the work environment there is a conflict between shared ownership (hot-desking) and user customisation; the former suggests separation between user and space (storage often becomes the intermediate buffer) while the latter implies integration and identification of spatial boundaries (which may be shared). The accommodation of visual and acoustic privacy is at the heart of successful shared occupancy where collaboration and concentration need to coexist.

DS10 Increase interactivity

The two building characteristics related to the increase interactivity design strategy are outlined in Table 9.10, together with the associated design tactics and case studies that exemplify them.

Increase interactivity promotes the design of spaces that are physically and visually connected which can increase the possibilities for their use (CAR43). Good physical linkage (CAR50) promotes legible, efficient and multiple connections that encourage growth. Circulation can often be more than a means of passage (CAR43) and should aid in the permeability between spaces and of the building and its surrounding context. Similarly visual linkages (CAR51) promote better communication, interaction and flexible working environments. For example, informal breakout spaces near staircases with natural light from above can reduce the need for formal meeting rooms.

Incorporating wherever possible spaces that are half one thing and half another, places where you can overlook one space but feel like you're part of a crowd and on your own as well.

Table 9.10 Associated elements of DS10 Increase interactivity

DS10 INCREASE INTERACTIVITY use of physical and visual connections to increase a sense of awareness creating a more legible place	CAR50	Physical Linkage	physical connections between spaces
	CAR51	Visual Linkage	visual connections between interior spaces and interior and exterior spaces
	Design tactics		DT45–6, 106, 117–20
	Case studies		A5, A9, A10, A13 and A15

DS11 Aesthetics

The five building characteristics related to the aesthetics design strategy are outlined in Table 9.11, together with the associated design tactics and case studies that exemplify them.

Aesthetics as a design strategy makes use of the building's image, form and narrative as a way of appealing to the users' and society's appreciation. Several projects discussed the use of colour (CAR52) to cleverly highlight design features, delineate circulation routes (way finding), mark different areas of the building, define ownership, increase legibility and ultimately create value by

What do you do, you take a white wall and you paint it, apply some vinyl to it and all of a sudden you've got something that is striking simply for that, regardless of the building or the rest of the space.

Table 9.11 Associated elements of DS11 Aesthetics

DS11 AESTHETICS use of the building's image, form and narrative as a way of appealing to the users' and society's appreciation	CAR52	Attitude and Character	use of colour and graphics to provide a level of character to the building
	CAR53	Spatial Quality	a unique spatial character
	CAR54	Building Image	the exterior image offers a level of familiarity or uniqueness
	CAR55	Quirkiness	spatial or physical anomalies that add to the character of the building
	CAR56	Time Interwoven	an historic narrative embedded into the design or through aged material
	Design tactics		DT51, 106, 121–6
	Case studies		A4, A8, A9 and A10

If an ugly building is empty … it's virtually impossible for anyone to make a case to keep it. So design quality is always good.

[CAR55] It's those spaces that are always engineered out of buildings that make the difference and that's why we like old buildings 'cause you come across something that's a bit of a quirk and you say 'Oh, this is nice, I can just hide myself here'.

[CAR57] We've learnt from history, we try and make a point of always building on transport nodes because some of our product has become obsolescent because you have to drive to work.

The adaptability of buildings in some way has to be tuned into the adaptability of the place and the degree of adaptability you would build into a building in an unadaptable place should be less.

simply adding a bit of extra vibrancy. Spatial quality (CAR53) can be established through a variety of fundamental aspects such as formal composition, accenting vertical circulation, an abundance of natural light (CAR37), use of warm, durable materials (CAR10), visual and physical connections between spaces (DS10) and vegetation.

There were two somewhat opposing trends with the building characteristic building image (CAR54) – *universal image* (familiar, not tied to a particular use or user) and *striking image* (unique, identifiable). Easy replacement of the elevation (CAR1) is an important aspect of adaptability because tenants expect the building to look 'up to date' or different if they're to continue to pay market rates. The use of low maintenance, durable and familiar materials can provide a strong and quality building image. On the other hand, change is often easier in the strange or unfamiliar as society can be protective of changing something that is familiar.

Quirkiness (CAR55) finds value in the spaces of unresolved geometries or 'hidden' spaces large enough for just one. It suggests spaces that may be difficult to use, but can provide character to a building, overcoming the inefficient use of space through the user's appreciation. The perimeter walls of the new extension for the Queens Central Library have been thickened to promote the use of the large window sills as reading nooks and intimate social spaces (Figure 9.8).

A common practice of time interwoven (CAR56) is to embed a local narrative into the building, whether it occurs as part of the physical architecture, through the materials chosen or through the building use. Additionally, time can be interwoven in a 'forward' manner – e.g. the intentional incorporation of materials that will age over time in a purposeful manner (materials that weather naturally such as copper or brass panels and timber cladding). A material surface over time can become imperfect or a form of patina.

DS12 Multiple scales

The four building characteristics related to the multiple scales design strategy are outlined in Table 9.12, together with the associated design tactics and case studies that exemplify them.

The multiple scales design strategy goes beyond the building to include aspects of the site and surrounding area. For example, the width of a street is important to the quality of a location (CAR57) and its ability for the street to accommodate a variety of purposes. Density and connectivity is important to the sustainability and adaptability of buildings given their demographic demands.

Important considerations when considering how to relate contextually (CAR58) are shape, scale and material. In addition, spaces between buildings, how they are exploited and how they can support one another are important. In this sense, buildings don't have to look similar or be of the same size, but simply have an understanding of neighbouring buildings. This includes the ways in which buildings link to the surrounding area (CAR59) that may come from the designer's own initiative or be part of a master plan that ties multiple developments together.

▲ Figure 9.8

Inhabitable niches at the Children's Library Discovery Center, Queens Central Library

Courtesy Michael Moran/OTTO for 1100 Architect

Table 9.12 Associated elements of DS12 Multiple scales

DS12 MULTIPLE SCALES consideration beyond the building to include aspects of the site and surrounding area	CAR57	Good Location	multiple transportation options, a favourable climate and ample density
	CAR58	Contextual	exploits and relates to its surrounding environment
	CAR59	Circulation (neighbourhood)	established physical connections to surrounding area
	CAR60	A Communal Place	a multifunctional, shared space that provides a place for gathering
	Design tactics		DT21, 32, 127–35
	Case studies		A2, A3, A4, A8 and A10

Provided you have the place, it's the place that's important and not the individual building within it.

A communal place (CAR60) embodies a mixture of other characteristics (similar to multifunctional space and isolatable). There are several types of communal space including atrium, public square, courtyard, roof space, landscaped garden and an open ground floor. They are typically large open plan spaces (CAR20) with no specific function in mind (CAR43) sometimes within the building (for the building's occupants) and other times exterior and open to the wider community. These spaces often provide a mixture of furniture, warm durable finishes, oversized circulation, good daylighting and suitable access. Establishing a level of symbolic ownership can be important as well in establishing a communal sense of place, enabling different groups to share an attachment with the building through its image or some form of decoration (CAR47).

9.2 Relationship of CARs to building layers

The building characteristics display four types of relationships to the layers, namely (1) concentrated, (2) dispersed with a focus, (3) dispersed without a focus and (4) too few instances. Table 9.13 lists each characteristic (rows) against the building layers (columns) to visualise the relationship types. Characteristics of the first and second type are heavily linked (i.e. almost 60 per cent) to one or two layers (yellow cells). The other two types (3 and 4) are not linked to any layers specifically; for example two characteristics spread across all the layers – *multifunctional spaces* (43) and a *communal space* (60).

Looking across the layers, all linked well to at least one characteristic, as summarised in Table 9.14. The *space plan* layer was clearly linked to more characteristics than any other layer while the *skin*, *structure* and *space* layers linked to a handful of characteristics.

This mapping is based on a sample of designs in our case studies. The patterns are therefore only indicative. Nevertheless, the large sample size provides generic insights and therefore the mapping can be helpful to designers by identifying the building layers that may be affected by a specific building characteristic, or by highlighting potential adaptability characteristics when designing a particular building layer.

Table 9.13 Characteristics (CAR) mapped against layers (L)

ID	Characteristics	SOCIAL	SPACE	STUFF	SPACE PLAN	SERVICES	SKIN	STRUCTURE	SITE	SURROUNDINGS	Total
1	REVERSIBLE		1	3	4	1	9		2		20
2	MOVABLE STUFF			12	5	1			1		19
3	COMPONENT ACCESSIBILITY				3	7					10
4	FUNCTIONAL SEPARATION				6	1	2	5			14
5	SERVICE ZONES					2					2
6	CONFIGURABLE STUFF			16	4	3	6	1		1	31
7	MULTIFUNCTIONAL COMP			1	1						2
8	NOT PRECIOUS			1	1	1	1				4
9	'EXTRA' COMPONENTS						1				1
10	DURABILITY			1	1		3	1			6
11	MATURE COMPONENT				2	1	2				5
13	GOOD CRAFTMENSHIP										0
14	OVERDESIGN CAPACITY		1	2	5	1	3	10	1	1	24
15	READILY AVAILABLE MATERIALS						3	1			4
16	STANDARDISED COMPONENTS			6	8	6		9	4		33
18	OFF-SITE CONSTRUCTION				1			1			2
19	SIMPLE CONSTRUCTION MET				3	1	2	3			9
20	OPEN SPACE	1	5	1	10			6	2		25
21	SUPPORT SPACE	4	6		7		3	1	4		25
22	OVERSIZE SPACE	1	7		14			3			25
23	TYPOLOGY PATTERN				1		1				2
24	JOINABLE/ DIVISIBLE SPACE		1	1	11						13
25	MODULAR COORDINATION				2	1	3				6
26	CONNECT BUILDINGS				1	1	1		3	3	9
27	STANDARD ROOM SIZE(S)		3		4						7
28	SPATIAL VARIETY	2	5		3					2	12
29	SPATIAL AMBIGUITY		1	1	4	1	1	1	2	1	12
30	SPATIAL ZONES			1	8	3		1			13
32	SIMPLE PLAN		7		6	2	1	2			18
33	STANDARD GRID		2					5			7
34	SIMPLE FORM				1	1	3	2			7
35	MULTIPLE VENTILATION STRA				3	1	4		1	1	10
36	SHALLOW PLAN DEPTH				3						3
38	BUILDING ORIENTATION										0
39	GOOD DAYLIGHTING	2	4		4	1	11	2	2		26

(Continued)

Table 9.13 (Continued)

ID	Characteristics	SOCIAL	SPACE	STUFF	SPACE PLAN	SERVICES	SKIN	STRUCTURE	SITE	SURROUNDINGS	Total
40	SPACE TO GROW INTO		1		4		6	7	6	3	27
41	PHASED										0
42	USER CUSTOMISATION			1	5	3	3	3	1		16
43	MULTIFUNCTIONAL SPACES	5	10	7	15	5	5	2	8	1	58
44	USE DIFFERENTIATION	2		1	3	3		2			11
45	MIXED DEMOGRAPHICS	2		1	1	1			1		6
46	MULTIPLE/ MIXED TENURE	1			1	2					4
47	SHARED OWNERSHIP	8	4		4				3		19
48	ISOLATABLE		1		1				1		3
49	MULTIPLE ACCESS POINTS	2	2		2		1		2	2	11
50	PHYSICAL LINKAGE	2	2		5	1	2		1		13
51	VISUAL LINKAGE	2	3		3	1	4	1	2	1	17
52	ATTITUDE & CHARACTER	1	1	3	3		3				11
53	SPATIAL QUALITY		2	1	2		2		1	1	9
54	BUILDING IMAGE				1	1	9				11
55	QUIRKINESS										0
56	TIME INTERWOVEN				1		3				4
57	GOOD LOCATION									4	4
58	CONTEXTUAL						1	1	2	1	5
59	CIRCULATION (neighbourhood)								1	2	3
60	A COMMUNAL PLACE	8	4	1	4	2	4	1	6	2	32
		43	73	61	181	56	102	71	59	24	

	Concentrated
	Dispersed w/ a focus
	Dispersed w/ no focus
	Too few instances

Table 9.14 Characteristics that linked well with layers

Layer	No. of CARs	Characteristics (IDs)
Social	2	47, 60
Space	6	21, 22, 27, 28, 32, 43
Stuff	2	2, 6
Space plan	16	4, 16, 19, 20, 21, 22, 24, 27, 29, 30, 32, 35, 36, 42, 43, 50
Services	1	3
Skin	7	1, 10, 15, 35, 39, 54, 56
Structure	5	4, 14, 16, 19, 33,
Site	3	26, 43, 60
Surroundings	3	26, 57, 59

9.3 Links between CARs and adaptability types

The characteristics can also be associated with the adaptability types via the solutions implemented in the case studies. Table 9.15 illustrates the relationships where all but two relate to between 1 to 3 adaptability types (number of x's across a row).

Table 9.15 Characteristics (CAR) mapped to adaptability types (AT)

	Design Stratergy		Characteristics	Adjustable	Versatile	Refitable	Convertible	Scalable	Movable	
1		MODULARITY	REVERSIBLE	X	X	X		X	X	5
2			MOVABLE STUFF	X	X				X	3
3			COMPONENT ACCESSIBILITY			X				1
4			FUNCTIONAL SEPARATION		X		X			2
5		DESIGN 'IN' TIME	SERVICE ZONES			X	X			2
6			CONFIGURABLE STUFF	X	X				X	3
7			MULTIFUNCTIONAL COMP		X					1
8			NOT PRECIOUS		X					1
9			'EXTRA' COMPONENTS	X	X		X			3
10	PHYSICAL	LONG LIFE	DURABILITY			X	X		X	3
11			MATURE COMPONENT			X				1
12			EFFICIENT SERVICES				X			1
13			GOOD CRAFTMENSHIP				X			1
14			OVERDESIGN CAPACITY				X	X		2
15			READILY AVAILABLE MATERIALS			X		X		2
16		SIMPLICITY & LEGIBILITY	STANDARDISED COMPONENTS	X	X	X		X	X	5
17			STANDARDISED COMP LOCATIONS			X		X	X	3
18			OFF-SITE CONSTRUCTION			X			X	2
19			SIMPLE CONSTRUCTION METHOD			X		X		3
20	SPATIAL	LOOSE FIT	OPEN SPACE		X		X			2
21			SUPPORT SPACE			X	X	X		3
22			OVERSIZE SPACE			X	X	X		3
23			TYPOLOGY PATTERN				X			1
24		SPATIAL PLANNING	JOINABLE/ DIVISIBLE SPACE			X	X			2
25			MODULAR COORDINATION			X	X			2
26			CONNECT BUILDINGS				X	X		2
27			STANDARD ROOM SIZE(S)			X	X			2
28			SPATIAL VARIETY			X	X			2
29			SPATIAL AMBIGUITY			X				1
30			SPATIAL ZONES			X	X			2

(Continued)

Table 9.15 (Continued)

No.	Design Stratergy		Characteristics	Adjustable	Versatile	Refitable	Convertible	Scalable	Movable	
31		PASSIVE TECHNIQUES	SPATIAL PROXIMITY		X		X	X		2
32			SIMPLE PLAN		X		X	X		3
33			STANDARD GRID		X		X	X		3
34			SIMPLE FORM				X	X		2
35			MULTIPLE VENTILATION STRATEGIES		X		X			2
36			SHALLOW PLAN DEPTH				X			1
37			PASSIVE CLIMATE CONTROL				X			1
38			BUILDING ORIENTATION				X			1
39			GOOD DAYLIGHTING		X		X			2
40		UNFINISHED DESIGN	SPACE TO GROW INTO				X	X		2
41			PHASED				X			1
42			USER CUSTOMISATION		X	X	X			3
43			MULTIFUNCTIONAL SPACES		X		X			2
44		MAXIMISE BUILDING USE	USE DIFFERENTIATION				X			1
45			MIXED DEMOGRAPHICS				X			1
46			MULTIPLE/ MIXED TENURE			X	X			2
47			SHARED OWNERSHIP	X	X					2
48		INCREASE INTERACTIVITY	ISOLATABLE		X		X			2
49			MULTIPLE ACCESS POINTS		X		X	X		3
50			PHYSICAL LINKAGE		X		X			2
51			VISUAL LINKAGE (views)		X		X			2
52	CHARACTER	AESTHETICS	ATTITUDE & CHARACTER				X	X		2
53			SPATIAL QUALITY				X			1
54			BUILDING IMAGE				X			1
55			QUIRKINESS				X			2
56			TIME INTERWOVEN				X			1
57	CONTEXT	MULTIPLE SCALES	GOOD LOCATION				X			1
58			CONTEXTUAL				X			1
59			CIRCULATION neighbourhood				X			1
60			A COMMUNAL PLACE		X		X	X		3
				6	30	16	45	14	8	
				1	3	2	4	2	0	

The interactions occur at three levels: *key characteristics* relative to a particular adaptability type are illustrated by an orange cell, based upon their prevalence and crucial role suggested by the data to enable the type's fulfilment. The remaining characteristics (plain X) can be considered 'nice to have' where they are likely to enhance the capacity of the adaptability type. Lastly,

Table 9.16 Number of CARs related to each adaptability type

Type	Key	Nice to have
Adjustable	1	5
Versatile	3	27
Refitable	2	14
Convertible	4	41
Scalable	2	12
Movable	0	8

unmarked characteristics are *not necessary* as they are unlikely to enhance the particular adaptability type. The vast majority of the latter relationships are not considered harmful, although it should be recognised that, depending on a particular solution, the achievement of some characteristics for one adaptability type may hinder another. Table 9.16 summarises the number of key and nice-to-have characteristics for each adaptability type. The spatial types of adaptability (versatile and convertible) are clearly spread across more of the characteristics.

As above, this mapping is only indicative but gives generic insights and can therefore be helpful to designers by identifying the adaptability types that may be affected by a specific building characteristic, or by highlighting potential adaptability characteristics when aiming for a particular adaptability type.

The useful life of any building is governed by a number and coincidence of several different factors.

Chapter 10

Unravelling contextual contingencies (CONs)

Israelsson and Hansson (2009) suggested that when people think about adaptability they tend to focus on the physical factors. However, the broader context in which buildings are designed, constructed and used mean that adaptability is more than just about the physical product itself. The degree to which buildings are designed to adapt, and the ways in which they are subsequently adopted and then adapted, are influenced by a complex mixture of social, economic and political factors: what we describe here as 'contextual contingencies' (CONs), reflecting the fact that context influences, whether any one factor has a positive or negative influence on adaptability. Only by unravelling these CONs can you begin to take them into account and understand their impact at different stages of the building life cycle.

You can't change them, you can't control them, you can't tell your client to shut up. Your job as an architect is to make sure that all these things are balanced.

In this chapter we discuss four types of CONs: stakeholders, rules, phases and economics. Table 10.1 summarises the matters we have identified under these headings. It is worth noting that these do not relate exclusively to adaptability and play a role in the broader design consciousness – they produce the underlying synergies and tensions that influence how buildings are designed, constructed and used. Organising the contingencies into these four groups aids clarity; however, during the course of this chapter we will also try to highlight the interrelationships between them.

Table 10.1 Categories of contextual contingencies

Stakeholders	Rules	Phases	Economics
1 Client mindset	6 Building regulations	11 Fragmentation	16 Business models
2 Architect mindset	7 Taxation	12 Brief(ing)	17 Valuation practices
3 End users	8 Heritage protection	13 Procurement	18 Market forces
4 Other stakeholders	9 Planning regulations	14 Management	19 Funding methods
5 Culture	10 Industry standards	15 Occupation	20 Risk

Then the human side kicks in and all sorts of weird things happen.

10.1 Stakeholders

Client mindset (CON1)

Enthusiastic and engaged clients are critical to developing appropriate adaptability solutions specifically, but also good buildings more generally. Table 10.2

Table 10.2 Positive and negative views of client attributes

Attribute	Positive view	Negative view
Mindset	Open	Rigid
Intended user	Client, known user	Speculative
Time perspective	Long-term	Short-term
Familiarity	Unfamiliar	Formulaic
Churn rate	Low	High
Organisational complexity	Single individual or group	Multi-headed
Relationship	Established	New
Enthusiasm	Design champion	Lack of care
Responsibility	Architect and client	Client only

We always start by asking all the questions even if some of them seem ridiculous, there's a sort of why not rather than, you know, trying to consider everything and not being bound by well normally this happens and normally that happens.

provides a list of client attributes that we found to be influential in having a positive or negative influence.

Clients who were more willing to engage in a conversation about design tended to be more open to suggestions by an architect regarding the quality of the design. Their willingness to engage in the design process openly allows a fluid response to issues that arise. In the UK for example, publicly funded hospitals operate within the general National Health Service (NHS) framework; however, while some will take a flexible approach to implementing national guidelines others will interpret them more rigidly. A sophisticated client will understand that they do not know what they need and want to manage that understanding rather than pretend to know the future. This may involve considering a broader market position rather than just their own particular situation, for instance by commissioning a neutral container, that can be occupied and de-occupied more quickly, rather than a purpose-built facility.

The client's enthusiasm and attitude more generally towards the project is important. A client may not care and simply want to finish the project as quickly as possible, whereas one who is happy for the supply team to investigate matters and develop alternative solutions is invaluable. Thus, a client interested in 'good' architecture is important. And, for some clients, this extends past the building itself into the public realm – reinforcing a broader value proposition.

We really enjoy being with a very demanding client, because you tend to get better buildings. They know what they want, but they're not quite sure how to get there and you've got to help them.

Architect mindset (CON2)

An architect's attitude and openness to change in both the process and product can have an important influence on adaptability. There is a danger of an architect becoming too attached to a particular vision, such that s/he doesn't allow it to evolve for better or worse. In contrast, some architects exhibit a fluidity that allows the architecture to adapt to its context and factors at play in the building development process. The latter approach sees forces as opportunities rather than constraints, through an open-ended approach to design.

Openness also enables the development process to take architects in interesting directions that are not restricted by their own vision or desires, and

A fluidity of thinking and a fluidity of what the building needs to do, both spiritually and emotionally as much as functionally. It is an interesting approach to adaptability, which is non-physical but it leads to a very specific physicality at the end.

allows the design to become better suited for the users' needs. This could be enhanced by setting up a simple design strategy, or parti, that allows the design (both brief and solution) to evolve in response to the issues/changes that will arise during the development process and hence is able to respond better to future changes. In other words, the architecture is adaptable because it is adapting to context and situations as opposed to (*merely*) having movable walls. Retaining the flexibility of the scheme for as long as possible allows the building to be more in tune when it reaches market, at which point more informed decisions can be made.

Fluidity is also reflected in the realisation that the architect is only one of many in the building development process. An architect's role is time-bound – s/he enters at one point and exits at another – which means that their role is not to control the process but to help enable it and allow for changes to occur – both good and bad. This may be easier said than done, as there is a general culture of fear among designers that users might do something to a building or space outside of their vision or control. For example, one building we encountered was empty and not generating income, so the facilities manager wanted to change several aspects to make it more lettable. However, the architect who designed the building fought every change as it was 'his building' and he didn't want the 'concept' of his building to be destroyed. Regardless of whether or not the proposed changes were appropriate, by retaining a rigid vision of the building the architect had limited the possibilities for how the building could adapt. Additionally in this case, the unwillingness to adapt an alternative solution also strained the client–architect relationship, an issue discussed further below. Hence, fluidity in the designer's mindset needs to extend beyond development into the occupation process. This, in essence, is about the designer's capacity to 'let go'. Architects who have the experience of working with older buildings tend to be more embracing of the idea of the building evolving over time – stressing *experiential design* over *form-based*.

Having a good client–architect relationship allows ideas to bounce around and for knowledge to be shared. A nurtured relationship builds trust and belief in the project and allows ideas to occur as part of the process – not a forced act of power. Sometimes it takes multiple projects to understand the process and it is easier to transfer lessons between projects than between clients. Having a good working relationship was also found to enable compromises to be made more easily.

A good relationship requires effective communication but the requisite skills take time to acquire and often require methods other than drawings, such as physical models, to help communicate design ideas. It is important for an architect to understand their client's language although their mutual understanding is often constrained by established industry practices, competing stakeholder priorities and fragmentation in the building life cycle.

The responsibility for determining the level of adaptability in a building can rest with:

- both the architect (push) and the client (pull);
- the client primarily, with the architect providing the solution; or

I would be perfectly happy if it completely changed use. I would consider it a great success if it changed.

We would like to be in a more productive relationship between client and architect that does go beyond the completion of the building and maybe we need to think about that a little bit more.

- the architect, either because of a sense of responsibility to society and/or an interest in the long-term legacy of the building.

In some cases there may be a tension between the short-term interests of the client and the longer-term interests of the architect. For example, the developer in a residential case study didn't want to create underground car parking, so the ground floor of the building contains car parking space wrapped in metal mesh screens. In this example, the cost to create underground car parking and allocate the ground floor for community uses wasn't seen by the developer to be economically viable. The architect's 'lost' desire to create a better sense of place (CAR60) is linked to long-term thinking and society's appreciation of a place. Elsewhere, several architects felt while they had a responsibility to illustrate to the client possible options on how things might change, at the end of the day it is the client's decision and their willingness to buy into that foresight. Other architects were more extreme, suggesting that a covert approach is required to smuggle in adaptability.

On the whole, designing for adaptability is done by stealth rather than by the brief. Most clients, when the issue of adaptability is discussed realise it is a good idea, but that aspect does not yet seem to influence the value of the project to them.

End users (CON3)

Unlike most other products, buildings can only be tested when built because there are no prototypes. Even so, learning from existing buildings is something that's woefully neglected in the building industry. Post-occupancy evaluations and other performance monitoring techniques have become more common, but feedback from buildings in use is still uncommon, ad hoc and informal, for instance through discussions with clients or by revisiting a building.

Understanding how users appropriate buildings is an important way of learning about what works and what does not work in terms of adaptability. User appropriation is a reflection of the fact that:

As an architect you only really learn once the people walk in the front door and start using the building.

1 a building is only a best guess at how users will go about using the building once it is occupied;
2 user needs aren't universal (they vary from person to person); and
3 nor are they static (they vary over time).

Users can themselves be very adaptable and will often adapt their buildings in ways that were never envisaged by the designers, but the process of user appropriation can also be facilitated by designing buildings that have an affordance for being adapted. However, while some architects embrace user appropriation, others struggle with (and against) it – they see 'their' building as being 'complete'. In essence, this is about attitude towards change – how an individual or organisation perceives change and to what extent are they open to it or not (CON1). Designing for adaptability requires people to look at buildings in a much more open way and appreciate that they are much more complicated when viewed from other stakeholder perspectives.

Issues around user appropriation often raise the question of whether it is better to finish a speculative space to a particular specification (e.g. Building Council for Offices (BCO) specifications) or to leave an empty canvas (CAR41,

CAR42). On the other hand, users do not always have the know-how or the care to understand how a building works. One example from a developer who despite putting together a user manual and spending time talking to all the occupiers, found that tenants would still place their desks directly over a floor grille and complain about the space temperature. A happy user is far more likely to be a) tolerant to inefficiencies and b) have a greater appreciation of the building and how it operates.

Other stakeholders (CON4)

Buildings are a product of a variety of stakeholders – including clients, funders, developers, architects, engineers, planners, contractors, valuers, quantity surveyors and manufacturers – each of whom have different, and sometimes conflicting, motives and values. This can result in design compromises, especially in the case of adaptability, because the costs are often borne in the short term by one group of stakeholders, whereas the benefits tend to be realised in the longer term by a different group. For instance, developers look to minimise risk and maximise profit by investing in projects they consider to be safe and predictable; in contrast architects are often motivated by the opportunity to design high quality, long-lasting and innovative buildings. The consequence is a very different value system and perspectives on what constitutes a good building. Local authority officers were portrayed to be more interested in whether the design complies with regulations than if the design quality was good or improved the quality of the area – a mindset viewed to hinder design innovation and creativity.

Constructing a more adaptable built environment will require a change in stakeholder mindsets. Hartenberger (2008) attributes the slow uptake of sustainability to a 'circle of blame' (Figure 10.1), whereby constructors do not produce greener buildings because they claim that developers do not want them, who in turn claim that investors will not fund them because there is no demand from occupiers. The same logic can be applied to the business case for developing more adaptable buildings, which is unable to break out of this circle of blame (Pinder *et al.*, 2013).

We will not do buildings where the engineer comes along and takes our drawings and puts a structure on … [the team] starts at the beginning and goes all the way to the end.

Adaptability is also dependent on the coordination of systems that are often controlled by different disciplines. We found that getting the right people together, with a positive and creative mindset, is seen to be a prerequisite to developing buildings with an appropriate level of adaptability. Collaboration provides stakeholders with a chance to engage with other perspectives and to challenge their own in an effort to enhance the design. Good collaboration can be fuelled by getting team members on board as early as possible, allowing for increased possibilities, greater influence and less rework. Co-location can also enhance collaboration.

Designers gave us interesting examples of who they liked to collaborate with on projects – from artists and philosophers (concept, image) to manufacturers and subcontractors (construction quality). The latter were seen to facilitate adaptability by creating a more legible construction system. Collaborating with subcontractors and manufacturers as early as possible allowed components

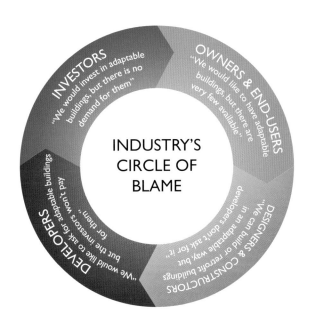

INVESTORS
"We would invest in adaptable buildings, but there is no demand for them"

OWNERS & END-USERS
"We would like to have adaptable buildings, but there are very few available".

INDUSTRY'S CIRCLE OF BLAME

DESIGNERS & CONSTRUCTORS
"We can build or retrofit buildings in an adaptable way, but developers don't ask for it".

DEVELOPERS
"We would like to ask for adaptable buildings but the investors won't pay for them".

to play a greater role in shaping the building rather than the building simply being shaped by an idea or form. Not only did this improve the quality of the construction, but it also reduced construction costs by around 20 per cent because the supply chain was engaged earlier in the process. However, this type of collaboration is still not common practice.

Culture (CON5)

Culture has an important influence on adaptability at national, sector and organisational levels. At a national level, differences in culture play an important role in influencing what type of buildings are constructed as well as how, where and when – but also by influencing the fate of the existing building stock. A country's stage of development will play a critical role in the materials, policies, mindsets, conversations, etc. that will each reflect a unique situation for adaptability. British culture puts a huge value on older residential buildings – even if they're leaking, cost more to run and in need of more maintenance. Such cultural discourses are often reinforced or legitimised through government regulations, taxes and incentives (CON6, CON7 and CON8).

The culture sector can influence the meaning of adaptability and how this manifests itself in terms of building design. For instance, practitioners operating in retail tended to distinguish between pre- and post-completion adaptability, the former being about enabling changes to the building during construction and the latter about accommodating the requirements of a range of retailers. Their emphasis on pre-completion adaptability is a reflection of the long lead times of large retail schemes, during which market conditions and retailers' requirements may change. These practitioners tend not to equate adaptability with change of use, largely because planning restrictions (CON9) precluded such changes. Similarly, organisational culture can set user tolerances and

What's nice is that we work quite closely with the manufacturers, they're influencing the design, we're influencing the construction. And it is a very dynamic process.

Adaptability in China, it is hard to have a straightforward conversation. They have different expectations about what the architect is delivering. There is almost a feeling that they will deliver what they can and hopefully the architect can produce some magic to make it all look wonderful.

behaviours when it comes to how spaces can be used and what is a 'culturally' acceptable use of space.

10.2 Rules

Building regulations (CON6)

Regulation is one of the primary mechanisms through which governments can influence and control the development of the built environment. The role of regulation is to promote and safeguard a better built environment for society (which may not always come through market forces) by specifying desired actions (prescriptive regulations) or minimum standards (performance-based regulations) that are backed up by legislation and subsequently enforced through some form of inspection regime (May, 2003). Some people argue that an increase in statutory requirements is necessary to get clients to address the issue of adaptability, while others believe existing legislation is a limiting factor and advocate its removal or loosening because such tick-box approaches create strong constraints that everyone has to commit to (good or bad) regardless of the specific context of a project.

If you want change in the industry it almost [always] has to come through regulation then there is no choice in the matter.

The degree to which government regulations influence how buildings are designed for adaptability varies from country to country. In the UK, government regulations do very little to encourage adaptability in new buildings, aside from occasional references to the issue in local planning policies and design guides. However, there was no indication of how this guidance would be implemented or enforced. Elsewhere most references to adaptability in national and local government building codes tend to relate to accessibility and inclusive design in housing, although again this often takes the form of good practice design guidance rather than mandatory standards. In England all new publicly funded housing must be built to Lifetime Homes standards, a set of 16 criteria for ensuring that houses can meet the changing needs of a diverse range of households. Government regulations and standards tend to have a greater influence on how buildings can be adapted post-construction. From a government (and societal) perspective, regulating the adaptation of the existing buildings is a convenient and necessary way of raising the performance standards of the country's building stock.

Some architects explained how they were able to interpret regulations to provide owners and/or occupants with a more adaptable building. For instance, one explained that because regulations dictate that every home needs to be provided with a parking space, his design allows for the space to be used for parking or as an additional front garden. Another designer explained that because plot ratios in the city were fixed based on the gross floor area he decided to move all the vertical service elements outside of the building envelope, which allowed him to negotiate an extra 20 per cent of floor area in the building. This was a very logical approach to a regulation that created financial benefits, a simple, versatile floor plate (CAR20 and CAR32) and easy to change services (CAR3).

It is a waste of resource and energy because we're putting all this stuff in to every building for a small minority of what might happen.

In some cases, policies aimed at encouraging adaptability were undermined by a lack of a joined-up approach between government departments. For example, a local authority planning department required developers to show how micro-flats for university students could be converted into family accommodation (i.e. a group of six or seven micro-flats can be connected by removing non-load-bearing partitions to form one conventional two-bedroom or three-bedroom apartment; CAR24). A planner explained that his department would request a set of plans at the planning approval stage, but confessed to not having the proper knowledge to verify the technical capacity for that to happen and that by the time the building was built the design could have changed. In other words, all the planner was doing, at a very early stage in the design process, was checking to see if partition walls between apartments were non-structural, whereas, a building control officer could have followed up later in the process to ensure that this was still the case.

Additionally, when regulations are applied to specific projects they can find themselves in tension (lack of overall congruence) and while making one aspect of the design 'better' worsening another aspect – i.e. unforeseen knock-on consequences. Acoustic requirements for classrooms were viewed to be important, but at the same time limited the visual connectedness of the spaces. The slow speed and timing at which regulations generally change can also hinder adapting buildings efficiently.

Taxation (CON7)

Governments use taxes to raise revenues but also to influence behaviour. Taxation policy can influence the form and density of the built environment: for instance, land value taxes have been used in some jurisdictions as a means of stimulating property development on vacant sites, with varying degrees of success.

Taxation policy tends to have a more substantive impact on how buildings are adapted post-construction, rather than influencing the way in which they are designed in the first place. A recent example from the UK concerns the reintroduction of business rates on empty buildings, to encourage their return to productive use. In reality the tax has led to owners knocking their buildings down and often using the land for parking, whereas in previous downturns they kept their building for as long as possible, finding alternative uses and sub-letting them until the next development cycle. The advantage of this from the city's perspective is that vacancy rates stay low, which allows rent rates to remain stable.

The cost of demolishing a building in the UK remains lower than in other European countries and there is a push to introduce/increase waste and demolition taxes in order to provide more incentive to adapt existing buildings. In addition, value added tax (VAT) promotes redevelopment as organisations don't pay this tax on a new building but do pay it on alterations to an existing building. Taxation policy can also have a positive impact on adaptation, for instance in the UK property owners can claim tax allowances when

It is a little bit of a dinosaur already … the latest Part L for example wouldn't allow us to build this building anymore because it is an all glass office building that's air-conditioned.

The landlords now turfed all these out, ended all their leases, got them out the buildings, then they found they have to pay council tax on the vacant buildings so they knocked the buildings down.

We are not allowed to fix anything to the existing building.

installing certain types of movable partitions because they are classed as plant rather than as part of the building. However, this is down to a legal ruling rather than a conscious policy initiative.

Heritage protection (CON8)

The protection of heritage buildings can create contradictions as they are valued enough to be preserved (CON3) but preserving those qualities limits the types of interventions (CON6), and hence the capacity of the building to adapt. In such cases, adaptation to a listed building will have to preserve aspects of the building found integral to the building's character, which can restrict construction methods, material choices and spatial possibilities. In a unique case an architect worked with English Heritage (EH) to assure that the building they designed with a grade I listing did not become 'frozen', EH recognised that the building was about its ability to change.

The building was designed to be totally adaptable and totally flexible, and now you can't even add partitions.

They'll wait for the right person to come along with the money to do it who's got the passion, commitment, but it is a problem because those buildings aren't getting any younger and they're not repairing themselves.

Listing a building can also force adaptation, even when this is challenging and the building is out of date. This highlights the need for conservation officers to strike a balance between full conservation and market requirements, otherwise such buildings will simply remain empty.

Planning regulations (CON9)

Planning approval can have a significant influence on how or whether buildings can be adapted and, therefore, the degree to which they are designed to be adaptable in the first place. For instance, in the UK the planning system tends to be prescribed and exclusive rather than inclusive (e.g. it can only be A not B, C or D), which means that changing the use of a building can be a costly and time-consuming process. Recognising this, the government introduced new permitted development rights in 2013 that allows offices to be converted to residential accommodation without the need for planning permission. The local authority planning professionals that we interviewed during our research were in favour of designing buildings for adaptability but were also very sceptical about the degree to which they could influence clients and developers to design for change.

I can say the materials you're using clash with surrounding materials, if it's high enough or if it's interfering with air traffic. But I can't turn round and say that building isn't sufficiently adaptable for a future that I can't anticipate.

It was suggested to us that the majority of planners and policy makers had moved away from mono-functional zoning and become more open to mixing uses and allowing for changes in use. Indeed, planning policies now tend to require developers to include a mix of uses – usually, retail, leisure and residential. However, this still falls short of what might be termed *flexible planning consent*, in which minimum and maximum areas for each use can be set and improves the ability to blur boundaries between uses. This flexible approach can also be implemented on a larger area, allowing a development to be set by the market by providing flexibility regarding building shape, size and function.

Industry standards (CON10)

Standards can have both a positive and negative influence on adaptability in buildings. For instance, the standard specifications that have developed over time in the office and retail sectors include parameters that allow buildings to be more easily reconfigured to meet the needs of a variety of tenants. Elsewhere, the UK's Lifetime Homes standard provides guidance on how homes can be designed to accommodate the changing needs of residents over time. However, such guidance tends to be based on a narrow view of adaptability in which changes occur solely within a particular use class, rather than between them.

Industry standards can also be so prescriptive that they limit design innovation and result in buildings being designed to satisfy the minimum requirements. While standards are necessary to protect against a lower than acceptable quality of design, they should not be a substitute for good design. There is a danger of designing to a standard without considering the client's actual needs. For example, the design and construction of publicly funded schools and hospitals in the UK is heavily influenced by government published standards that cover a wide range of design issues. While many standards were viewed to have good intentions, people found issues with a lack of detail (no real strategic direction), a lack of power to implement them and a lack of follow-through to confirm compliance.

Nobody comes back to you and says this is a great piece of room data sheets. Good architecture makes the standards invisible.

10.3 Phases

Fragmentation (CON11)

Fragmentation is revealed to be twofold – between stakeholder mindsets and stages in time – suggesting the need for improved communication and cross-over between stages. There is an enormous gap between the procurement and construction of a building and the business cycles that operate within it. Thus, the long length of the procurement process itself was seen to create fragmentation with operational, legislative and staff changes as well as most stakeholders not being involved in the entire process.

Many stress the fragmentation between stages of the process particularly between design (architect), construction (contractor) and use (FM) this being frequently cited as a reason why a particular building was not constructed to be as adaptable as it could have been. This disconnect was particularly felt early on in the process through poor briefing, which itself is partly a product of the procurement route and particularly those that exacerbate entry/exit points of team members. Figure 10.2 illustrates the potential fragmentation across stages and stakeholders.

The transition between procurement and use is a critical transfer with little stakeholder carry-over. Possible solutions include Facility Managers (FM) being involved much earlier in the process or the architect's involvement to include a facilities management service. While a crossover between FM and design teams is important, the way fees are traditionally structured creates a barrier to this, e.g. where buildings are funded with capital expenditure separate from

[Architect] guilty of feeling phew I've got rid of that one, I'll move on to the next one.

The client wants us out of the way and they want to get on with what they do.

There is an acoustic problem in the foyer, I'm sure if we had had a good FM team in here originally they would have picked up on that.

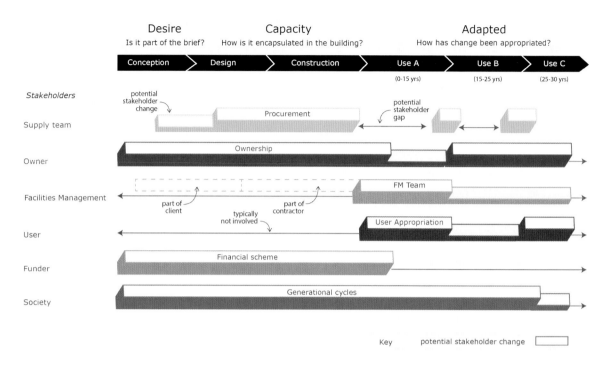

Desire
Is it part of the brief?

Capacity
How is it encapsulated in the building?

Adapted
How has change been appropriated?

| Conception | Design | Construction | Use A | Use B | Use C |

(0-15 yrs) (15-25 yrs) (25-30 yrs)

Stakeholders

potential stakeholder change

Supply team — Procurement — potential stakeholder gap

Owner — Ownership

Facilities Management — part of client — typically not involved — part of contractor — FM Team

User — User Appropriation

Funder — Financial scheme

Society — Generational cycles

Key   potential stakeholder change

▲ Figure 10.2

Fragmentation model (M8)

The worst projects are where the briefs are done before you start working; the best one is where you write the brief as you go … the building will match the brief perfectly.

The procurement process has been hijacked away from architects by people like project managers and what they're interested in doing is finding what's measurable because they can deal with measurable things, but they can't deal with immeasurable things.

the revenue streams used to operate and maintain the building (CON19). But it is disappointing to report that while PFI was perceived to provide a greater incentive for the contractor to take a long-term perspective, tying them to an FM role, it is felt that this does little in the way of providing more adaptable solutions (see CON13 below for more details).

Brief(ing) (CON12)

The brief (noun) was expressed as a written document that outlines or specifies the needs of the client. The document(s) could be very simple (a single page) with a list of terms or intractably complex with pages of room descriptions and dimensions. Devising a brief (briefing) is a key part of the building development process, allowing the design team to understand how the building can better meet the client's needs and adapt to those in the future. The purpose of this process is to draw out all the things the client doesn't know they know. Understanding which parameters should be challenged is an important skill. Indeed, some suggested that the quality of a brief depends on how far people are willing to go through a process of expanding their understanding of what they want and don't want. Without this process, adaptability tends to be an umbrella term 'thrown in' without clear understanding of how and to what extent it is needed. We found a consensus that the industry does not generally do a good enough job at developing briefs and this has a significant impact on adaptability.

Procurement (CON13)

We heard critical comments in relationship to the shifting nature of procurement routes – from a more traditional method where the supply side is led by the architect to more modern routes where the contractor has the leading role. In general, Private Finance Initiative (PFI) and design/build (D&B) contracts were considered negatively, described as a change in who controls the process and creating a shift in primary values. Construction is seen more as a numbers game with a much narrower focus on specific goals – 'it is about programme and cost, rather than about quality'. The fact that the client (contractor) is no longer the end user sets a particular value chain in place that is more about risk management than use. Thus, many declared the process itself as yielding bad results, while others felt it came down to the people involved (CON4). Thus acceptance of the PFI process was premised on if they were 'lucky' to have a long-standing relationship with the contractor and as a consequence were able to produce a good building. Others were completely dismissive of the process altogether as a waste of money and energy where a bidder loses.

Despite PFI contracts tying the contractor to the building for (usually) 25 years, many feel they take a limited long-term perspective and contractual limitations hinder the capacity to adapt the building. The two procurement processes (PFI and D&B) are also thought to limit design time and dialogue with consultants, this being detrimental to the build-up of trust (CON4). Advocates for long-term design strategies believe the structure limits their capacity to communicate with clients as all client conversations involve the contractor and have concerns with the timing when designers come on board. However, there is recognition that having the contractor involved early can allow a fuller dialogue and reduce surprises and value-engineering later.

Framework contracts are positively regarded in relation to adaptability in that the architect and developer can grow together through a relationship established over a period of time and they incentivise performance to maintain the relationship. On the other hand, once on the framework, teams get jobs because they 'just happen to be next on the list', placing designers in set processes that can result in a lower quality of work

The negative views of alternative procurement routes are seen by many to perpetuate the problem, although it was said 'we have to get into their [contractor] mindset and offer a best value to them as well as to the view understanding where their priorities lie'. Moreover, some see alternative routes such as partnering positively, for example in one case a client set the budget and asked each team to propose what they could delivery for that budget. The architect commented that, 'it utterly transformed the way everybody's thinking about it – how can we make the building so flexible and so simple that actually you can afford to introduce into the design all the things that you otherwise wouldn't have got'. In other words, the best chance of winning the competition is to produce the best quality building for a particular budget, rather than finding the cheapest building that fits the criteria.

If you're 1m² over for your PFI contractor, the classroom doesn't work because it doesn't work in what they want to pay for that classroom.

There is no understanding of where you are; the things that make you feel comfortable in a space are missing; and it is the process that causes that.

[PFI] The school is not allowed to use Blu-Tack because it takes the paint off and if they wanted to reconfigure some of the spaces, the penalties involved meant they couldn't do that in terms of the contract.

We are quite choosy about our building managers and it is trying to nurture that feeling almost like a hotel … they take a bit more active a role in trying to make sure the tenant is happy, there's lots of feedback going each way.

Management (CON14)

Delivering good management is seen as key to creating adaptable buildings. High tenant satisfaction (CON3) has led to buildings accommodating change well – e.g. businesses who have switched spaces because they did not want to leave the business park. Indeed one architect went further by describing their building as architecturally bland but, the tenant support during regular reviews has kept occupation high – management is responding to their evolving needs. As one developer put it, 'tenants are by far the best ambassadors for the scheme', enhancing the adaptability of the building by transferring positive feedback to new tenants. Good management creates regular feedback loops that refresh a building.

Occupation (CON15)

Some designers take a philosophical view that adaptability principles can be applied across building types, but others feel that each type will have its own set of conditions that influence adaptability and deploying adaptability strategies universally could compromise the building's first use. Thus we found views that affirm the view that the building should be designed specifically for first use, while others feel that despite the different optimum sizes and change demands, a more universally appropriate system could be applied to a band of typologies of similar building form (Figure 10.3, level 02). Regarding the definition and blending of uses, an additional link can be made to culture (CON5) – both at a national level and at an organisational or user level regarding tolerances.

The optimum office building would have a depth from the core to the window of 18 metres which is hopeless for residential 'cause it is too deep … so fundamentally, to change that building you've got to either chop off a bay, if you like, to thin it out or you've got to put a big hole in the middle of it.

10.4 Economics

Business models (CON16)

From a client's perspective, if adaptability is perceived not to add value (or is not mandated by legislation), then it is unlikely to rank highly on their list of priorities. They will only feel inclined to invest (time, effort or money) in an adaptable design solution that brings them a net financial return or other business benefit. Indeed, two contrasting client value systems were evident in our research: short-term merchant developers and long-term investment developers.

[The client is] saying there is no value in the market today for any of it. So there's no impetus for him to spend money, extra money, on things that are perceived to be sustainable in order to add value to his buildings.

The former are less likely to be concerned with how long the building will last or how it might need to change in the future and less likely to find value in deploying adaptable strategies and tactics. This is usually reflected in a very simple value equation – immediate economic return (selling price) over capital costs.

For a merchant developer, who develops buildings to sell, not only is it cheaper to build this way (non-adaptable) but the added realisation is they don't want people to adapt their homes anyway, they prefer them to go out and buy a new one. Thus despite the potential benefit, they intentionally construct redundancy into their developments as part of their business plan i.e.

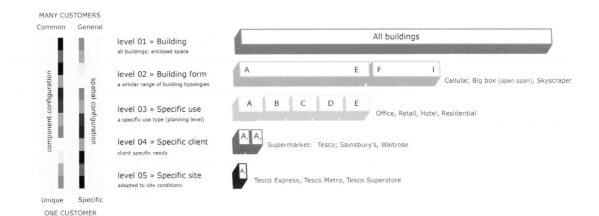

MANY CUSTOMERS

Common   General

component configuration | spatial configuration

Unique   Specific

ONE CUSTOMER

level 01 » Building
all buildings; enclosed space

level 02 » Building form
a similar range of building typologies

level 03 » Specific use
a specific use type (planning level)

level 04 » Specific client
client specific needs

level 05 » Specific site
adapted to site conditions

All buildings

A   E F   I
Cellular, Big box (open span), Skyscraper

A B C D E
Office, Retail, Hotel, Residential

A₁ A₂
Supermarket: Tesco; Sainsbury's, Waitrose

A
Tesco Express, Tesco Metro, Tesco Superstore

▲ Figure 10.3
Building specification model (M9)

it is not simply an issue of awareness, but of business models/values. When adaptability is considered from a short-term perspective, it is to appeal to the broadest tenant base with the highest net lettable floor space possible. While clients are becoming more responsive regarding green agenda items, they do not necessarily make the connection to designing for adaptability. In such cases designing for adaptability can often become a covert operation.

On the other hand, clients who value (and often are tied to) a longer-term perspective of the building are both proactive in suggesting adaptable design tactics and also more amicable to their suggestion. It fundamentally changes the way architects specify materials. Adaptability becomes about how they are going to use the space, i.e. operational as well as business-oriented. There is value in finding a balance between the division of 'buildings for use' and 'buildings as investment units' – balancing investment criteria and functional criteria – as swaying too much in either direction may result in a building that is unusable or in administration (both diminishing future efforts).

If we are to make assessments of the value of adaptability, we need an appropriate definition of value that also differentiates the concept from that of human values (i.e. motivational goals). Thomson et al. (2003) provide such clarification and have demonstrated that most definitions are in the form of a trade-off between benefit (worth) and cost. Mills and Austin (2014) present a more refined definition of value as the trade-off between 'what you get' and 'what you give' where this is clearly stakeholder dependent. This can be expressed as outputs of (benefits less any sacrifices) versus resource inputs (not necessarily just cost) – see Figure 10.4 (a).

Investment developers are interested in adaptability because they will be the ones responsible for running costs and material upkeep and ultimately in 20 years the ones who deal with the building when it begins to fall apart. This perspective evidences well the more complicated value system of this type of client which in addition to capital costs will include rental income, operational costs, depreciation and legacy. But don't think that investment developers are not interested in maximising their profits; the fact that they are invested well into the operational period of the building allows for a broader interpretation of how the building will generate value, which includes use and cultural value.

Sometimes we are trying to get something into a project that the client might not actually want if he knew enough about it. … Because if you have that dialogue with them they are going to be thinking well is he more interested in somebody else or me? I am paying you to do a service why are you talking to me about somebody else's interest 30 years down the line.

$$\text{(a) Value} = \frac{\text{benefits - sacrifices}}{\text{resources}}$$

$$\text{(b) Merchant developer}_{\text{(short-term interest)}} = \frac{\overset{\text{(business value)}}{\text{selling price}}}{\text{capital costs}}$$

$$\text{(c) Investment developer}_{\text{(long-term interest)}} = \frac{\overset{\text{(use value)}}{\text{rental income}} + \overset{\text{(business value)}}{\text{selling price}} - \text{depreciation} + \overset{\text{(cultural value)}}{\text{legacy}}}{\text{capital costs} + \text{operational costs}}$$

Clarity regarding the additional elements varies – rental income, operational costs and certain aspects of depreciation (materials) are reasonably calculable; while other aspects of depreciation and legacy (society's appreciation) are more difficult to gauge. One university client asked an architect to explore a 400-year lifespan for their new building from experience of their existing buildings, whereas rebuilding every 60 years was considered too costly an endeavour.

While it can be a costly thing to do, the client, in this case, knows the benefits, because flexibility allows them to let the building easily, so the smart developers, that's what they do.

Figure 10.4 (c) caters better to adaptability; however, its immediate market value is weak (or zero) and is reduced to within-use rather than across uses (funding silos). Hence, the deployment of adaptable strategies often means clarifying or expanding a client's value system (gross development value); this was suggested in many cases to be extremely difficult and seen to perpetuate adaptability as an additional design quality rather than a functional necessity – keeping it at the margins. The added value sought could come through local appreciation and use.

But you could, and arguably should, go further. Expressions (b) and (c) remain largely an assessment of tangible outputs, in other words revenue. Products also provide many intangible benefits and this is certainly the case with adaptability. These can then feed in to a much broader indication of value, as expressed by equation (a) in Figure 10.4. There are a variety of ways to capture these, but put simply in this context, they can be found by repeatedly asking the question 'why do you want adaptability' until you work down through the replies until you reach their end goals, as visualised in the benefit mapping model (Figure 10.5). This is a type of FAST diagram (Function Analysis System Technique) where the logic also works in the opposite direction (to the left) to reveal *how* such an end result can be achieved. The application of such an approach is discussed further in Chapter 11, section 11.5.

Furthermore, there is a difference depending on knowing who the user will be and whether or not they are the client. Designing adaptability for a speculative user demands a more generic, market-based approach that allows the user to customise or finish the space to suit their needs. Whereas designing for a specific client inherently suggests a more nuanced approach to adaptability. If the user is speculative, the desire is to appeal to the widest user base with a generic 'common-denominator' container (possessing the

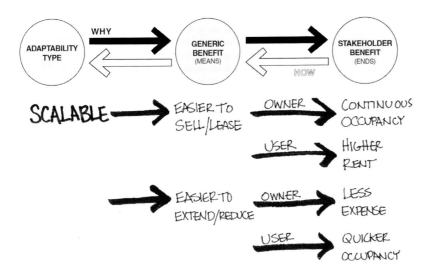

WHY

ADAPTABILITY TYPE → GENERIC BENEFIT (MEANS) → STAKEHOLDER BENEFIT (ENDS)

HOW

SCALABLE → EASIER TO SELL/LEASE → OWNER → CONTINUOUS OCCUPANCY

USER → HIGHER RENT

→ EASIER TO EXTEND/REDUCE → OWNER → LESS EXPENSE

USER → QUICKER OCCUPANCY

highest net lettable space). While designing for a known user allows the designer to focus their attention on how they operate (a tailored approach), from an adaptability perspective it can allow a broader band of working methods or uses to be accommodated that does not necessarily conflict with the current mode of operation. When a known end user is different from the client (e.g. estates management), user workshops and tactics are important to seek their perspective, addressing the gap that typically exists between the different stakeholder value systems to develop a more adaptable solution.

Regarding the size of the budget there were two perspectives revealed by our research – the budget often restricts the amount of adaptability you can design for and, in contrast, a tight budget ignites designer creativity, which creates a more adaptable solution (CON2). The latter fits with the perception of adaptability as trying to do more with less, which might mean:

1 trying to enclose as much space for the minimum amount of cost;
2 importing things that are extremely cheap and making the most of them; or
3 providing a 'light touch' building that does not become an overly designed object with precious materials (CAR8, CAR22 and CAR42).

Defining a simple system not only helps to keep costs down, it adds to the adaptability as well (CAR19). It forces the designer to know where to spend the money and not to try and design everything anew. Moreover, many architects acknowledged the discrepancy between client aspirations (CON1) and the limitations of the budget as a starting point. In this sense, the briefing process becomes a very important part of prioritising needs over wants (CON12).

The opposing angle is that a lot of adaptability solutions are counteracted by the budget – if everything is measured by cost per square metre it becomes very hard to build-in spatial adaptability. As mentioned earlier, educational

If you know the user, the more you're forced to focus on exactly how they work and that tends to lead you into thinking about how that might change.

The most serious level of adaptability seems to come when people are working really hard, to think really hard about what the problems are because they don't have any money, they don't have any time, they're under a lot of pressure.

buildings are allotted budgets based on their floor area and the UK government is trying to reduce the capital cost per square foot (15 per cent for secondary schools and 5 per cent for primary schools). Taller floor heights and longer structural spans will carry an associated cost that many clients do not want to pay for. The often initial enthusiasm for adaptable tactics is constantly reduced to the point that they are no longer viable through the design process. This confrontation is also linked to the PFI procurement route (CON13) where the contractors are the primarily guardians of the budget. In a case study example, the architect designed the ground floor circulation to include a clerestory with roof lights (CAR35 and CAR39) but the contractor chose to remove them – leaving a conventional single-storey building reliant on artificial systems. The example illustrates how a contractor can provide the cheapest solution for the client's needs without being concerned with the quality of the space – which is counterintuitive to trying to maximise what the client can get for a particular budget.

Valuation practices (CON17)

The way in which we give value to buildings, land and their uses influences the adaptability of a building. One way is through labels and the market favours straightforward and definable classifications (CON18). This is the driver for the Building Council for Offices (BCO) fit-out categories (CON10) establishing quality standards that provide value to the lease (tenant) and in turn provide value to the building (owner). This is increasingly important with shortening lease lengths that move from a 'lease and forget' mentality to one of 'lease and lease again' requiring a stronger commitment to maintaining the value of the space. In one project, the developer moved to a flexible leasing policy that allowed companies to grow/shrink their space within the building as their needs changed and there would be no red tape in doing so – tenants had already taken advantage of this policy within the first three years of the building being in use (CAR24). Continued value was perceived to be partially defined by assigning the flexibility (versatility) label. In this sense, the theory of flexibility adds or extends value to the space because rather than it being one thing (e.g. one spatial arrangement) it can be 'three' things and you've thus reduced the risk of obsolescence by making it appealing to a larger market (CON20).

Another example illustrates how an unnecessary solution is added to allow the building to be labelled a higher standard (providing a future user a ventilation choice; CAR35) – whereas if it is only naturally ventilated, it would be labelled a lower quality office space (the additional cost for mechanical ventilation was one-third of the increased value). In a contrasting case, the desired versatility was not of value to the developer, so the architect had to fight hard to have an additional room at the front of the house on the ground floor that could be used to run a business. The room was kept when it was decided it could be labelled a bedroom adding clear economic value to the developer.

Another tension is between land value and building value – if the former is significantly greater there will always be the tendency to knock the building down and build something new, particularly if the building value is low. If a building is to be adaptable (despite its physical capabilities) it has to maintain or reach a certain level of value in relationship to the land – a 'cheapness' threshold. Thus, the attractiveness of such an adaptability tactic will vary depending on the location of the building.

Value is not static – things go from being worthless to very valuable through subtle changes in boundary conditions or legislation. One legislative example is that as soon as a property obtains *planning permission* (CON9) the value of that site shoots up. The market perception of a commercial building's life cycle is important and getting shorter. The 20-year life cycle is seen as a critical decision point from an owner's perspective of how to handle the building (Figure 10.6). Projects often get steered towards demolition and redevelopment purely because value is defined by the *capital cost of construction* as opposed to the *gross development value*. However, the environmental impact, questions of social sustainability and continuity of community and residents is generally absent from this discussion. At the same time, if a building can live beyond a certain point, society tends to regain interest in it – it becomes representational of an era and we begin to assign value back to it. This also relates to cultural perceptions and how a space can be used (or labelled) – urban gentrification is an example of this.

Lastly, many discuss building value as simply determined by the size (sqm) and use of a space. In this narrative, adaptation is a result of spatial limits. And, if possible, the adaptation is not of continued use, but of a change of use where the same amount of space in today's market is worth a lot more as an alternative use (e.g. residential over office space). Thus, in this case, the decision to adapt is determined by the amount of buildable space and the use of that space before even looking at the building's physical capacity to adapt. Another problem with valuing buildings by the square metre is that the ratio of capital cost to market value is not always 1:1. For example, a

People go around and assess these buildings about whether they are or are not adaptable. And the criteria that they use is quite interesting, a lot of it is about location, not about specification, having gone over the location issue, is it in the right place for their people, we then get onto is it the right size and the right shape. [CAR57]

▼ Figure 10.6
Critical decision model (M12)

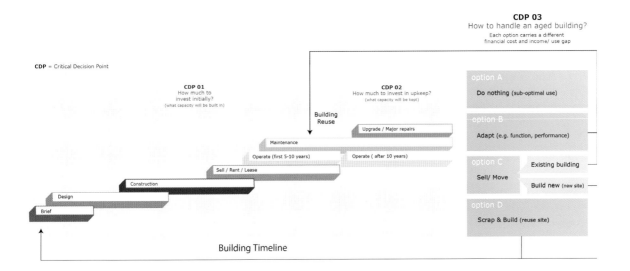

Almost all of the buildings, the office buildings I can think of around London where they've kept a 20 or 30 year old building and refurbished it rather than replacing it, was a second choice after they discovered they wouldn't get another one even bigger.

At the height of the market, there was lots of easy money … There was a notion at the time that if you build something really good then you create your own market.

Some buildings are adaptable to those, kind of, requirements [change of use], but you have to find the circumstances of the right building, the right location and the right [market] cycle in order for that exchange to take place.

The fact that the building might have to be pulled down after 30 years is immaterial, if it can make a good profit within the year 20, and for 5 years turn in a huge profit, then that's enough.

developer had a hard time understanding that by taking advantage of the way in which the houses were assembled and delivered, the floor area could be increased at a fraction of the cost in relation to the increased sales price. In this example, the exterior panels were constructed off-site and delivered to the site. The original size of the panels left 2m empty on the truck that could be 'filled' at a small cost of extending the size of the panels. In another project rather than reduce the capital costs by selecting cheaper materials, the team increased the floor area slightly to allow for additional residential units to be added, which raised the annual income significantly and bolstered the client's business plan.

Market forces (CON18)

The supply–demand context is seen to be largely driven by cultural trends (CON5). The recipe of physical features for each building will be different depending on the demand. After discussing several ways in which they have looked at adapting theatre spaces an architect admitted, 'But what we keep coming up against is there's no market, there's no real function'. So despite a physical capacity to adapt (and an owner's desire to) the lack of demand leaves the space unused and the designer's ideas on paper. Correspondingly, the point in the market cycle effects the ability to develop and occupy different types of buildings. Some think that in a buoyant market there's less incentive to adapt since there are more development and occupancy options; whereas in a downturn, instead of moving to a new building people start looking at refurbished buildings or improving where they are.

A supply shortage (high demand) often works against the inclusion of adaptable features, a situation referred to by a handful of architects regarding the UK housing market, resulting in a lack of quality. In such a case, the producers don't have to pay too much attention to what the market wants because they can pretty much sell anything. Limited availability of space also puts commercial owners in a strong position for high rent returns (law of supply–demand).

In addition, many tied the market to location (CAR57) – what is viable in one (market) location may not be in another given viable capital costs are heavily linked to the rents or selling price an owner can charge – i.e. what might be a common practice in London will have little viability in Newcastle. Thus, often it was considered very difficult for the market to regenerate on its own in some locations and it was presumed to partially be the role of government policies to ignite/support market forces (CON6).

Funding methods (CON19)

The banking system also causes difficulties as developers generally do not fund their own projects. Funders (pension funds, insurance companies, investment trusts and commercial banks) need convincing that an adaptable building is worth constructing. They often deal with a single building type and such silos see little value in a building that can adapt to a variety of uses. Moreover, funding is often split between phases (M6) particularly organisations that fund the development (secured through other assets, overdrafts, nothing in the height of the market) and those that fund the use or management of the building (secured by the value of the building itself). In an effort to keep the risk down, most development loans seek to minimise the gap between phases and keep additional expenditures at a minimum operating on a short-term return plan (e.g. three years). Furthermore, most management funding performs at five-year intervals generating perpetual short-term goals that again work against consideration of long-term benefits.

In a UK public funding example, schools only receive finance if there is a shortage of space or something is seriously wrong with the existing fabric. This need is then translated into a square footage by a standard formula (Building Bulletin 98) and the school receives funds based on a cost per square foot. This formulaic approach to funding is viewed by some to discourage adaptability. As with most public projects there is a detachment between capital expenditures and revenue streams for operation and maintenance (CON11), which suggests that a stream of smaller lump funding based on delivery of a continual service is more appropriate than the conventional lump sum funding based on delivery of a product – Figure 10.7. Switching to a more long-term financial scheme would also have effects regarding tenure. This approach could be supported from a tenant's perspective with flexible leasing giving tenants additional options (CON16).

The challenge also extends to the tension between capital and long-term costs or whole life costing. Industry still does not understand or have the proper data to analyse over a whole life well, making it hard to evidence the long-term cost benefits to a client. The lump sum approach to funding means the client has X amount of money to make the building work today and often

We operate with a 10-year life so a lot longer than most companies, most start-ups have to show returns very quickly otherwise the backers wouldn't want to pump in any more money – most business models do not look long-term.

▼ Figure 10.7
Funding method model (M13)

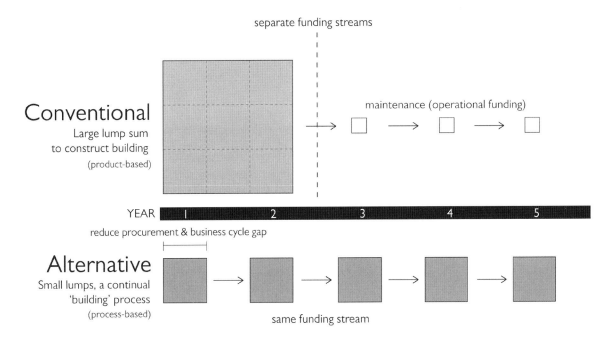

What's more important is making the school work for the money at the time isn't it?

doesn't have the luxury of considering the impact of future costs. In such a case, adaptability is slowly eroded over the priority of getting the building up and running for today. The situation is made worse by the supply team's general involvement between briefing and occupation as a one-off design, leaving little consideration for post-occupancy costs (CON11). The irony is that later down the line budget restrictions are often the main reason why a client chooses to adapt an existing building over constructing a new one – reinforcing the economics of today rather than tomorrow and the conventional view that a new building suited for today's needs is always the preferred choice.

Risk (CON20)

You can never take all risk out of it as risk and reward are inextricably linked.

The construction industry is conservative and always seeking to minimise unpredictability. There is a tension between the designer's creative desires and a quantity surveyor's view that this brings unknown developmental risks – thus standard business models are not good for innovation or driving adaptability and flexibility (CON16). Risk management protects time and money, but often at the expense of quality. This short-term view works against long-term planning risks often resulting in a building that doesn't allow for change well.

Private development is all about finding a formula that worked and replicating it as much as you can, in essence taking a lot of the risk out of it.

Unforeseen costs create anxiety among mortgage lenders and insurers (CON19). This is exemplified by a tenant who wanted to use the space as a lab rather than an office. While the building itself could accommodate this change the insurance in place hindered the process. In summary, the uncertainty, time and cost that risk management attempts to capture is both a reason to develop more adaptable buildings (counter-measure), but also a reason not to, because the benefits of adaptability are uncertain (unnecessary expenses).

Chapter 11

Design resources

The literature often links the capacity of a building to adapt to the design decisions undertaken early on; it is therefore imperative that the design team embed the consideration of adaptability into the design process, as part of a wider sustainability agenda. This chapter offers a selection of 12 resources for designing, communicating or evaluating adaptability. They are presented here consecutively for simplicity, although in practice such tools are intrinsically linked. We anticipate that individuals and organisations will select those that appeal and meld them into their existing processes.

11.1 Design guidelines (DR1)

Design guidelines act as 'design instructions' for the adaptability types. In an effort to organise the range of guidance, we have identified 24 specific types of guidance that can be placed into four typological groupings (Table 11.1): components (e.g. shape, scale, material), component relationships (e.g. interfaces, divisions), spaces (e.g. dimensions, proportions) and spatial relationships (e.g. access, proximity).

Components

Guidance on *components* considers the number, their configuration, capacity, characteristics and capabilities. Components that are of standard shapes, well interfaced and an appropriate size and weight (ease of handling) are beneficial (CAR16). When considering where to divide elements, Utida (2002) presents a comprehensive list: standard shapes, durability level, function, corresponding usability, types of constructor, construction process, logistics, price and stakeholder ownership. Guidance on the number of functions a component should provide is contradictory. Hashemian (2005) like Utida suggests components should be 'functionally autonomous' (CAR4), while others like Guy and Ciarimboli (2008) suggest, 'doubling and tripling the functions that a component provides helps dematerialise the building' (CAR7). This multiplicity is consistent with the literature that suggests minimising the number of and type of components as a means to aid changeability by simplifying the design (Schneider and Till, 2007). The contradicting challenge then is to minimise complexity (minimum parts) while allowing for sufficient capacity for a system to change with as little disruption as possible (functional separation).

component a group of parts that can be identified as a constituent of a system.

component relationships how two components relate to each other either structurally, spatially or through service flows – e.g. visualised through product structures.

space the physical void inside, between, and outside the physical bits. Spatial characteristics include size, proportion, height, depth, etc.

spatial relationships how two spaces relate to each other through access, proximity or separation (e.g. visualised through bubble diagrams).

Table 11.1 Types of design guidelines

Components		
1	Component configuration	where and how components are divided
2	Capacity of component	oversize components with a dormant capacity
3	Number of components	minimise number of parts
4	Additional components	'extra' components
5	Type of component	materials/components chosen
6	Capability of component	components which enable user control
Component relationships		
7	Type of interaction	connection method; components which can be moved, removed, replaced
8	Number of interactions	reduce component interaction between systems or layers
9	Component records	maintain accurate design/construction records
10	Component coordination (in location)	component morphology and coordination
11	Component coordination (in time)	logistics/construction process
Spaces		
12	Spatial dimensions	loose spaces (slack space)
13	Spatial form	transformational spaces (scalable space)
14	'Support' spaces	additional spaces not in the brief (soft space)
15	Spatial quality	unfinished spaces (raw spaces)
16	Spatial barriers	blurred boundaries between spaces (buffer zones)
17	Spatial uses	multiple/temporary uses for spaces (polyvariant spaces)
18	Spatial orientation/form	naturally lit and ventilated spaces
19	Spatial sizes	standardised and variant spaces
20	Empty space	Plot density (leave space for growth)
21	Unconstrained space	open spaces
22	Spatial identity (place)	a community/narrative (identity to place)
Spatial relationships		
23	Spatial relationships	location of spaces (relationship between spaces and outside)
24	Spatial circulation	circulation plan (e.g. multiple configurations, alternative access points)

The minimisation of components is made more confusing by suggestions to supply additional components to enable easy growth or reconfiguration (CAR9), particularly relative to service elements (see Cowee and Schwehr, 2009). Despite the suggestion for simplistic and durable components (CAR10), many also advise components that enable user control and comfort – i.e. components that can be adjusted (e.g. operable windows, lighting, services) or moved (e.g. furniture, equipment, partitions) (Iselin and Lemer, 1993) – which can encourage easier facilitation of change, but also tend to be more complicated and less durable (CAR2, CAR6).

The type of component suggested also provided some contradictions. Some prefer prefabricated or engineered components to aid interchangeability (CAR18; see Gorgolewski, 2005), while others suggest avoiding engineered components as overly specialised (Leaman and Bordass, 2004). The most common advice is to oversize components (CAR14), providing a dormant capacity to help to mitigate against change propagation. The majority of cases pertain to structural (foundation, live loads, columns) elements that allow for holes to be cut in the slabs, additional floor(s) to be added, or a change of use (increased live loads) (see Gold and Martin, 1999). Excess service capacity and surplus branch distribution and connectors are also mentioned, enabling an increased service demand (see Geraedts, 2006).

Component relationships

This guidance is concerned with the type and number of interactions, documentation and the coordination of components that are interdependent due to location (product) or time (process). The intent is to minimise the damaging effect to both components – connections should be exposed (easily accessible), reversible (easily separated), universally recognised and non-penetrating (CAR1, CAR3). Minimising the number of interactions between components is critical, and is consistent with designing an architecture of hierarchical layers as a means to help define which relationships are most critical to resolve or remove problems (see Brand, 1994). Component morphology and coordination is a substantial consideration for adaptability, so divisible, nested and coordinated grids – starting with a regular and wide structural grid – are often deployed (CAR25, CAR33). Thus, understanding how components relate to grid lines aids adaptability by increasing the legibility of the design (CAR17). The preferred location of elements varies. For example, 3D Reid (2005) suggests positioning the core at the perimeter of the floor plate to allow for additional lifts and risers to be added easily if needed; while others such as Russell and Moffatt (2001) suggest a central location to maximise access, subdivisibility and use of the core for lateral bracing (CAR24, CAR31). Coordinating components to make sure they are accessible is, however, consistently recommended. Therefore, documenting as-built drawings with element locations through photos, sketches, and explanations of design rationale can make future changes easier.

Spaces

Many support designing spaces beyond their functional minimum in plan and in height (CAR22). This 'looseness' supports different uses, servicing strategies, technologies and activities (CAR43). Suggested optimum storey heights vary from 3.3m to 4.9m (see Iselin and Lemer, 1993). Enlarged spaces are often accompanied by 'unconstrained space' generally in the form of a wide framed structure, where optimum spans vary between 6m and 10m (CAR20). Loose-fit spaces are often considered in conjunction with either the standardisation of room sizes or spatial variety (CAR27, CAR28). Non-hierarchical standard room sizes avoid many bureaucratic issues allowing for improved interchangeability, yet providing different sizes of spaces as suggested by Lynch (1958) can support a larger variety of activities. When considering this interplay we note Rabeneck *et al.*'s (1973) suggestion of avoiding 'extremely large or small sizes', and Hertzberger's (2005) plea for spaces that are dimensioned appropriately for the functions intended.

Simple floor plans are common with regular, generic shapes consistent with guidance on providing transformational spaces (CAR32) – of divisible depth and length (see Lynch, 1958). Moreover, plan depth serves a dual role in supporting naturally ventilated and lit spaces (CAR35, CAR36, CAR39). The provision of extra spaces is seen as valuable, as are 'soft' spaces with lower intensity use that can be relocated to expand high-intensity adjacent spaces (CAR30). The interchangeability of space is also recommended through the provision of functionally neutral spaces by designing rooms without labels (see Schneider and Till, 2007) and offering little overt expression of room function (CAR43) – e.g. standard furniture and windows (Rabeneck *et al.*, 1973). Indeed, leaving some spaces unfinished to allow user customisation is to be encouraged (CAR42; see de Neufville *et al.* 2008).

Spatial relationships

The last category considers the location and relationship of spaces, particularly circulation. Guidance is straightforward on the relationship between spaces, between spaces and the exterior and between neighbouring buildings. Important considerations for circulation include good access and flow, minimised travel distances, multiple paths and support for multiple configurations (CAR50). Two apparently contradictory recommendations with the same intent are 'providing no "circulation" space by allowing each room to act as an antechamber to the next' (Rabeneck *et al.*, 1974) and 'enlarge circulation spaces to allow for different functions to take place' (Schneider and Till, 2007). Both are trying to achieve multifunctionality of spaces, but from opposite directions (CAR43).

design parameter different units or decisions that make up the building; e.g. height, width, material, colour.

11.2 Critical (design) parameters (DR2)

You can improve a building's capacity to accommodate change by considering a subset of design parameters that influence the capacity to adapt a building. One way to understand the importance of a design parameter with regards to adaptability is its *inability to be changed*. Boyd and Jankovic (1992) provide a relatively comprehensive set of 24 such factors, related to six aspects, five of which constitute the building itself (e.g. internal form, envelope) and the sixth the site (including planning and building regulations). For example they identify building orientation, floor shape, foundation, load transmissions (frame, wall), grid and floor-to-ceiling height as impossible to change. Douglas (2006) also identifies parameters that are 'incorrectable': poor location, inadequate building morphology (e.g. ceiling heights), restricted site, and unsatisfactory microclimate (spatial configuration). Douglas also explains under what conditions these parameters make adaptation difficult, e.g. low floor-to-ceiling height, awkward plan shape, close column centres and deep-plan buildings.

Another approach is to recognise parameters that are *most likely to change* or *costly to be changed*. Gann and Barlow (1996) adapt Boyd and Jankovic's list of design parameters and cite 'ease of access to services' as being most critical, since up to 60 per cent of adaptation costs can be from stripping out and installing new equipment. They also highlight 'depth of floor plan' as being critical regarding service distribution in the case of residential buildings. Kincaid's (2000) extensive study of building adaptations also found 'servicing elements' as the most frequent elements changed (air-con, heating and ventilation). Secondary were means of escape, building access and cladding. However, the most important factors that influenced the marketability (interest and willingness to adapt) represented a different set of parameters – building character, storey height and window size.

From the literature, there appears to be a clear relationship between the parameters and their associated building layers – those that cannot be changed (structure, site) and ones where change is often and potentially costly (service, skin). Thus, the majority of the critical parameters are related to the longer lifespan components, re-emphasising the significance and controlling nature of the building's more permanent layers. Design parameters, however, do not exist in isolation as Blyth and Worthington (2001) highlight the contingent nature of the parameters, e.g. storey height affects servicing strategy and options for natural ventilation and light (plan depth and windows). In addition, disparities between stakeholder priorities are common. Bottom *et al.* (1998) illustrate the gap between supply and demand where two parameters were considered important to adaptability: spatial flexibility ranked 12th out of 39 features from the demand side and 27th from the supply side; while inversely, storey height ranked 36th by the client and 7th from a supply perspective. Stakeholder disparities like these often lead to compromised solutions as a result of poor communication (CON12).

There are two types of design parameters – ranges (continuous design variables) and options (design choices). Table 11.2 lists the design parameters (organised by parameter type and building layer) against the six adaptability types. A design parameter relevance to an adaptability type is either significant (1), linked (0.5) or blank (no link found).

Three industry examples mobilise the critical parameters. One team evolved five design principles over several projects to create a typology (CAR23) that they believe represents the future of office design: concrete structure, tall ceilings, deep plan, smart servicing and simple passive façade (Figure 11.1). The exposed concrete frame (CAR19) maximises thermal storage (CAR37), provides a pleasing aesthetic feel (CAR53), allows floor bays to be removed (connect multiple floors, CAR50), offers 4m floor-to-floor heights (CAR22) and the concrete 'upstand' perimeter wall eliminates the need for perimeter columns. The design includes a compact core of lifts and stairs along with fire sprinklers so the space can remain open and connected (CAR20 and 51). The taller floor heights

Table 11.2 Design parameters mapped against adaptability types

Adaptability types	Structure				Space				Services		Space plan				Site			Structure	
Ranges (continuous design variables)	Storey height	Number of storeys	Structural morphology	Floor loadings	Plan depth	Plan Shape	Plan width	Total floor area	Capacity of services	Location of services	Fire design (max. travel distance)	Max. distance to core	Core location	Corridor locations	Block spacing	Plot density (solid/void)	Building orientation	Stuctural system	Foundation design
Adjustable																			
Versatile			1		0.5	0.5	0.5	0.5		0.5			0.5	0.5					
Refitable	0.5	0.5			0.5	0.5			0.5	0.5									
Scalable	0.5	0.5		1	0.5				0.5	0.5	0.5		0.5	0.5	1				1
Convertible	1		1	1	0.5				0.5	0.5	1	0.5	1	1	1				
Movable																0.5		1	1

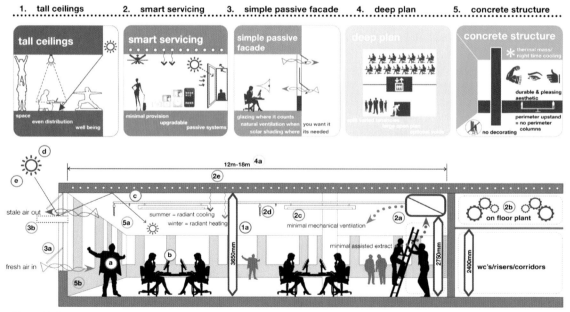

1. tall ceilings 2. smart servicing 3. simple passive facade 4. deep plan 5. concrete structure

▲ Figure 11.1
White Collar Factory's critical parameters visualised
Courtesy AHMM

| Options (design choices) | | | | | | | | | | | | | | | | | | | | | | | |
| Skin | | | | | | | Services | | | | | | | | | Space plan | | | | | | Stuff | |
Cladding system	Roofing system	Shading system	Window (type, size, shape)	Door (type, size, material)	Moisture protection	Thermal protection	Ventilation system	Communication system	Water system	Heating/ cooling system	Security system	Fire system	Power system	Sanitation system	Drainage system	Lighting system	Acoustic design	Wall Partitions	Ceiling system	Flooring system	Wall finish system	Furniture system	Fixtures
																						1	1
								1								1	0.5	1				1	0.5
1		0.5	1		0.5	1	0.5	1								0.5			1				
0.5	0.5																						
0.5		0.5					1	0.5		1	0.5					0.5							
0.5																							

allow for on-floor plant to be contained in the core space above the WC where lower ceilings are okay (2.4m). The size of the floor plates (12–18m to core) are dictated by the amount of natural light (CAR39) and potential for natural ventilation (CAR35). The size, position and location of windows are adjusted for solar orientation (CAR38) removing the need for expensive shading devices (CAR37). The windows are operable by the user (CAR6) and are positioned above desk height. Chilled water pipes are cast into the bottom of the floor slabs (integrates structure and services) and cool the space as the hot air rises reducing the need for air conditioning (CAR37). The base building additionally includes universal artificial lighting throughout the space (CAR9).

Another example provides rules of thumb for developing good space for speculative office developments that can change use. The designer identified standard dimensions for different uses with the intent to identify overlaps in the codes to generate a notional set of adaptable design rules. For example, *plan depth* should not exceed 5x the *ceiling height* (5h) and should be in a 1.5m module, which is the BCO recommended planning module (CAR25). *Storey heights* are suggested at a module of 0.15m to coordinate easily with *stair height* (CAR25). Figure 11.2 illustrates the ability to stretch the plan depth

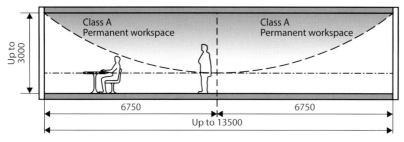

TOTALLY FLEXIBLE SPACE - all well daylit

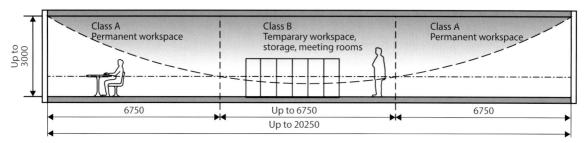

MAXIMUM DEPTH OF USEFUL SPACE - up to 33% class B support space

based on defining two spatial zones (CAR30; permanent workspace and temporary workspace). Finally, the *space between buildings* (w) should be at least one-third of the total *building height* (3w) – it is suggested that 18m between buildings provides for a *good public realm* (CAR60).

A last practice-based example (Figure 11.3) illustrates the ability of a generic frame – 7.5m standard grid (CAR33), 15m plan depth (CAR36) and 4m storey height (CAR22) – to accommodate a range of conventional uses. The uses are defined by standard dimensions for critical parameters. The illustration shows different floor-to-ceiling heights, façade patterns (size of window openings) and materials and spatial configurations (open plan – cellular) which require different beam depths and servicing strategies.

Scenarios attack a design from so many directions that gaps and oversights are likely to show up.

change scenario a narrative for how the building could change; provides a measure for envisaging and testing adaptability strategies.

11.3 Scenario planning (DR3)

Change scenarios ask the 'what if' (demand) or 'how can' (supply) questions that help to resolve future possibilities. The key to scenarios is thinking about what could change and what is fixed under more than one future condition to accommodate multiple futures. Such scenarios can be presented as social (cause, why) as demonstrated by Rabeneck *et al.* (1974) who describe change in family make-up, family activities; fashion and quality of the home. Scenarios can also reflect the physical effect (how) of those social causes, as illustrated by Altas and Ozsoy (1998) who consider a residence's capacity to adapt: capacity to add space(s), change between interior and exterior space, subdivide larger spaces and move activities. Consequential scenarios therefore

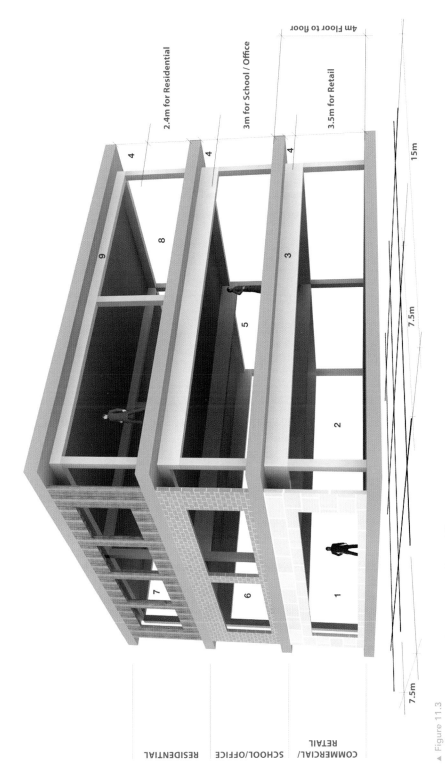

▲ Figure 11.3
Section illustrating generic solution accommodating different use types
Courtesy Buro Happold

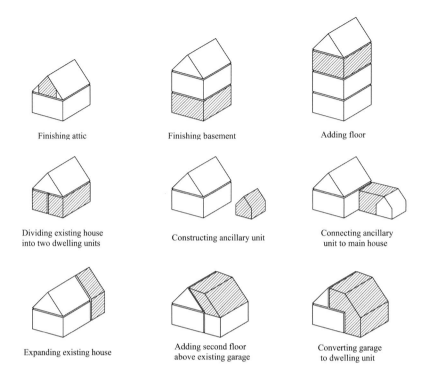

Finishing attic

Finishing basement

Adding floor

Dividing existing house
into two dwelling units

Constructing ancillary unit

Connecting ancillary
unit to main house

▶ Figure 11.4
Various residential scenarios
Courtesy Avi Friedman

Expanding existing house

Adding second floor
above existing garage

Converting garage
to dwelling unit

generally evolve around a set of basic transformative actions as proposed by Durmisevic (2006): elimination, addition, relocation and substitution of the element. Different actions (verbs) can be seen as equivalents or combinations of these actions (e.g. reconfigure). Friedman (2002) presents a series of change scenarios to an existing home based on events in time creating new requirements – Figure 11.4.

If clients do think about change it is usually in the short term, as reflected in the most common reference to scenarios being multifunctional spaces (CAR43) as a quick and simple method to confirm that a space can be reconfigured to accommodate a variety of working conditions, activities and demands. This is conventionally done by laying out furniture and equipment in plan with standard spatial dimensions for operation illustrating a handful of layout options. For example, Figure 11.5 shows eight spatial configurations for a theatre space.

Particular uses will be more prone to dynamic typologies given the complexity (healthcare), marketability (offices) and cyclical nature (schools) of a use – Table 11.3. Other more static typologies have evolved more dramatically recently with electronic technology such as theatres and libraries. For example, libraries were about a place to store books or to study quietly, but have now opened up to creating broader learning experiences – a place to meet, work and socialise – intertwined with an array of modern methods for obtaining and processing information – cafés, sofas, computer stations.

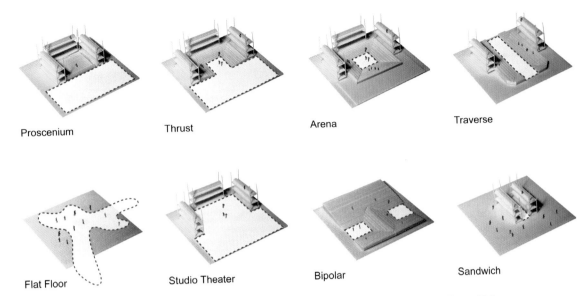

Proscenium

Thrust

Arena

Traverse

Flat Floor

Studio Theater

Bipolar

Sandwich

▲ Figure 11.5
Theatre spatial configurations for Dee and Charles Wyly Theatre
Courtesy REX Architecture for Dee and Charles Wyly Theatre

Table 11.3 Dichotomy of uses

DYNAMIC USES (80–90%)*		PRESUMED STATIC (10–20%)	
MEDICAL	LABORATORIES	MUSEUMS	CIVIL BUILDINGS
OFFICE	EDUCATIONAL	LIBRARIES	TRANSPORTATION
RETAIL	MANUFACTURING	MONUMENTS	
HOUSING	RESTAURANT	CEMETARIES	

*PERCENTAGE OF BUILT ENVIRONMENT

Change scenarios are not typically linked to the different types of change (adaptability types) or specific implementation level (design tactics). Figure 11.6 maps the change scenarios to the six adaptability types helping link them back to the broader client needs and Table 11.4 identifies typical types of change(s) that commonly occur across six use types along with a handful of solutions (design tactics) in response to those changes and the motives for why those changes occur.

Another helpful differentiation between scenarios is – *specific scenarios* that are tuned to the client's nuanced needs and come from the client, and *market scenarios* that the designer can provide based on their experience and understanding of industry standards, allowing them to extend adaptability to things that may not be within the client's current mindset. This suggests there is a certain amount of predictability in adaptability that should be built in and the rest should come from the specifics of the client limiting the range of scenarios that are applicable. For example a speculative office developer may want to look at different ways of dividing a floor plate or the requirements

Even though it wasn't required ... I think that's what makes a building adaptable is thinking beyond its specific role and thinking more of its ability to do other things.

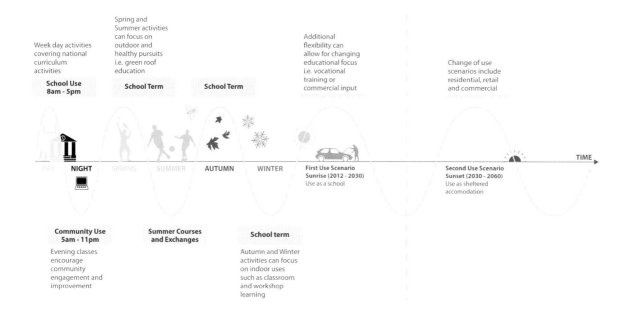

Spring and Summer activities can focus on outdoor and healthy pursuits i.e. green roof education

Week day activities covering national curriculum activities

School Use 8am - 5pm

School Term

School Term

Additional flexibility can allow for changing educational focus i.e. vocational training or commercial input

Change of use scenarios include residential, retail and commercial

DAY **NIGHT** SPRING SUMMER **AUTUMN** WINTER

First Use Scenario Sunrise (2012 - 2030) Use as a school

Second Use Scenario Sunset (2030 - 2060) Use as sheltered accomodation

TIME

Community Use 5am - 11pm
Evening classes encourage community engagement and improvement

Summer Courses and Exchanges

School term
Autumn and Winter activities can focus on indoor uses such as classroom and workshop learning

▲ Figure 11.7
Building timeline
Courtesy Buro Happold

through possible futures will better prepare the building for its unpredictable future.

11.4 Other time-based resources (DR4/5)

Scenario planning is a good example of integrating time into design thinking. Films (DR4) add time to the representational medium and thus are well suited to communicating the life of the building whether over a day, week, year or decade. They can tell a story of change through a combination of photographs, maps, sound bites and illustrations (Figure 11.8). Everyone enjoys watching films, unlike conventional architectural representations that can appear quite unreadable to the layperson. In this respect, films can supplement conventional forms of representation well, because they can convey a clear message through the dimension of time.

'Active' drawings (DR5) is a style of illustration that includes people and stuff to show how the building could be used (Figure 11.9). They are like visual scenarios to help imagine use possibilities and are sometime referred to as a graphic manual for the building.

We draw the objects and the human mess in the space ... it's far more exciting drawing shelves with all the stuff on it because you can't judge how those shelves are working until you see the thing as a living, breathing, useful apparatus.

11.5 Benefit mapping (DR6)

In Chapter 10 (section 10.4) we discussed the implications of various business models and ultimately how adaptability can be valued. The value equation model (Figure 10.4, M9) gives examples of how value can be expressed in terms of a cost–benefit analysis. Of these, the most general is (a) benefits minus sacrifices over resources.

As explained, the advantage of such a definition is that it can take account of the many intangible, subjective benefits of a product (or service) including making a building more adaptable. If identified, they can be weighed against

Medieval Market Town

◀× 0:05 / 3:11

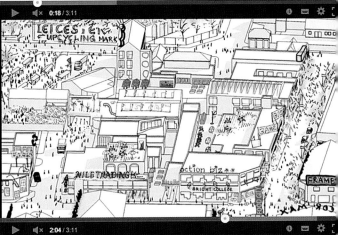

▶ ◀× 0:18 / 3:11

◀× 0:52 / 3:11

▶ ◀× 2:04 / 3:11

▲ Figure 11.8
Snapshots of Leicester Waterside
film
Courtesy Ash Sakula Architects

▼ Figure 11.9
'Active' drawings for Leicester
Central Bus Depot
Courtesy Ash Sakula Architects

Customisation to every artist's needs

Meeting and break out space

the resource input. The latter is often the additional capital cost, but could also be in terms of the higher cost of making a change more expensive if not designed in. Figure 10.5 presented the benefit mapping model (M11) to show how a type of FAST analysis can help to identify the ultimate (ends) benefits and associated beneficiaries. This can be done top-down, from a perceived need for a particular adaptability type to flush out the benefit, or bottom-up from the required benefit to identify the associated type of adaptation. It is also possible to capture any downside of a particular situation in terms of a sacrifice (that is a disbenefit).

It is worth emphasising that contrary to the view that a project has shared goals, we believe value is in the eye of the beholder and thus unique to each interested party. We have used two approaches to help a project team pinpoint each stakeholder's benefits, which can loosely be regarded as inductive and deductive. In the first, the project team starts with a blank sheet of paper and uses a suitable technique to collectively, or in groups, identify the potential benefits of a particular adaptability type (see Figure 10.5). You can get to the ultimate goals by repeatedly asking the question, *'why do you want this?'*

The alternative approach is to use your experience to create a predetermined list of potential benefits (Figure 11.10). Participants can then be prompted to tease out those relevant to their organisation. As with any activity aimed at identifying a set of features of a product or process, there are pros and cons to each approach. A blank sheet reduces the risk of unduly influencing the participants, requires deeper thinking and gives a sense of ownership to the end result. On the other hand substantial experience is required to build a checklist, but it is quicker to administer, can capture learning by embedding

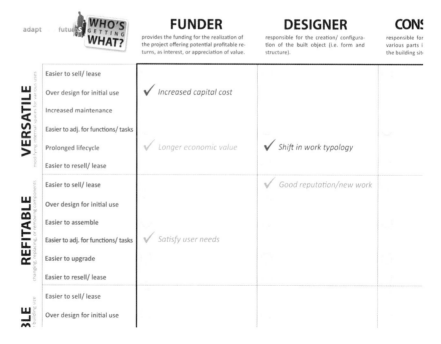

▶ Figure 11.10
Result of a project team brainstorm of stakeholder benefits

OWNER *has the rights to the building; investing in the building as an asset (a finished leasable/ useable object)*

REFITABLE *changing or removing components*

Easier to sell/ lease
Continuous Occupancy ⟶ Continuous cash flow

Over design for initial use
Increased cost ⟶ More initial capital

Easier to assemble
Cheaper price ⟶ Lower initial capital

Easier to adjust for functions/ tasks
Larger market base ⟶ Increased rent opportunites
Less 'large' costs ⟶ Less expenses/ more profit

Easier to upgrade
Uncoupled layers ⟶ Cheaper maintenance
Lifetime compatibility ⟶ State-of-the-art facility
Longer value ⟶ Increased profit over time

Easier to resell/ lease
Longer investment value ⟶ Better return on investment
Higher occupancy rate ⟶ Continuous cash flow

SCALABLE *increasing/ decreasing the building size*

Easier to sell/ lease
Continuous Occupancy ⟶ Continuous cash flow

Over design for initial use
Increased cost ⟶ More initial capital

Suits future change in size of use
Prolonged value ⟶ Increased profit over time

Easier to extend/ reduce
Less expense ⟶ Less capital needed

Prolonged lifecycle
Increased longevity ⟶ Increased use/ profit over time

Easier to resell/ lease
Longer investment value ⟶ Better return on investment
Higher occupancy rate ⟶ Continuous cash flow
Faster sales ⟶ Less 'down time'
Lower management/ admin. costs ⟶ Less expenses

new ideas and may catch benefits that might otherwise be missed. Both can prompt interesting conversations. In our view it doesn't matter how you do it – the important thing is to go on the journey and make some attempt to value the incorporation of adaptability into a building. Each stakeholder will then have a set of benefits with which they can judge the design and weigh against the cost.

Figure 11.11 illustrates the checklist approach being used for design assessment rather than briefing. In this case the stakeholder indicates to what degree a benefit is desirable or not on an H,M,L scale (larger bold text headings) as well as making a judgement on whether the benefit is delivered by the proposed design (criteria in smaller text below headings).

▲ Figure 11.11
Stakeholder checklist of predetermined benefits

11.6 Evaluation tools (DR7)

Evaluation tools are techniques that can objectively evaluate the potential to adapt a design or an existing building. Two types emerged from our studies: those which *assess the level of adaptability a design accommodates* and those used for the *financial assessment of converting buildings* from one use to another. An example of the first type is Larssen and Bjorberg's (2004) software tool that examines flexibility (functionally), generality (spatially) and elasticity (overall size) by associating them with physical parameters (e.g. structural span, heating capacity, building size) rating them on a four-point scale (see Table 11.5 for an example, where 0 is best). However, the included

Table 11.5 Scoring examples of two parameters

Storey Height	Floor Span
grade 0 (>3.9m, flat ceiling)	grade 0 (>18m)
grade 1 (>3.6m few beams in one direction)	grade 1 (>16m)
grade 2 (>3.0m)	grade 2 (>14m)
grade 3 (>3m, beams and crossing secondary girders)	grade 3 (>12m)

Larssen and Bjorberg (2004)

factors are limited to the building itself neglecting any financial or location effects.

Geraedts and de Vrij's (2004) *New Transformation Meter* broadens the evaluation criterion to include location (social image, amenities, public transport) and non-physical variables (e.g. acquisition and operational costs). The approach focuses on evaluating the conversion of vacant office buildings to residential units by assessing a hierarchy of items with three instruments (a quick scan, feasibility meter and checklist). The methods start with a quick evaluation that requires limited special knowledge prior to deeper forms of assessment, ultimately weighing the financial costs of the conversion against the financial benefits. While the parameters are amendable, the evaluation criteria are tailored for office to residential conversions (in Rotterdam).

A final illustration is the use comparator by Kincaid (2002) which is a decision framework for the viability of adapting buildings to auxiliary, mixed or new uses through functional (regulatory framework), technical (physical capacity to change) and economic criteria. The two-stage software-based process initially converges on a set of possible uses by matching 5 of the 13 design parameters identified as important (e.g. tenure, floor-to-floor height, floor strength). The characteristics are measured by selecting one of the predetermined choices (either a numerical range or an option) and then compared with the demand characteristics of the 77 possible uses in the software's database to produce a suitable list. The second stage employs the remaining eight characteristics to produce a more detailed financial appraisal and a list of options that can be evaluated financially (e.g. conversion to X will cost this amount, while conversion to Y will cost this). The software provides an analysis for matching supply characteristics (existing buildings) with new demands.

All the evaluation tools investigated used design parameters to evaluate a building's capacity to adapt. They, however, neglect the contingent relationships between parameters and thus offer little insight into how change would propagate.

11.7 Other resources (DR8–12)

Several other design resources came up throughout our investigation, many of which are not specific to adaptability but were applied in various projects to communicate or design for adaptability. We've chosen to include some examples here to illustrate the variety of applications. For example, an organogram

▲ Figure 11.12
Existing resident's self-customised fireplace
Courtesy FAT Architecture

(DR8) can be used to explore spatial demands and dependencies (CAR30). Like physical dependencies, such knowledge can help to conceive which spaces can be joined or separated in the future to allow for different ways of using the building.

The use of project precedents (DR9) can illustrate what has or has not worked in a specific context. The application of precedents is to understand the fundamental principles of what makes certain buildings work and stand the test of time which can be a very convincing piece of evidence. Photographs of existing conditions can visualise DIY transformations and help designers understand how users have accommodated certain changes over time (a reconfigured kitchen, overlaying of personalised decoration) and ways in which they could not (redefined circulation path off the living room) – Figure 11.12. Analysis of the photographs and conversation can become an important source to develop a brief.

A parti (DR10) is a simplified visualisation to illustrate a basic scheme or design concept. Figure 11.13 communicates the financial benefit of a versatile plan (multiple configurations) compared to a rigid plan (single configuration).

The success of a building can often be the result of engaging stakeholders from an early point in the design process. Workshop exercises (DR11) can provide an informative way to gather information and get people to

▶ Figure 11.13
Conceptual diagram for Dee and
Charles Wyly Theatre

*Courtesy REX Architecture for Dee and
Charles Wyly Theatre*

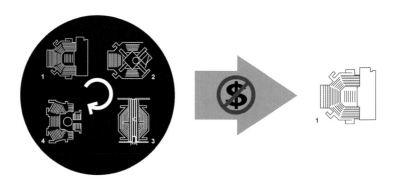

Potential Flexibility   **De Facto Rigidity**

*A simple architectural
diagram can set a very
rigorous system of
working.*

*Though they're [end
users] not trained
architecturally, they know
what they want, they just
don't know how to put it
together.*

define, visualise and agree upon various aspects rather than designers making assumptions on how users will appropriate the space. Furthermore, developing methods to stay in contact with users to enable a feedback loop for the building's performance can be especially important regarding adaptability. One communication method used was through websites or social media tools (DR12) as a tool to grow over time and track the development of the building.

Chapter 12

Meta-models

This chapter presents seven meta-models that link together key elements of multiple models. They can therefore help communicate and visualise important cross-concept relationships, and hence consider deeper aspects of adaptability and its contingencies.

12.1 Adaptability types, layers and stakeholders

The heart of this tabular model (Figure 12.1) visualises the linkages between the two fundamental models of adaptability types (M6 in the rows) and building layers (M4 in the central columns). The model also identifies on the left the cause (social) and effect (physical) of the six types of adaptability, and on the right the key stakeholders (on the supply and demand sides). This may help project teams communicate the differences between the types in simple terms – and visualises the often-cited gap between who pays for adaptability and who benefits from it.

The links between the adaptability types and building layers were established by analysis of the adaptable solutions identified in the case studies and are classified in terms of probability of occurrence as either *high*, *medium*, *low* or *not recorded*. Several patterns are discernable if we assume the *site* layer and movable adaptability type are strongly correlated and excluded as a special case. The two *spatial* adaptability types (versatile and convertible) affect most layers – versatile spreads across all five and convertible four (not *stuff*) and both have a strong relationship with the *space plan* layer. On the

▼ Figure 12.1
Linking meta-model (M14)

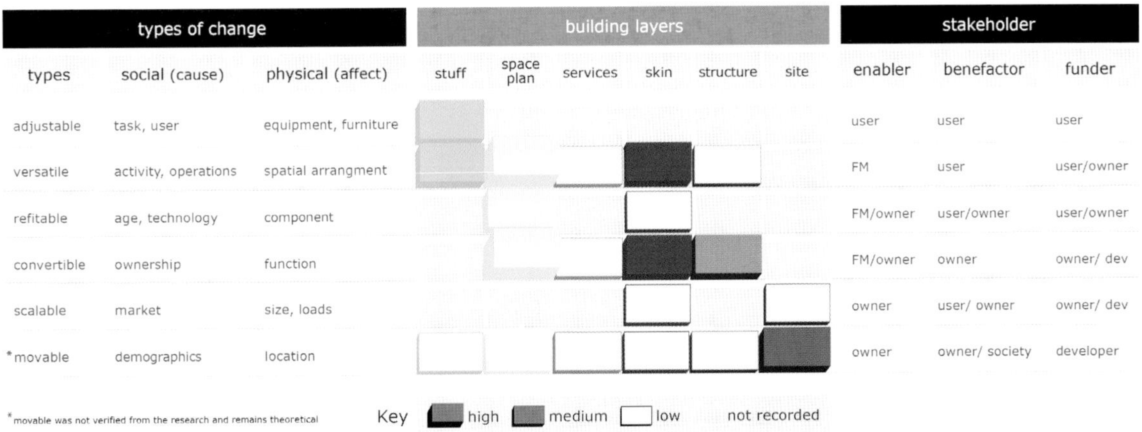

types of change			building layers						stakeholder		
types	social (cause)	physical (affect)	stuff	space plan	services	skin	structure	site	enabler	benefactor	funder
adjustable	task, user	equipment, furniture							user	user	user
versatile	activity, operations	spatial arrangment							FM	user	user/owner
refitable	age, technology	component							FM/owner	user/owner	user/owner
convertible	ownership	function							FM/owner	owner	owner/ dev
scalable	market	size, loads							owner	user/ owner	owner/ dev
*movable	demographics	location							owner	owner/ society	developer

*movable was not verified from the research and remains theoretical

Key ■ high ■ medium □ low not recorded

other hand, *physical* adaptability types are less influential – adjustable on just the *stuff* and *space plan* layers, scalable the *skin* and *structure* layers, while refitable spread across *space plan, services* and *skin.* Interestingly, from a layers perspective the *skin* layer had the widest dispersion being spread across four adaptability types – the exception being adjustable.

The links can help to focus conversation and design efforts by associating client aspirations with the physical object. If a particular adaptability type is desired, the model can indicate which layer(s) the design team should consider. The adaptability could also be augmented by focusing on linked building characteristics (CARs) – either through the specific adaptability type or layer.

12.2 Framecycle

The Framecycle meta-model (M15, Figure 12.2) integrates the adaptability type model (M6, large coloured text), design tactics (dark grey text) and stakeholder benefits (M11, lighter grey text around inner circle) in a time-based orientation. The model is centred on our definition of adaptability with the six motivational goals (adaptability types) moving, clockwise, from relatively high-frequency changes on a daily scale (adjustable) to those that occur, if at all, over decades (movable).

The purpose of the model is to make explicit the nature of adaptability that is desired – to improve on the imprecision in language identified in the

▼ Figure 12.2
Framecycle meta-model (M15)

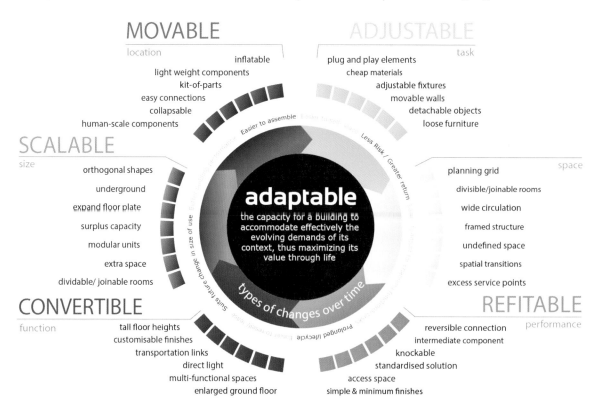

literature and our interviews, as stakeholders often struggle to articulate their goals through the design process. Such a comprehensive vocabulary can assist briefing and clarify goal-setting.

12.3 Sources of know-how

The Sources meta-model (Figure 12.3) places the adaptability types (M6) in a broader contextual spectrum of information inputs and controls that must be drawn upon when designing for adaptability (contextual contingencies).

Thus, the sources of know-how explain where our information, knowledge, resources and constraints of adaptability come from – factors that hinder, enable and/or accommodate change. They include: *culture* (artefacts, values), *design intelligence* (philosophy, experiences), *rules* (services, structure), *policy* (e.g. planning and building regulations, taxes), *market* (financial schemes, land values) and *products* (standard details, national standards) organised in relation to their permanence or fluctuation – ranging from more timeless, enduring behavioural and value aspects (intelligence, culture) to time-bound, physical factors (products, market) in a greater state of flux.

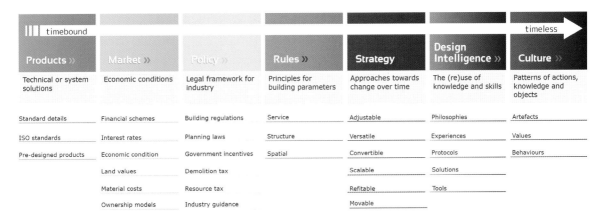

Products »	Market »	Policy »	Rules »	Strategy	Design Intelligence »	Culture »
Technical or system solutions	Economic conditions	Legal framework for industry	Principles for building parameters	Approaches towards change over time	The (re)use of knowledge and skills	Patterns of actions, knowledge and objects
Standard details	Financial schemes	Building regulations	Service	Adjustable	Philosophies	Artefacts
ISO standards	Interest rates	Planning laws	Structure	Versatile	Experiences	Values
Pre-designed products	Economic condition	Government incentives	Spatial	Convertible	Protocols	Behaviours
	Land values	Demolition tax		Scalable	Solutions	
	Material costs	Resource tax		Refitable	Tools	
	Ownership models	Industry guidance		Movable		

▲ Figure 12.3
Sources meta-model (M16)

12.4 Design process

The time-relatedness of the Sources meta-model (M16) can be visualised as part of the project process. The idealised illustration (Figure 12.4) suggests a sequential condition between the sources in time (starting from 12 o'clock moving clockwise).

The model delineates the influence and timescale of each element with separate coloured lines, emphasising the continuous impact of design intelligence and culture (green). Our experiences along with built and unbuilt solutions feed into our intelligence as we move on to new projects. The model thus illustrates how successful, and indeed unsuccessful, design ideas (i.e. lessons learnt) can be embodied into future projects. These range from replicating specific physical systems to less tangible know-how, with organisational standard solutions in between.

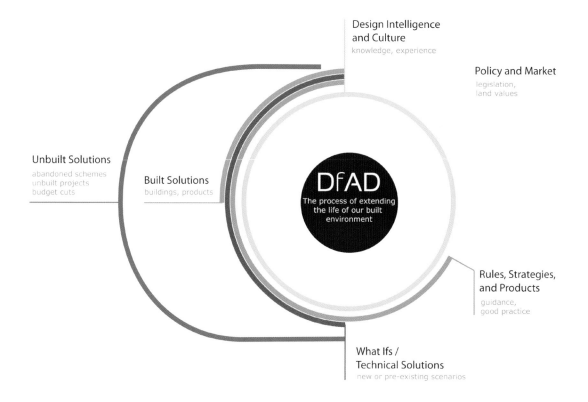

Design Intelligence
and Culture
knowledge, experience

Policy and Market
legislation,
land values

Unbuilt Solutions
abandoned schemes
unbuilt projects
budget cuts

Built Solutions
buildings, products

DfAD
The process of extending
the life of our built
environment

Rules, Strategies,
and Products
guidance,
good practice

What Ifs /
Technical Solutions
new or pre-existing scenarios

▲ Figure 12.4
Design process meta-model (M17)

12.5 Causal links

Chapter 10 discusses many of the elements listed in the Sources model (M16; e.g. market, policy, culture) as contextual contingencies (CONs), while Chapter 9 presents the desirable building characteristics (CARs). These two perspectives have for the most part been presented separately to this point for ease of communication. However, they make up a complex world in which adaptability must be communicated, designed, deployed and eventually implemented. We can piece together a more holistic picture as we discuss the associations and causation and whether the relationship is positive or negative.

The Causal links meta-model (M18, Figure 12.5) exemplifies the relationships between characteristics (purple) and contextual contingencies (black) established from the case studies and describes their positive/negative nature. The model illustrates why designing for adaptability is not a straightforward task but tied up in complex design, construction and use processes. It does not represent all the interactions between characteristics and contingencies, but examples found in our case studies.

The general pattern is for a contextual contingency to influence one or more building characteristics; however, there are instances where characteristics influenced contingencies creating relational loops (and hence potential iterations). One interesting example is the uncertainty that the market (CON18) creates, emerging as a significant contingency to developing more adaptable

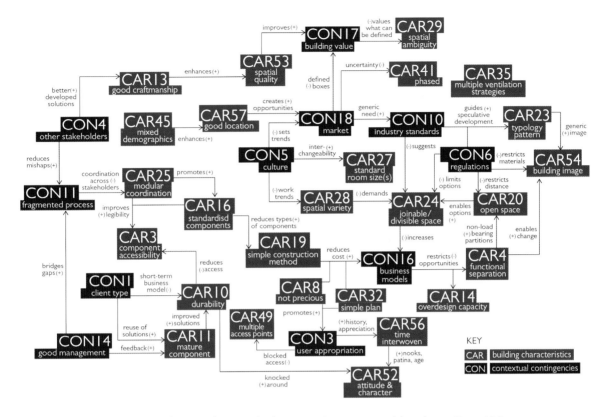

▲ Figure 12.5
Causal links meta-model (M18)

buildings. The data revealed a paradox, in which uncertainty was considered to be both a reason to develop more adaptable buildings but also a reason not to, because the benefits of adaptability were uncertain – suggesting an interesting interplay between cost (CON16) and uncertainty and how risk (CON20) is handled through the chosen solutions.

12.6 Cost certainty

The interplay between cost and uncertainty is visualised in this quadrant model using examples of solutions collected from the building case studies (Figure 12.6). The model explores relative costs and frequency of change, suggesting indicative locations for each solution.

In the bottom left-hand corner are examples of what could be termed 'good buys' – low-cost solutions that are almost certain to be used in the future, such as demountable partitions or raised floors in an office building (CAR24, CAR3), or the overprovision of power outlets in a retail scheme (CAR9). In contrast, some low-cost solutions, 'cheap tricks', might be worth investing in, even if they might not be used to support future adaptation, because they add little to the cost of construction but mean that the building could be adapted more easily and cheaply in the future should the need arise. For instance, the lintels of 85 Southwark (Chapter 14, A2) will allow for new openings to be made more easily in the future with a marginal additional cost.

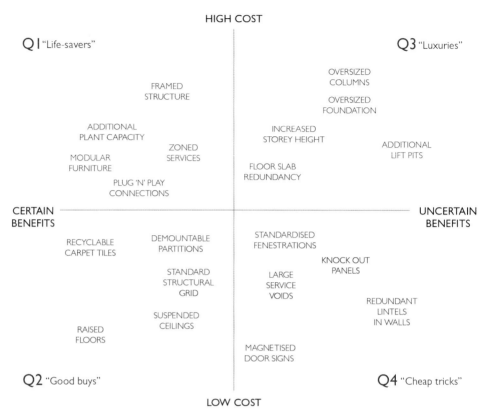

HIGH COST

Q1 "Life-savers"   Q3 "Luxuries"

OVERSIZED
COLUMNS

FRAMED   OVERSIZED
STRUCTURE   FOUNDATION

ADDITIONAL   INCREASED
PLANT CAPACITY   STOREY HEIGHT   ADDITIONAL
                    ZONED   LIFT PITS
MODULAR   SERVICES
FURNITURE   FLOOR SLAB
        PLUG 'N' PLAY   REDUNDANCY
        CONNECTIONS

CERTAIN   UNCERTAIN
BENEFITS   BENEFITS

                                STANDARDISED
                                FENESTRATIONS
RECYCLABLE   DEMOUNTABLE   KNOCK OUT
CARPET TILES   PARTITIONS   PANELS

                STANDARD   LARGE
                STRUCTURAL   SERVICE   REDUNDANT
                GRID   VOIDS   LINTELS
                                                IN WALLS
                SUSPENDED
                CEILINGS
RAISED
FLOORS
                                MAGNETISED
                                DOOR SIGNS

Q2 "Good buys"   Q4 "Cheap tricks"

LOW COST

▲ Figure 12.6
Cost certainty meta-model (M19)

The top-left quadrant contains examples of 'life savers', which more expensive design solutions that are worth the investment because otherwise adapting the building at a later date may be technically impossible, prohibitively costly or disruptive to the occupants. For example, providing additional plant room capacity to support an increase in the number of building users is a common solution (CAR14). Meanwhile, the design solutions in the top-right hand corner could be described as 'luxuries', because they are expensive and there is a high level of uncertainty as to whether they will ever be exploited for future adaptability. Examples include oversized foundations and increased storey heights (CAR14; CAR22).

The common perception that adaptability equals extra costs will continue to hinder adaptability until stakeholders broaden their limited understanding of what it constitutes. One example that combats this perception is the characteristics that were cited to reduce costs – simple construction method (CAR19), simple plan (CAR32) and use of non-precious materials (CAR8).

12.7 Pathways

This meta-model maps the 12 design strategies (on the left, supply side) and six adaptability types (on the right, client demand) to three elements of the theory. Figure 12.7 shows how identifying the appropriate *building*

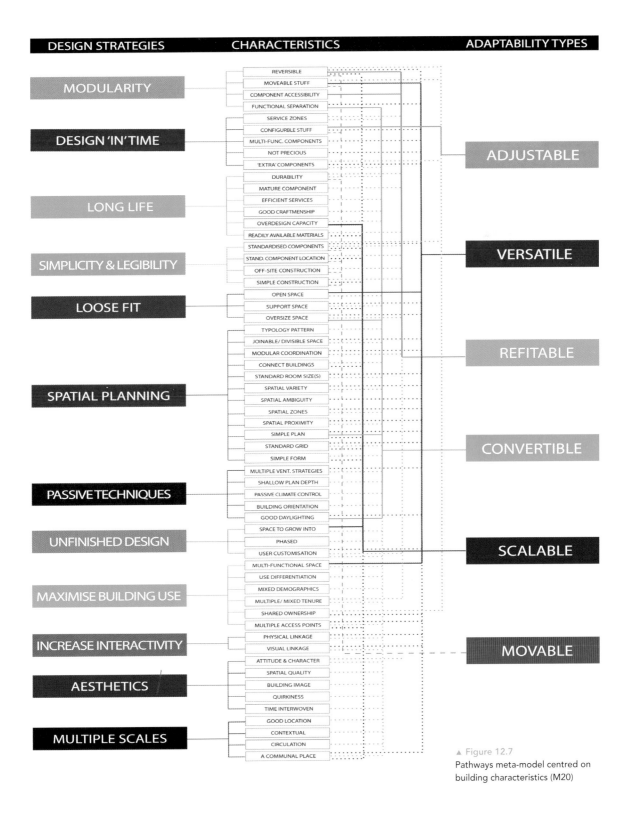

DESIGN STRATEGIES	CHARACTERISTICS	ADAPTABILITY TYPES

MODULARITY

- REVERSIBLE
- MOVEABLE STUFF
- COMPONENT ACCESSIBILITY
- FUNCTIONAL SEPARATION

DESIGN 'IN' TIME

- SERVICE ZONES
- CONFIGURBLE STUFF
- MULTI-FUNC. COMPONENTS
- NOT PRECIOUS
- 'EXTRA' COMPONENTS

ADJUSTABLE

LONG LIFE

- DURABILITY
- MATURE COMPONENT
- EFFICIENT SERVICES
- GOOD CRAFTMENSHIP
- OVERDESIGN CAPACITY
- READILY AVAILABLE MATERIALS

SIMPLICITY & LEGIBILITY

- STANDARDISED COMPONENTS
- STAND. COMPONENT LOCATION
- OFF-SITE CONSTRUCTION
- SIMPLE CONSTRUCTION

VERSATILE

LOOSE FIT

- OPEN SPACE
- SUPPORT SPACE
- OVERSIZE SPACE

REFITABLE

SPATIAL PLANNING

- TYPOLOGY PATTERN
- JOINABLE/ DIVISIBLE SPACE
- MODULAR COORDINATION
- CONNECT BUILDINGS
- STANDARD ROOM SIZE(S)
- SPATIAL VARIETY
- SPATIAL AMBIGUITY
- SPATIAL ZONES
- SPATIAL PROXIMITY
- SIMPLE PLAN
- STANDARD GRID
- SIMPLE FORM

CONVERTIBLE

PASSIVE TECHNIQUES

- MULTIPLE VENT. STRATEGIES
- SHALLOW PLAN DEPTH
- PASSIVE CLIMATE CONTROL
- BUILDING ORIENTATION
- GOOD DAYLIGHTING

UNFINISHED DESIGN

- SPACE TO GROW INTO
- PHASED
- USER CUSTOMISATION

SCALABLE

MAXIMISE BUILDING USE

- MULTI-FUNCTIONAL SPACE
- USE DIFFERENTIATION
- MIXED DEMOGRAPHICS
- MULTIPLE/ MIXED TENURE
- SHARED OWNERSHIP
- MULTIPLE ACCESS POINTS

INCREASE INTERACTIVITY

- PHYSICAL LINKAGE
- VISUAL LINKAGE

MOVABLE

AESTHETICS

- ATTITUDE & CHARACTER
- SPATIAL QUALITY
- BUILDING IMAGE
- QUIRKINESS
- TIME INTERWOVEN

MULTIPLE SCALES

- GOOD LOCATION
- CONTEXTUAL
- CIRCULATION
- A COMMUNAL PLACE

▲ Figure 12.7
Pathways meta-model centred on building characteristics (M20)

characteristics (CARs) should be a central goal of a project. As noted earlier, the relationship between the design strategies and building characteristics is nested (1:many), while the adaptability types is categorical (many:many) and so we distinguish between primary links (solid line) and secondary links (dotted line). The second part of the model (Figure 12.8) shows how the *building layers*

▼ Figure 12.8
Pathways meta-model centred on building layers (M20)

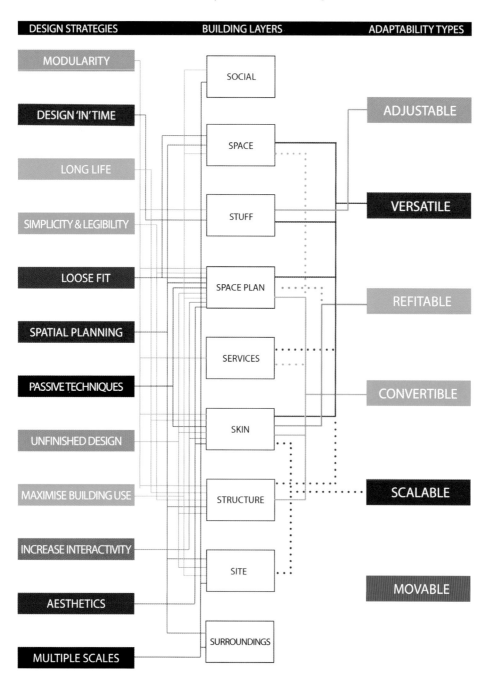

(M4) mediate between adaptability goals and design strategies while the third (Figure 12.9) does the same for the *design guidelines* (Table 11.1). This meta-model can be used by designers to check or establish pathways of interest, or

▼ Figure 12.9
Pathways meta-model centred on design guidelines (M20)

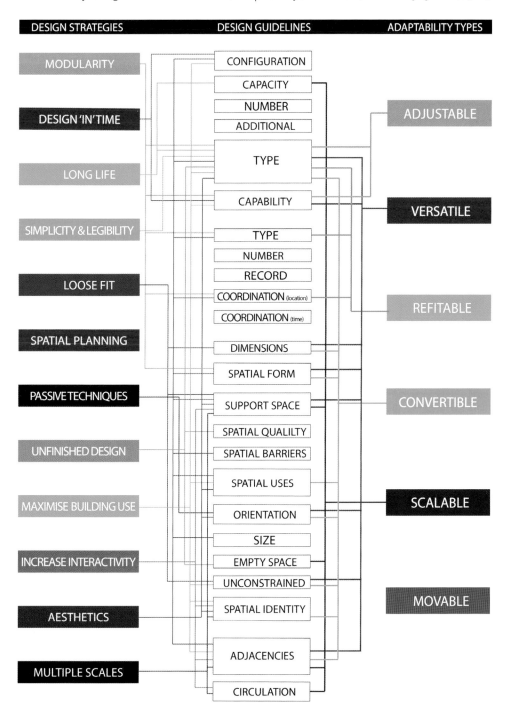

DESIGN STRATEGIES	DESIGN GUIDELINES	ADAPTABILITY TYPES
MODULARITY	CONFIGURATION	
	CAPACITY	
	NUMBER	
DESIGN 'IN' TIME	ADDITIONAL	ADJUSTABLE
	TYPE	
LONG LIFE		
	CAPABILITY	
SIMPLICITY & LEGIBILITY		VERSATILE
	TYPE	
	NUMBER	
	RECORD	
LOOSE FIT	COORDINATION (location)	
	COORDINATION (time)	REFITABLE
SPATIAL PLANNING	DIMENSIONS	
	SPATIAL FORM	
PASSIVE TECHNIQUES	SUPPORT SPACE	CONVERTIBLE
	SPATIAL QUALILTY	
UNFINISHED DESIGN	SPATIAL BARRIERS	
	SPATIAL USES	
MAXIMISE BUILDING USE	ORIENTATION	SCALABLE
	SIZE	
INCREASE INTERACTIVITY	EMPTY SPACE	
	UNCONSTRAINED	
	SPATIAL IDENTITY	MOVABLE
AESTHETICS	ADJACENCIES	
MULTIPLE SCALES	CIRCULATION	

with the client to highlight the design intent or possible conflicting demands that need resolution.

12.8 Chapter summary

The intent of the adaptability models is to embody important theoretical concepts of adaptability in accessible, user-friendly visualisations. They demonstrate that the ability to deliver an adaptable solution often goes beyond what is seen as the 'final' product and is tangled within a complex web of contextual contingencies. These can challenge good design, but experience and understanding of alternative ways will mitigate the constraints if you can identify the synergies and tensions of designing a building in a particular way.

The models can be used in two forms – either as presented in the book to explain a particular concept of adaptability or a stripped-down version to be reconstructed by stakeholders to make it project specific. As an example, Figure 12.10 shows the appropriation of a blank version of the Framecycle model (M15) in a design workshop. The models can thus become thinking or design tools throughout the project process (see Figure III.2 at the start of Part III).

▼ Figure 12.10

Appropriation of the Framecycle model (M15)

Part IV

ADAPTABILITY IN PRACTICE

Chapter 13

Linking theory to case studies

13.1 Design strategies and building characteristics

Table 13.1 maps the characteristics (rows) across the primary building case studies (columns). It shows that nine of the characteristics were embedded in most of the projects (highlighted in pink across the table). Multifunctional spaces (CAR43) was the only characteristic to be deployed in every building. The nine characteristics cut across eight design strategies (five spatial, two physical and building character). At the other end of the eight characteristics that make up the bottom quartile five are physical characteristics (highlighted in purple).

The number of characteristics embedded in each project ranged from 17 to 41 with an average of 31 – i.e. approximately half of the characteristics. The residential project of Carl Jacobsens vej (A8) deployed the most and The King's School Theatre (A13) the least, which is to be expected as the latter project only entailed a section of an existing building. Given the explicit intent to design for adaptability in many of these projects, it would suggest accommodating all 60 characteristics in a single project is not necessary (i.e. wasteful), reflecting the untenable ideal of universal adaptability.

Radar charts for each project were constructed to illustrate patterns associated with particular approaches to designing for adaptability (Figure 13.1). A project's accommodation of a strategy was determined as the number of building characteristics embedded as a percentage of the total number of characteristics for that strategy. It is immediately apparent that the overall 'shape' of each project is unique but some areas of the radar repeat. This supports the finding that every project will require its own mix of strategies and characteristics. For example:

1 Vodafone Headquarters (A14) displayed a *broad tripartite form* highlighting modularity (DS1), passive techniques (DS7) and increase activity (DS10).
2 However, many of the projects (projects A7, A9 and A13) displayed *thin forms with points* accentuating one or two particular strategies – e.g. Bio Innovation Centre (A7) with simplicity and legibility (DS4) and loose fit (DS5).
3 CRPL (A4) and The Cube (A10) illustrated similar shapes with a much heavier tendency with regards to the strategies on the left side of the chart creating *lop-sided shapes* – emphasis on building scale and spatial characteristics (DS8–12).

Table 13.1 CARS mapped against case studies

	Design Characteristics	A1	A2	A3	A4	A5	A6	A7	A8	A9	A10	A11	A12	A13	A14	A15	
1	REVERSIBLE	X					X		X			X		X	X	X	7
2	MOVABLE STUFF		X	X				X		X	X		X	X	X	X	9
3	COMPONENT ACCESSIBILITY	X	X	X	X	X	X	X	X		X		X		X	X	11
4	FUNCTIONAL SEPARATION	X	X	X	X	X	X	X	X		X		X		X	X	12
5	SERVICE ZONES		X	X	X	X	X	X	X		X				X		7
6	CONFIGURABLE STUFF	X	X	X	X	X	X	X				X	X	X	X	X	11
7	MULTIFUNCTIONAL COMP	X	X		X									X	X		3
8	NOT PRECIOUS	X												X	X		2
9	'EXTRA' COMPONENTS	X						X				X		X		X	4
10	DURABILITY		X		X				X	X	X			X	X	X	8
11	MATURE COMPONENT	X			X	X						X		X	X	X	3
12	EFFICIENT SERVICES				X	X						X			X		4
13	GOOD CRAFTMENSHIP								X			X				X	3
14	OVERDESIGN CAPACITY	X	X			X	X	X	X	X	X	X	X		X	X	12
15	READILY AVAILABLE MATERIALS		X				X		X	X					X	X	4
16	STANDARDISED COMPONENTS	X	X				X	X	X			X	X		X	X	8
17	STANDARD COMP LOCATIONS								X			X					2
18	OFF-SITE CONSTRUCTION										X	X					2
19	SIMPLE CONSTRUCTION METHOD		X			X	X	X	X	X	X	X			X	X	7
20	OPEN SPACE	X	X	X	X	X	X	X	X	X	X	X		X	X	X	13
21	SUPPORT SPACE	X	X	X	X	X	X	X	X	X		X			X	X	11
22	OVERSIZE SPACE	X	X	X	X	X	X	X	X	X	X	X	X		X	X	13
23	TYPOLOGY PATTERN				X		X	X		X	X				X	X	6
24	JOINABLE/DIVISIBLE SPACE	X			X		X	X	X	X	X			X	X	X	10
25	MODULAR COORDINATION		X				X		X								3
26	CONNECT BUILDINGS		X			X	X	X	X				X		X		6
27	STANDARD ROOM SIZE(S)	X		X	X	X	X	X	X						X	X	8
28	SPATIAL VARIETY		X	X	X	X	X	X		X	X		X	X	X	X	10
29	SPATIAL AMBIGUITY	X	X	X	X		X			X	X	X	X		X	X	8

PHYSICAL (rows 1–19) / SPATIAL (rows 20–29)

Table matrix (criteria × case studies). The left column lists the item number and criterion; the final column gives the per-row total. The category labels CHARACTER and CONTEXT run vertically alongside the lower rows. Per-column totals are given in the final row.

#	Criterion	Total
30	SPATIAL ZONES	10
31	SPATIAL PROXIMITY	2
32	SIMPLE PLAN	13
33	STANDARD GRID	11
34	SIMPLE FORM	9
35	MULTIPLE VENTILATION STRATEGIES	6
36	SHALLOW PLAN DEPTH	4
37	PASSIVE CLIMATE CONTROL	4
38	BUILDING ORIENTATION	2
39	GOOD DAYLIGHTING	14
40	SPACE TO GROW INTO	10
41	PHASED	3
42	USER CUSTOMISATION	8
43	MULTIFUNCTIONAL SPACES	15
44	USE DIFFERENTIATION	9
45	MIXED DEMOGRAPHICS	11
46	MULTIPLE/ MIXED TENURE	11
47	SHARED OWNERSHIP	10
48	ISOLATABLE	7
49	MULTIPLE ACCESS POINTS	8
50	PHYSICAL LINKAGE	10
51	VISUAL LINKAGE (views)	13
52	ATTITUDE & CHARACTER *(CHARACTER)*	12
53	SPATIAL QUALITY *(CHARACTER)*	6
54	BUILDING IMAGE *(CHARACTER)*	9
55	QUIRKINESS *(CHARACTER)*	5
56	TIME INTERWOVEN	5
57	GOOD LOCATION *(CONTEXT)*	10
58	CONTEXTUAL *(CONTEXT)*	10
59	CIRCULATION (neighbourhood) *(CONTEXT)*	6
60	A COMMUNAL PLACE *(CONTEXT)*	10

Column totals (left to right): 34, 35, 31, 38, 32, 32, 30, 41, 26, 35, 27, 22, 17, 39, 31

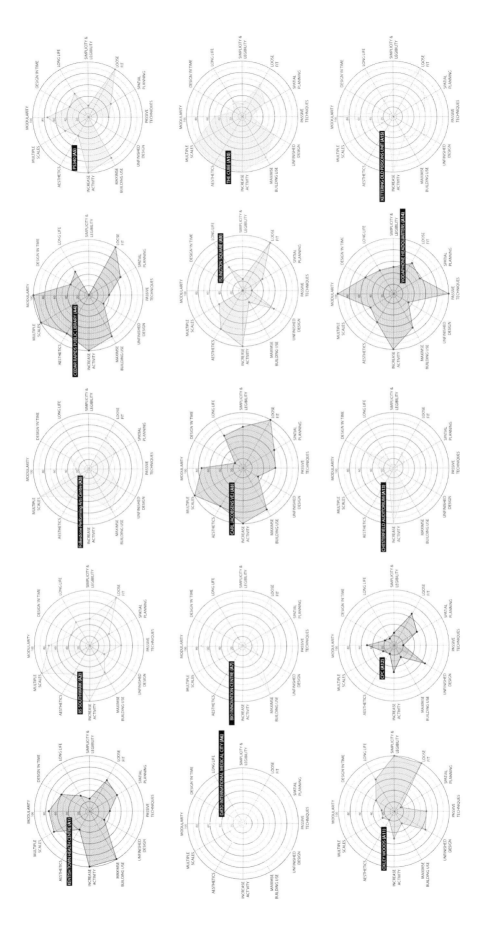

4   On the other hand, DOIMC (A6) and Bio Innovation Centre (A7) designed by the same architectural practice (different geographical locations/offices) and to a broader extent KOPU (A15) present similar *shaped 'pulls' with multiple strategies* suggesting a common ethos within the practice centred around modularity (DS1), loose fit (DS5), spatial planning (DS6) and maximise building use (DS9).

5   Overall, design 'in' time (DS2) and long life (DS4) appeared to be the two strategies utilised least holistically, while many of the projects displayed strong 'pulls' with regards to loose fit (DS5) and increase activity (DS10).

13.2 Linking adaptability types

The adaptability types are applied to the 15 case studies (A1–A15) in two ways: (1) did the building meet all of the key characteristics for an adaptability type; and (2) what percentage of all the relevant characteristics ('key' + 'nice to have') did the building meet? Regarding the first question, Table 13.2 illustrates how the case studies map against the 12 key characteristics (x). The cells are coloured yellow when a case study meets all the key characteristics for an adaptability type, e.g. case study A1 satisfies adjustable, refitable and convertible.

Table 13.2 A case study's fulfilment of key CARs

ADJUSTABLE	A1	A2	A3	A4	A5	A6	A7	A8	A9	A10	A11	A12	A13	A14	A15
CONFIGURABLE STUFF	X	X	X	X	X		X				X	X	X	X	X
VERSATILE	A1	A2	A3	A4	A5	A6	A7	A8	A9	A10	A11	A12	A13	A14	A15
MOVABLE STUFF		X		X	X		X		X				X	X	X
OPEN SPACE		X	X	X	X		X	X	X	X	X	X	X	X	X
MULTIFUNCTIONAL SPACES	X	X	X	X	X	X	X	X	X	X	X	X	X	X	X
REFITABLE	A1	A2	A3	A4	A5	A6	A7	A8	A9	A10	A11	A12	A13	A14	A15
REVERSIBLE	X			X		X		X			X			X	X
COMPONENT ACCESSIBILITY	X	X		X	X	X	X	X		X		X		X	X
CONVERTIBLE	A1	A2	A3	A4	A5	A6	A7	A8	A9	A10	A11	A12	A13	A14	A15
FUNCTIONAL SEPARATION	X	X	X	X	X	X	X	X		X		X		X	X
OVERSIZE SPACE	X	X	X	X	X	X	X	X	X	X	X	X			X
SIMPLE PLAN	X		X	X	X	X	X	X	X	X	X	X	X	X	
GOOD DAYLIGHTING	X	X	X	X	X		X	X	X	X	X	X	X	X	X
SCALABLE	A1	A2	A3	A4	A5	A6	A7	A8	A9	A10	A11	A12	A13	A14	A15
OVERDESIGN CAPACITY	X	X			X	X	X	X	X	X	X	X		X	X
SPACE TO GROW INTO		X	X	X			X	X	X		X	X			X

Looking at the relevant characteristics for each adaptability type, Table 13.3 shows the percentage each case study achieved for the more expansive set of characteristics, e.g. case study A2 contains 3 of the 6 relevant adjustable type characteristics (50 per cent). Projects over 60 per cent are highlighted in blue.

◀ Figure 13.1 (OPPOSITE PAGE)
Case studies visualised

Table 13.3 Adaptability types embedded as a percentage of relevant characteristics

ADAPTABILITY TYPE	A1	A2	A3	A4	A5	A6	A7	A8	A9	A10	A11	A12	A13	A14	A15
ADJUSTABLE (AT1)	83	50	33	67	33	50	67	50	0	17	67	50	50	83	83
VERSATILE (AT2)	80	57	60	73	57	63	60	63	37	60	47	47	47	70	77
REFITABLE (AT3)	50	50	31	44	47	63	25	75	38	50	60	25	13	56	44
CONVERTIBLE (AT4)	56	60	58	67	60	53	56	71	49	64	36	36	31	64	49
SCALABLE (AT5)	57	64	43	50	50	71	57	93	50	36	60	50	14	79	64

In Table 13.4 we combine the two metrics to illustrate how the case studies faired with the provision of each adaptability type.

Table 13.4 Links between types and case studies

ADAPTABILITY TYPE	A1	A2	A3	A4	A5	A6	A7	A8	A9	A10	A11	A12	A13	A14	A15
ADJUSTABLE (AT1)	83	50	33	67	33	50	67	50	0	17	67	50	50	83	83
VERSATILE (AT2)	80	57	60	73	57	63	60	63	40	60	47	47	47	70	77
REFITABLE (AT3)	50	50	31	44	47	63	25	75	38	50	60	25	13	56	44
CONVERTIBLE (AT4)	56	60	58	67	60	53	56	71	49	64	36	36	31	64	49
SCALABLE (AT5)	57	64	43	50	50	71	57	93	50	36	60	50	14	79	64
TOTALS	4	4	3	4	4	3	3	4	2	2	2	3	2	5	4

Fullfilled key characteristics and a high percentage of all relevant.

Fullfilled key characteristics, but not a high percentage of all relevant

Fullfilled a high percentage of relevant characteristics, but not the key characteristics

Didn't fulfil key characteristics or a high percentage of all relevant.

Table 13.4 reveals that:

- 11 case studies are strongly related (green) to at least one adaptability type
- 8 case studies have types with just a high percentage of relevant characteristics (blue), e.g. *versatile* – A1, A3, A6, A8 and A10
- 11 case studies exhibit types with just a high percentage of key characteristics (yellow)
- no project implemented the same pattern

Table 13.5 maps designer intent (X) against the fulfilment categories defined in Table 13.4. Eighty-six per cent of the desired adaptability types were fulfilled (X inside a coloured box) while 14 per cent of the desired types were not (X inside a white box). Table 13.5 also shows seven cases where the adaptability type was not explicitly desired but fulfilled through embedded design solutions (coloured box with no X), while the blank cells represent undesired and unfilled types (24 per cent of all cells).

Table 13.5 Designer intent (X) mapped against fulfilment of adaptability type

ADAPTABILITY TYPE	A1	A2	A3	A4	A5	A6	A7	A8	A9	A10	A11	A12	A13	A14	A15
ADJUSTABLE (ATI)	X	X		X			X					X	X		X
VERSATILE (AT2)		X	X	X	X	X	X	X	X	X	X	X	X	X	X
REFITABLE (AT3)	X			X		X	X	X			X				
CONVERTIBLE (AT4)	X	X	X	X	X	X	X	X		X		X		X	X
SCALABLE (AT5)		X		X		X	X	X	X		X	X	X	X	X

X	X	X	Desired and fullfilled
		X	Desired, but not fullfilled
			Not desired, but fullfilled
			Not desired, not fullfilled

Chapter 14

Primary case studies

A1 Kentish Town Health Centre

Building type: healthcare
Adaptability types: adjustable, versatile, refitable, convertible
Location: London, UK
Completion date: 2008
Architect: AHMM Architects
Website: www.ahmm.co.uk

The Kentish Town Health Centre (KTHC) is a local health clinic in London. Contextually, the architects referenced the brick and stucco of the neighbouring structures (CAR58) and had to work around the preservation of several listed trees on the site (CON8) giving the building an immediate connection to its surrounding context upon completion – Figure 14.1. The challenge for the

▶ Figure 14.1
Conserved trees on site
Courtesy Timothy Soar

architect was fitting several users and organisations under one roof (CAR46) while maintaining a sense of community. The building was constructed to as large a mass as possible given current planning and conservation rules (CON8, CON9).

The client as an owner-occupier was heavily engaged and enthusiastic throughout the project, and worked closely with the architect to convey the needs of the practice and how the building would be used (CON1). The strong engagement with the client allowed the architect to understand how to provide spaces that could work in a way that strongly meets the client's changing needs.

The overall design concept of Jenga (Figure 14.2) – the pushing and pulling of blocks – created several voids, balconies, terraces, light wells and other communicative and linking moments throughout the building to help to create a sense of community through transparency and connectivity (CAR50, CAR51). These 'extra' spaces – undefined in the brief – add to the overall comfort of place (CAR21). Careful consideration was also given to the vertical stacking of programmatic elements moving from more public spaces on the ground floor, consultant rooms on the first level, and teaching/private office areas above (CAR30). On the other hand, the geometry created by the Jenga concept (CAR53) created a greater level of rigidity with the ability to move interior partition walls. Despite the interior partitions being stud wall partitions, the complexity of the structural layer restricts alternative locations.

▼ Figure 14.2
Pushing and pulling form
Courtesy Timothy Soar

CAR11
mature
component

CAR6
configurable
stuff

CAR53
spatial
quality
(push and pull concept)

The circulation plan is driven by a 'main street' that acts as a visible axis through the building providing an open and legible path (CAR22, CAR50; Figure 14.3) and access from either end of its elongated form (CAR49) supporting the multiple tenants occupying either end (the clinic and NHS tenants, CAR46). The 4m wide corridor serves as a sub-waiting area and reception for diagnostic imaging allowing for informal communication and a sense of openness and comfort for the users (CAR22, CAR43).

The upper level corridors utilise a track system (top rail system) that allows community artwork to be hung and is changed regularly allowing for the community to identify with the building (CAR60; Figure 14.4). The standard solution (CAR16) is used as an intermediate component to allow the

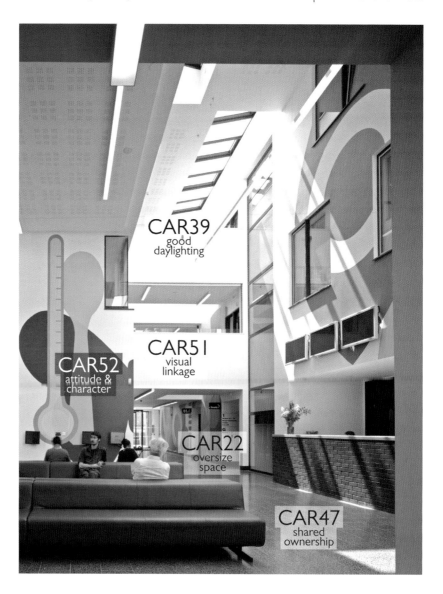

▶ Figure 14.3
Main street circulation corridor
Courtesy Timothy Soar

CAR16
standardised
components

CAR52
attitude &
character

separation between space plan and stuff layers to be eased. The system is comprised of two fixed rails that allow for a variety of objects (e.g. storage units, shelves, furniture, fixtures) to be suspended and moved around without any difficulty. The simplicity of the system allows users to change the use of rooms without the need of facilities or special tools (CAR42). Architecturally, the system required a stronger partition wall (CAR10; gypsum with ply-backing) to afford the additional strength to support the various objects (slight additional cost). The system is used throughout the building to maximise interchangeability in offices, consultant rooms, GP hot-desk area and corridors (CAR43).

The clinic shares consultation rooms since the normal clinical routine for a doctor is to work 8 out of 10 half-day sessions during a week. Rather than permanent name plates on the door, the facility has magnetic name strips that are stored in a shared office (each doctor has a portable tray with their name plate and personal instruments) and allows each clinical room to be shared and occupied daily (CAR47, Figure 14.5). The open office space has a hot-desking policy and is complemented with bookable rooms for privacy (CAR28). Locks were deliberately omitted on drawers to avoid people colonising them with personal items. Where equipment needs to be locked, (storage cupboards in consulting rooms) standard locks (CAR16) avoid the problem of people losing keys.

▲ Figure 14.4
Top rail system used to hang community artwork

▲ Figure 14.5
Magnetic name strips and
doctor trays

The treatment rooms, which are larger than the consultant rooms, allow them to be used as the latter if needed (CAR43). Furthermore, IPS (integrated plumbing systems) sink units were considered for the second floor office spaces to allow use as consultant rooms (CAR43). At the time, the extra cost was deemed a deterrent (CON19); however, now there is a demand for additional consultant rooms due to their premium charge. Nonetheless, access/ security would be an issue since currently the public is unable to access the rooms on this floor (swipe card).

The standardised consultant rooms (CAR27) are equipped with a variety of lights controlled by a panel of switches that allow the physician to carry out an array of tasks (CAR6; Figure 14.6). The rooms also consist of magnetic boards to easily change bulletins without damaging the walls (CAR1) and tables that have been configured to allow doctors and patients better informal communication and access to perform a mixture of tasks (CAR6). A common solution across healthcare facilities are refillable trays for stocking rooms with general supplies. The trays act as an intermediate component and are either delivered

178   PART IV ADAPTABILITY IN PRACTICE

▲ Figure 14.6
Consultation room

to the facility pre-stocked or (re)filled in a central store. The new trays are brought in and the partially used ones are removed from the cabinet. This allows all clinical spaces to be restocked quickly without having to check each room.

Despite not being a staple in modern commercial developments, operable windows (CAR6) are a common configurable element that provide natural ventilation (CAR35) and night cooling (CAR37). The proprietary window system used here is comprised of two parts: a large pane of inoperable glass and a smaller section of metal mesh with an operable shutter that can be open both horizontally to allow fresh air/light in and at the top to allow for ventilation (CAR7). The system was developed on a previous project, refined, and has been applied here (CAR11).

At the start the building had eight meeting rooms, five of which can be divided into three smaller rooms with acoustic separators (CAR2, CAR6). However, after occupying the building, the clinic decided they had too many meeting rooms, so two were allocated as counselling offices (CAR21 and 43) – this transformation was bolstered by the variety of furniture provided in the rooms which allows alternative activities such as meeting rooms or counselling offices.

Spatially, the architects positioned an access door inside the main entrance vestibule (CAR49) allowing controlled access to part of the building for after-hours use by the community (CAR44, CAR48; Figure 14.7). The

Separate access door inside
vestibule

community on various nights holds activities in a large partitionable space
adjacent to the entrance (CAR24). The space is supplied with stackable chairs
and tables (CAR6) and a sprung floor to enhance its ability to be used for a
wide range of activities (CAR43).

The project procured a generous budget for the building's graphics which
was used to increase legibility and present an overall feeling of increased
comfort (CAR52; Figure 14.8). While the dropped ceiling provides access to
the services above (CAR3), the services proved very difficult to change (CAR1),
because of how they were installed. A lack of coordination during construction

Way finding and signage
Courtesy Robert Parish

between stakeholders (CON4) and the inability of the architect to control the finished work (CON13) meant the legibility of the services remained poor.

A2 85 Southwark Street

Building type: office
Adaptability types: adjustable, versatile, convertible, scalable
Location: London, UK
Completion date: 2003
Architect: Allies and Morrison
Website: www.alliesandmorrison.com

85 Southwark Street is located on the site of a derelict garage in London. The building was designed by Allies and Morrison to accommodate their own studios. The simple cube-shaped concrete structure (CAR19) is a six storey office building including a basement tailored to the practice's changing needs, yet generic enough to be sub-let or sell (CAR54). A large lobby space, that is oversized for the building (CAR22, the building is 2,276m² with a lobby of 117m²) remains without a specific purpose, and is used to display the firm's work, for informal meetings, evening parties, book launches, lectures, concert recitals and formal dinners (CAR43; Figure 14.9). The basement, ground and first floor are linked by a spiral staircase that provides a special architectural moment within the lobby space (CAR52) while creating a linking and social experience between the three different levels (CAR21, CAR50).

▼ Figure 14.9
Oversized lobby space
Courtesy Allies and Morrison

The three studio floors include an atrium that provides a visual connection (CAR51); however, the structure can be extended if additional space is needed. The large exterior wall adjacent to the atrium is riddled with lintels allowing additional windows to be added easily by removing a panel at a minimal cost. It costs practically nothing (£20.00) to put a beam and day joint in as part of the initial construction, but can cost significantly more to do later on. Furthermore, whilst the current building is six storeys in height, planning permission was granted for an additional storey (CON9) relieving any future planning hurdles and the foundation/structure is designed to support the additional floor (CAR14). Given the tight urban condition the concrete wall adjacent to the neighbouring building, was built with a knock-out panel (CAR14) to enable combining the two buildings, which happened in 2013 (CAR26). Not only was the building designed to be scaled up, inward and outward, in a unique situation, the practice petitioned (and was granted by the city council) to close the small street behind the building which they have now extended into an additional (undefined) outdoor space (Figure 14.10) that has been repaved and filled with comfortable outdoor furniture and apple trees (CAR60).

▶ Figure 14.10
Various expansion spaces
Courtesy Allies and Morrison

The design implemented many BCO guidelines to assure quality and standards (CAR11). The studio spaces are open plan (32m × 6.5m) equipped with standard office furniture (CAR2, CAR16) that can be organised into blocks of six and grouped around team meeting tables and storage spaces or can be reconfigured based on team sizes from 3, 6, 9, 12 or more. The versatility is enhanced through the non-hierarchical allocation of space – everyone sits in the open plan (CON6) along with an ongoing shift from allocated to hot-desking space that reduces spatial demands and allows a variety of activities (CAR43).

There is a mixture of formal and informal meeting spaces, each floor having open space for informal meetings and enclosed formal meeting spaces while the ground floor lobby is typically configured with a loose arrangement of tables and chairs for quick meetings with consultants or product representatives. The top floor provides the largest meeting space with a full-height glazed wall overlooking the roof deck and a prominent roof light (CAR39) giving the space a special character (CAR53). Meetings can also take place on the roof deck itself or in the adjacent café on the ground floor that the practice owns (CAR47).

The building has a light well that stretches the length of the site and provides natural light to the workshop spaces in the basement (CAR37). The workspaces receive an abundance of light from the glazed façade to the north, and daylight sensors were installed to maintain the appropriate level of lighting in the space without relying on manual switches. Each workstation is also provided with a task light for personal control. Natural ventilation was discarded even with the building's shallow plan (CAR36) due to the amount of noise and traffic pollution from the main street (CAR57); however, some of the windows were made operable to increase user control and natural ventilation after hours (CAR6). The 'fractured' south-facing façade is a reaction to a complex 'right to light' regulation (CON9) and the shifting scale between the commercial street at its front and the residential behind (CAR58). The design takes advantage of the shift by providing a cascading garden for each studio (CAR51).

The concrete columns, soffits and walls are often left exposed (CAR37), with materials and connections within the building being simple and robust (CAR19). The services run horizontally under a raised floor (CAR3) and can be changed according to the workspace configuration (CAR2). Colour is used boldly and in bursts to punctuate the space (CAR52).

The exterior walls are conceptualised and constructed as three separately functioning layers: the outside one for the building's image (skin), the middle layer for weathering (services) and the inside layer (space plan) related to the versatility of the room. The separation of the wall functions allows each layer to be more tuned to the individual function and for them to act independently of each other. For example, the inner glazed layer uses a 1.5m module (in line with the 4.5m structural grid) so that the interior space can be partitioned every 1.5m to accommodate a variety of spatial layouts (CAR25). The glazed street façade provides a bright, colourful image by using lights located on the floors that turn on when its dark and bright yellow shutters can open like butterfly wings to multiply the light onto the streetscape (Figure 14.11).

The concept of adaptability can be scaled throughout the building and into the urban surroundings. Rather than entering directly off the street, the design cuts a single-storey, 4m wide pathway through the building – doors are provided on either side of the path. The entrance ties the building into the larger area circulation scheme (CAR59) from the residential area behind the building all the way to St Peter's Church on the other side of the Thames River. This was done through discussions with neighbouring building owners (CAR26), e.g. a new circulation path that is part of Tate Modern's extension).

A3 Folkestone Performing Arts Centre (FPAC)

Building type: cultural, office

Adaptability types: adjustable, versatile, convertible
Location: Folkestone, UK
Completion date: 2009
Architect: Alison Brooks Architects
Website: www.alisonbrooksarchitects.com

Over the last century, the centre of Folkestone has lost much of its vibrant life. The Creative Foundation was established in 2002 to spearhead an art-led regeneration programme for which the Folkestone Performing Arts Centre (FPAC) is a centrepiece as a new cultural hub and catalyst for an emerging arts quarter. The design concept stems from Renaissance myths, representing the scallop shell as a local symbol of the pilgrimage soldiers undertook down Main Street to the pier. Architecturally, this is embraced through the translucent curved façade panels painted a scallop shell pink and softly lit from behind in the evening reinterpreting the local architectural symbolism of the shells as architraves over windows (CAR56). The innovative aesthetic of the building changes with the cladding's unique pattern and texture depending on the time of day and quality of light reflecting the changing activities inside the building (CAR43, CAR54).

Proportions, height of floors and the overall building height all relate to the neighbouring Georgian buildings, but at the same time don't attempt to replicate the architectural style or materials (CAR58; Figure 14.12). Attention was also given to how the neighbouring sites would develop over time and how the building could complement new uses around it. For example, the neighbouring site (highlighted in yellow in Figure 14.12) is planned to become a new public square, which would serve as a forecourt to the building (CAR60). The public

▼ Figure 14.12
FPAC in context of neighbouring buildings
Courtesy Dennis Gilbert

space would link to events and performances and in effect scale the space and use of the theatre (CAR40). This reinforces the adaptability of the building by opening it up and bolstering community engagement and appreciation.

FPAC is thoughtfully designed to contain a mixture of spaces and be used in a variety of ways, combining cultural and commercial uses (CAR44, CAR45, CAR46). The design of the top floor has already allowed it to adapt to a change in the market (CON18). The openness of the space (CAR20) along with depth of the plan (CAR36), amount of daylight (CAR37) and high storey height (CAR22) allowed a large restaurant to easily become incubator offices with the addition of interior partitions (CAR24) – offering a range of business suites, meeting rooms and one large versatile space that can be leased out for special occasions or temporary use (CAR28). The space could be easily changed again, if there were to be another shift in the market, to be developed as residential units for example.

The theatre space was designed, used and intentionally labelled as a multi-purpose community space (Figure 14.13). The seats can be retracted for conferences, weddings and other events. The space could have catered to more uses if they had included a large window (natural light), but acoustical glass was outside the budget and thus the window lost (CON19). Another option that could be implemented later is exterior doors, allowing the space to open directly onto the street as an alternative entrance and operate as a separately secured facility (CAR48, CAR49).

▼ Figure 14.13
Theatre space
Courtesy Dennis Gilbert

The oversized circulation space (CAR22) on the ground floor typically serves as a gallery that is open to the public to wander into the building (CAR60) – the space is a reception when the theatre is active (CAR43), but can also hold events or be converted in the future e.g. retail. It allows the public to informally engage the building and its uses, not restricted by the conventional inside/outside boundary of a traditional theatre. The restaurant located on the first floor serves theatre events, but is also open to the community for regular hours. The varied and multiplicity of uses (CAR44) for the building establishes a vibrant life internally and externally, generating an intriguing overlap between how the building is used throughout the day, week and year.

Adaptability is enhanced through the nuance of labelling or the lack thereof and bolsters a shared sense of ownership and diversity of activities

A4 Cedar Rapids Public Library (CRPL)

Building type: cultural
Adaptability types: adjustable, versatile, refitable, convertible
Location: Cedar Rapids, USA
Completion date: 2013
Architect: OPN Architects, Inc.
Website: www.opnarchitects.com

In June 2008 a major flood devastated Cedar Rapids, Iowa, pouring water into hundreds of buildings including the 25-year-old Public Library and destroying much of its contents. In the search for a new site, the library wanted to maintain a downtown and street-front presence as well as be accessible to public transport (CAR57) – something renovating the existing facility could not provide. The new site acts as a bookend to the small central park opposite the Cedar Rapids Art Museum. Careful deconstruction of the existing building on the new site resulted in 95 per cent of the materials being salvaged – e.g. ceiling tiles, drywall, copper piping were all made available to companies specialising in reuse. The new building incorporated several reused materials (CAR11) including historic stained-glass windows and limestone panels from the exterior cladding of its previous home, salvaged bricks from the Sinclair smokestack (an iconic and historic industrial relic) were incorporated into a feature wall and inclusions of salvaged stained-glass windows from a demolished local landmark church (CAR56) – Figure 14.14.

The client was driven by a young, new director who envisioned moving library services very much into the future, treating it more as a retail book store than a traditional library (CON1). The library has no main circulation area as staff are located throughout the collections at small versatile kiosks (CAR2)

▼ Figure 14.14
Reclaimed materials from two local landmarks
Courtesy OPN Architects, Inc.

equipped with belt clips that can swipe cards and check out books for patrons (moving equipment from the stuff layer to the social layer).

The plan of the building is an extruded T with spatial and physical elements pushed and pulled to define undulations in the form. Three primary points of entry allow users direct access to appropriate areas of the building from varying modes of transport (CAR44, CAR49, CAR57). The southern portion of the site is currently surface parking and has been designated as an area for future expansion (CAR40) – extending the main line of circulation.

The architect clustered all the fixed items (toilets, mechanical room, elevators) into a single zone allowing for the majority of the space to be as versatile as possible over time (CAR30). The two large open collection spaces (35m x 48m each) are filled with a variety of adjustable furniture (CAR6), movable book shelves (CAR2), floating kiosks and include a wide column spacing of approximately 10m spans (CAR20; Figure 14.15). The second floor space also includes a raised access floor system to run cabling and add in the flexibility of the space (CAR3). The ground floor height is 5.6m high and the first floor height is 4.9m contributing to its persona as an open public space (CAR22, CAR60).

In addition, the building is organised as contemporary (highly active, noisy spaces) on the ground floor (laptop bar, café, youth areas) with more traditional, quieter areas on the second floor for periodicals, computers and meeting spaces. Shelving and furniture delineate uses and change according to the occupants needs (CAR29). The café inside is privately operated; however, the seating space is shared by the café and the library (CAR47) blurring the boundary (CAR29) and serving as a welcoming public interface for the library (Figure 14.16).

▼ Figure 14.15
Open collection space with a variety of seating
Courtesy OPN Architects, Inc.
(Figures 14.15–14.18)

The children's area includes 'lava tiles' that respond to pressure and coloured fluid reacts and changes the image underneath (CAR6, CAR52). The monumental public stair in the two-storey lobby conveys the activity of people moving up and down the stairs on to the translucent panels of varying depths with programmable actuators and sensors (Figure 14.17). At night, the undulating façade surrounding the protruding auditorium glows as 60 8' x 1' openings reveal a warm, inviting light (visible in Figure 14.18).

The library has several visual connections to neighbouring sites and exterior spaces to allow library activities to extend easily blurring the boundary of activities (CAR29). The large public plaza in front of the library is a series of plateaus which can act as tier seating for special events (CAR60) and is equipped with electrical outlets and urban furniture, both of which support the wireless library network broadcasts that extend into the park (CAR43; Figure 14.18). Red accent colours are used throughout the building – the central cylinder that stresses the height of the building as a legible landmark, signage, solar shading aerofoil fins, entrance ribbon and the art installation in the plaza (CAR52, CAR58).

The library has an outdoor roof space open to the public that can be used to host events, informal gatherings or individual reading (CAR43). A large section is planted providing a natural setting and integral storm water management system and rainwater storage which irrigates the vegetation and includes permeable pavers on the ground (CAR7, CAR12). The library was designed to exceed LEED platinum (CON11); heating and cooling is provided by a localised geothermal pump, while the orientation and shape of the library

▲ Figure 14.16
Café with shared seating
Courtesy OPN Architects, Inc.

▲ Figure 14.17
Lit panels respond to user steps
Courtesy OPN Architects, Inc.

▼ Figure 14.18
Aerial view illustrating plaza and rooftop space
Courtesy OPN Architects, Inc.

takes advantage of natural conditions (CAR37, CAR38). Additional technologies were implemented to reduce heat gains – e.g. high-spec lighting, highly efficient glazing assemblies and solar control glazing (CAR12). The majority of the library is clad with a rain-screen panel with exposed fasteners clipped to an inner layer of the structure that creates a thermal break and allows the panels to be switched out easily (CAR1, CAR4).

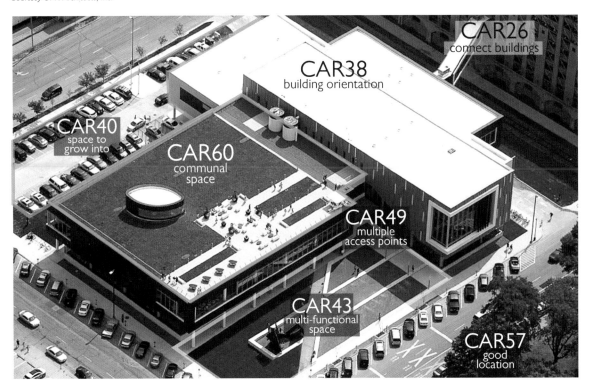

A5   PS340 Manhattan

Building type: school
Strategy: versatile, convertible
Location: New York City
Completion date: 1989 (conversion 2014)
Architect: MDSzerbaty Architecture
Website: www.mdsnyc.com

PS340 is the partial conversion of a 1989 hospital building situated in the centre of NYC. The demand arose for the new school with a large number of neighbouring residential conversions over the last ten years. With the hospital's medical services moving to a new building outside the city, the lower six floors of this 14-storey high-rise were left vacant and subsequently converted to house the new school while the remaining floors above remain in hospital use as administrative offices (CAR44, CAR46). The school benefits from its central and corner location which provides a number of public transportation options; however, students typically walk to school given the close proximity (CAR57). Despite being slightly taller than its older neighbouring buildings (7–8 storeys), the building shares commonality in its façade (material, proportions, window size and location; CAR58) and physical bulk (e.g. required setbacks; CON9).

The converted floors were stripped back to the steel frame structure which was slightly strengthened for its new use. The exterior walls were demolished to the back-up brick and reinsulated to meet energy code requirements (CON6). The majority of windows remained as they included low-e insulated glazing while views and daylight penetration were enhanced with new large window openings that contrasted the existing standard punched openings (Figure 14.19) – e.g. a multi-storey curtain wall was added to the southern facing rear courtyard. The typical floor-to-floor height is 4m which is slightly lower than school standards (4.3m–5m), resulting in a marginally reduced ceiling height of 2.8m. However, light penetrates deep into the interior through the introduction of numerous double-height spaces (lobby, library and stair), accomplished by removing sections of the existing floor framing.

The building has a simple rectangular floor plan (60m × 30m) with a standard structural grid of 7.6m × 7.6m (CAR32, CAR33). The floor plan includes a 9m rear setback that allows daylight deeper into the plan and for an exterior playground to be located on top of the lower roof (CAR39). Given the construction complexity a conversion project can afford, the design attempted to repeat details where possible to simplify the construction process (CAR19; e.g. glass partitioning, stairs, built-in furniture). Chosen materials are meant to have a 50-year lifespan exemplified by the interior gypsum partitions, use of an abuse-resistant core that provides greater resistance to surface indentation and abuse (CAR10). Windows are operable and include window shades, but because of school environmental requirements for air purity, humidification and temperature control, only custodians are able to open them (CAR6,

▲ Figure 14.19
School entrance located on the
smaller, less active street
Courtesy Jon Reis

*In 95 per cent of the
discussions with teachers
their response to the
question what is the most
important thing about
their classroom is the
flexibility of the space to
do a variety of things and
storage.*

CAR37). Services are accessible through drop ceilings and access doors provided at strategic locations in the walls and ceilings (CAR3).

Programme distribution in plan and section encourage interaction through the open, light-filled environment. Openness and transparency throughout the building connect internal school spaces as well as provide captivating views of the city (CAR51) – e.g. Figure 14.20 illustrates the openness of the library. The strategic configuration and placement of support and common spaces allow additional light to penetrate into the building and for the spaces to be used in a variety of ways (CAR43). The vertical organisation of shared common spaces encourage interaction amongst students, teachers and administrators (CAR30). To connect the vertical plans a major open and glass enclosed staircase extends from the main entry lobby to the topmost floor serving as a constant reference point as people move through the building (CAR50, CAR51). The stair varies in its location to allow maximum light penetration and is supported with adjacent niches to promote informal conversations and meetings (CAR21).

Student classrooms are of standard dimensions (7.6m × 9.2m; 70sqm) and fit-out to aid in their interchangeability (CAR27). The classrooms are set up with open areas in the centre with built-in objects around the perimeter (CAR20) – NYC's School Construction Authority (NYCSCA) requires book cases, lockers, computer desks and technology to be built-in infrastructure-wise. Space standards for the classrooms are, however, larger than most school standards to allow for the classrooms to remain versatile for a variety of activities (CAR22, CON10). In addition, breakout spaces and niches can be found throughout the

PART IV ADAPTABILITY IN PRACTICE

▲ Figure 14.20
Double-height library space with glazed openings to the corridor
Courtesy Jon Reis

corridors and are used 'impromptu' by teachers (CAR21, CAR28). The break-out spaces expand the basic corridor width to provide semi-private niches for small classroom groups and are strategically located throughout, e.g. outside the library. The carved-out areas also provide a connection to the exterior wall permitting natural light to flow into the central spaces (CAR39). The versatility of the spaces are enhanced by providing lightweight and mobile soft seating (CAR2). The entire school is wireless which allows the teaching environment to move freely throughout the school and enhances the use of the breakout spaces and niches. Colour features identify floor levels, grade levels and specialty classroom locations (CAR52) and extend from the corridor into the classroom to the exterior wall to tie the spaces together.

The large, open, double-height and street-level entry lobby provides a welcoming space that can be used to support both school and community activities. The main staircase incorporates a bright and identifying art wall that uses colours from the palette used in the school (Figure 14.21). The vertical layout of the school works well (CAR30) to accommodate community use during off hours as the lobby provides a direct connection to shared community spaces in a secure yet open plan – the dance studio, cafeteria, community room and lecture hall. Outside groups are encouraged to, and frequently use, these facilities in an open yet secure environment separate from school classroom and administrative facilities on the floors above (CAR43, CAR45, CAR48).

The split use of the building has required separate access with the hospital's entrance on the main road (6th Avenue) and the school's along the quieter 17th street which helps mitigate the dense urban conditions for a primary

Main circulation staircase with identifying art wall and large structural glass opening

Courtesy Jon Reis

school (CAR49, CAR58). With the exception of life safety systems (e.g. fire alarm, smoke exhaust) the two uses are completely separated and allow the school to monitor energy and water usage efficiently through a building management system (CAR12). Electric usage is coordinated and controlled through occupancy sensors and timer controls for lighting and power systems (CAR6). The school takes advantage of a common riser, but segregates use for each floor with their own air handling units which minimises duct runs (and sizes) and allows for more individualised control (CAR5; e.g. community use of lower floors). The conversion process was complicated by the 2008 building code revisions which required enhanced stair pressurisation and corridor smoke exhaust for the change of use (CON6). While not considered at the time, the school could potentially grow into the remaining eight storeys above if the hospital were to move out. In the end, the school was successful in achieving green status following the NYCSCA-adapted LEED Guidelines (CON10).

A6   Dato Onn International Medical City (DOIMC)

Building type: healthcare
Adaptability types: versatile, scalable, refitable
Location: Johor Bahru, Malaysia
Completion date: 2016 (phase I)
Architect: IBI Group, Inc.
Website: www.ibigroup.com

The Dato Onn International Medical City (DOIMC) is an iconic medical complex for KPJ, the largest healthcare provider in Malaysia. It is a mixed-use facility (CAR44) that will cater to the needs of a growing international medical market. The design consists of several wings or centres of excellence that will host different medical services (e.g. oncology, cardiology, CAR30) – each wing having its own identity (CAR54). The five-finger plan of the building enables phased development (Figure 14.22). The first phase provides a larger building than is currently necessary, finishing approximately (70 per cent) of three of the fingers completely and leaving 30 per cent unfinished (CON41) – the unfinished area will flex with the market as needed (CON17). The timescale for Phase II is unknown (five years was suggested), but they anticipate the short-term need of an additional 250 beds. The design team explored the idea of adding space later vertically (CAR40), but the client preferred the empty space, rather than tolerate the disruption later (CON1). A subsequent third phase would construct the remaining two fingers (CAR40).

The adjacent multi-storey car park was initially designed to maximise parking spaces providing the most efficient, economical solution given the compact nature of the site; however, the client asked the architect to adjust the

▼ Figure 14.22
Rendering of 'finished' complex
Courtesy IBI Group, Inc.

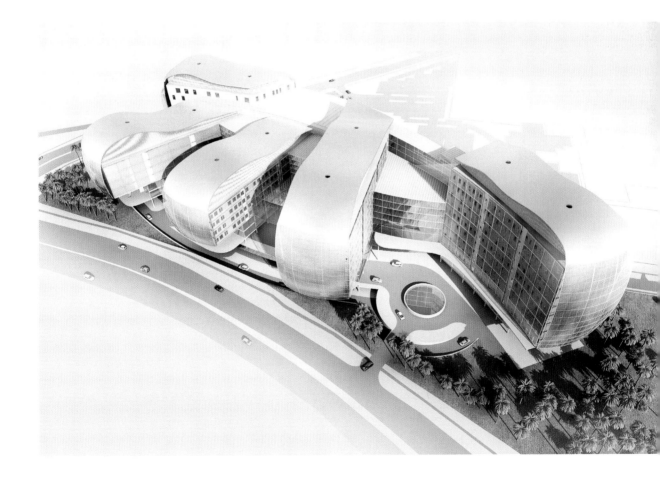

floor height to match the adjacent building (CAR43). In this case, the client was willing to reduce the number of car parking bays for a more convertible option; however, to be implemented other difficulties exist for this strategy such as how to handle the car ramp, vertical circulation and floor loadings.

Despite the client requesting each wing be unique (whimsical corridors), the grid pattern remains consistent across all wings and enough elements were standardised (e.g. location of permanent elements like plant room, vertical circulation) that with a flexible servicing strategy the wings remain interchangeable between wards and clinics (Figure 14.23; CAR23, CAR43). The width of the corridors is 2.4m which is defined by the movement of beds and provides ample space for service ducts (CAR22). The wings also incorporate soft space (e.g. storage, IT, administrative) at the ends, which can change use to allow expansion/contraction within, and potentially between, departments (CAR21, CAR29).

▼ Figure 14.23
Floor plan of a typical wing
Courtesy IBI Group, Inc.

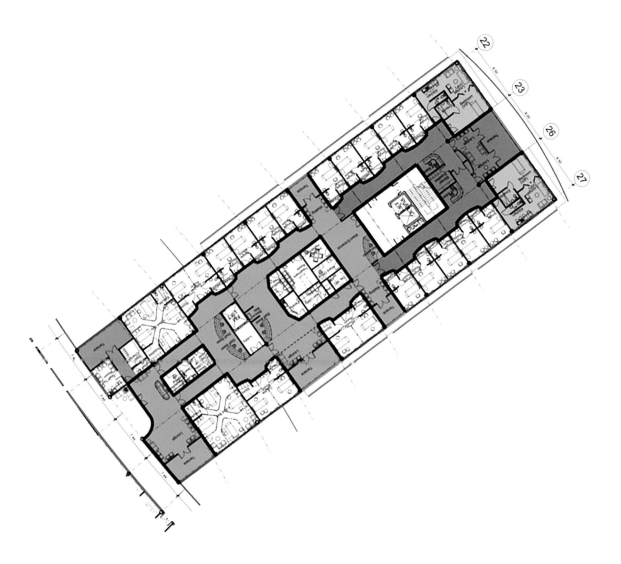

Rationalised room sizes (CAR27), standardised grid layout (CAR33; 8m × 8.5m) and modular façade design (CAR1, CAR16) all aid the legibility of the design and its capacity to adapt to changing needs. The double skin consists of a changeable curtain wall system with a bolted-on mesh screen positioned 1m away to hide individual air-conditioning units while providing an ample gap between inner and outer layers so the inner layer can be maintained easily (CAR1, CAR3). Windows are designed in strips whose size, material and connection enable changes in the use and configuration of rooms (CAR24, CAR43).

Floor heights are 4.5m with a down-stand beam structure (cheapest solution), though the architect would like a flat slab solution to free more space for service distribution and allow for lower floor heights (CAR19). Services are separated by each wing allowing smaller units and ducts while the air-conditioning system is localised on each floor to maximise individual control (CAR5). Conventional design of interior partitions in Malaysia (CON5) are masonry walls; however, the architect would prefer plasterboard partitions for the additional versatility (CON19).

Dedicated waiting areas were considered for each consultant but a centralised waiting space reduces the need for additional spaces and can support other activities if needed (CAR43). In addition, the facility contains a retail portion that requires separate access (CAR44, CAR49). At one point the scheme included a double-height supermarket, but local legislation made it unfeasible requiring a completely separate parking area (CON9).

A7 Bio Innovation Centre

Building type: labs, offices
Adaptability types: adjustable, versatile, scalable, convertible
Location: Liverpool, UK
Completion date: 2016
Architect: IBI Group, Inc.
Website: www.ibigroup.com

The Bio Innovation Centre will be a state-of-the-art lab facility and the first on site for the proposed 'Bio-campus', setting the stage for Liverpool to be recognised as a leading international centre for life sciences. The contemporary architectural language of the building's exterior does not communicate a specific use typology (CAR54; Figure 14.24) and comprises lettable office space primarily on the ground floor with two floors of chemistry and two floors of biology labs above (CAR44). The five-storey building uses a standard 6.6m grid (CAR33) which is divisible to the 3.3m window module (CAR25) and allows for the lab spaces to be subdivided into smaller spaces if desired (CAR24).

The long rectangular form (CAR32) locates structural, service and welfare cores on both ends (CAR30) with non-load-bearing partitions in between allowing the floor plates to be subdivided in a variety of ways to accommodate

▲ Figure 14.24
Exterior rendering
Courtesy IBI Group, Inc.

most commercial uses (CAR4, CAR20, CAR43). This is coupled with a generous 4.6m floor-to-floor height that is finished at 2.7m with a large 1.8m service void (CAR22). In addition, the single storey section has a foundation to withstand being increased to the full five-storey building height and has been designed to consider future connections as the bio-campus develops (CAR14, CAR40, CAR50). Vertically zoned M&E services allow for parts of the building to be operational 24/7 (labs) while other parts can shut down (offices) (CAR5, CAR45, CAR46).

The labs themselves are of a standard size (100m^2) and proportioned to facilitate a range of lab bench layouts (CAR27, CAR6). The labs offer a rational layout of service drops and runs to maximise versatility and are designed so that internal modifications to lab layouts do not affect the servicing strategy of the building. The ratio between lab and admin space can be easily altered based on the user needs and are suitable to be converted into office space (CAR24, CAR43; Figure 14.25).

The building potentially offers flexible leases as well that would allow occupation of labs to be as short as a month (CON14). The labs are supported with shared storage and meeting spaces (CAR21, CAR47) and have the capacity to be converted into office space if the market demands (CON18). Meeting rooms and the office module are kept constant so that uses can be interchangeable and meeting rooms have demountable folding screens so sizes can be varied (CAR24, CAR27). In addition to the lab and office spaces the building incorporates a seminar space and terrace which allows the building to cater to an array of social events (CAR28).

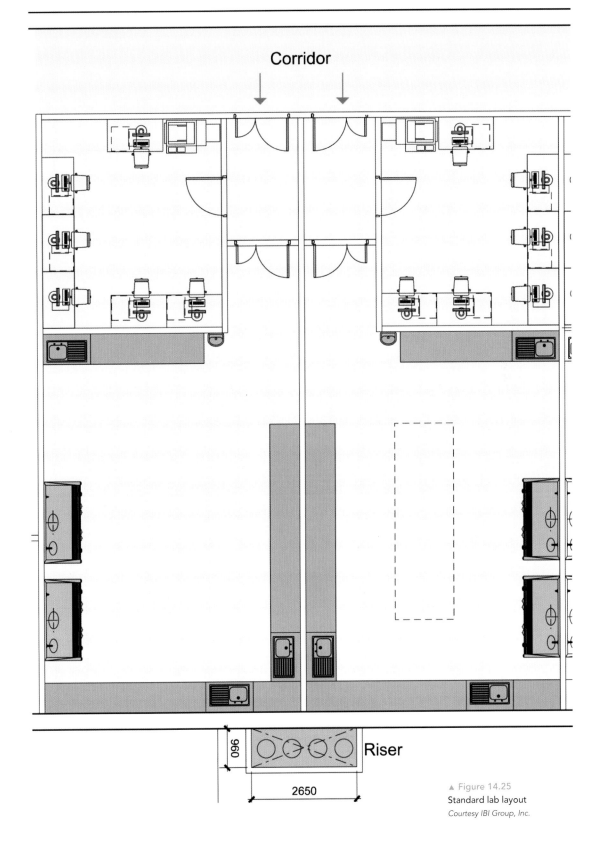

Corridor

960

Riser

2650

▲ Figure 14.25
Standard lab layout
Courtesy IBI Group, Inc.

The building's versatility is also enhanced with its undefined large open plan area on the ground floor that has the potential to exhibit work and engage the public in a variety of ways (CAR60). The security check point is intentionally set back from the entrance to allow the space to blur the inside–outside boundary and the building to engage the public (CAR29). Moreover, the service access has been located and designed to become a secondary entrance in the future if needed (CAR49).

A8 Carl Jacobsens vej

Building type: residential
Adaptability types: versatile, refitable, convertible, scalable
Location: Copenhagen, Denmark
Completion date: 2105
Architect: Vandkunsten Architects
Website: www.vandkunsten.com

The project is situated in a gentrifying, mixed-use and well-connected area of Copenhagen (CAR57) where redevelopment is focused on establishing the train station as a major hub. The project provides a mix of social (100m^2) and special needs (60m^2) housing and will also include a kindergarten, workshops and the residential apartments above (CAR44, CAR46). The scheme illustrates how adaptability can be achieved and limited at the same time as a conscious cost decision (CON19). The apartments have partition walls (CAR24) but the walls between units are load-bearing and restrict the ability to combine units (a common occurrence in Copenhagen).

The design couples the smaller residential units with common open plan spaces (CAR20) for varying activities depending on the time of day or day of the week. The ground floor comprises a common area, a courtyard, kindergarten space and semi-public, open roof tiers that provide seating and green spaces (CAR28, CAR43, CAR47, CAR60). Moreover, local planning policy requires one-half of a parking space per a residential unit (CON9); however, most social housing residents in Copenhagen don't own cars. So the architect designed the carport spaces so they can be a place of work or leisure (CAR43) and hence additional functional capacity for the less versatile residential plans.

Despite the conventional residential levels being of standard ceiling height, the design provides taller floor-to-floor heights in three other applications – ground floor (4m) for unspecified uses, first floor (3.25m) required by regulations for special needs housing and the top floor for the penthouse residences (CAR22). All the hidden service installations are ducted in vertical shafts located in standard grid locations (CAR17, CAR33). The structure has the extra load capacity to add an additional floor of apartments, but is limited by current policy (CON9, CAR14, CAR40). Standardised lightweight residences were designed to be located on the roof if planning regulations change.

The exterior image is strongly formed by its context with its geometry and exterior materials (brick) reflecting the surrounding buildings (CAR58). The universal image approach embodies a standard pattern across the façade utilising a standard cladding system, generic window pattern and a simple colour scheme of greys to accompany the brick exterior and enhance its universal applicability (CAR16, CAR54; Figure 14.26). Furthermore the project intentionally created a very rough exterior surface with irregular projecting bricks and untidied mortar to give the feeling of an aged building (CAR56). Two window types are used throughout (standard and bay) as a method of component standardisation (CAR16) and particular views are framed by providing larger than usual openings towards the roof terrace, courtyard and street. The large windows facing the street could support a variety of functions (e.g. retail; CAR43).

Circulation between apartments is along the inner exterior façade and is wider (2.5m) than required (1.3m) to allow the residents to appropriate the space for recreational or community use (CAR21, CAR42). Direct access to the tiered roof terraces reduces the need for vertical circulation cores which can be a floor plan restriction.

▼ Figure 14.26
Exterior image
Courtesy Vandkunsten Architects

A9 Islington Square

Building type: residential
Adaptability types: versatile, scalable
Location: Manchester, UK
Completion date: 2006
Architect: FAT Architecture
Website: http://fashionarchitecturetaste.com

The Islington Square project in Manchester consists of 23 two- to four-bedroom family homes as part of the larger New Islington development by Urban Splash. The project addressed trends in lifestyle changes, which have led to a more open plan approach (CAR20) – utilising the kitchen as a social-ising space and eating formally around a dining table, neither of which were accommodated in the resident's existing homes (CON5). The design reverts to pre-modern housing in that spaces lie somewhere between circulation space and living (without a dedicated corridor) and merges positive qualities of sub-urban semis into a dense, central urban area (CAR57; Figure 14.27).

The overall plan is an L-shaped, open plan configuration (Figure 14.28) that blurs the boundaries between living, circulation, dining, kitchen, front and back garden and can be subdivided easily to create a variety of spatial and

▼ Figure 14.27
Open L-shaped kitchen plan
Courtesy FAT Architecture

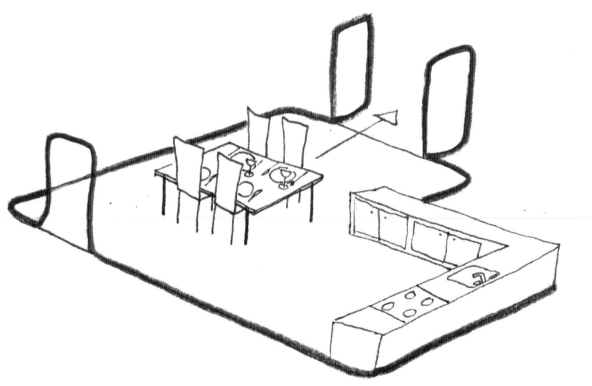

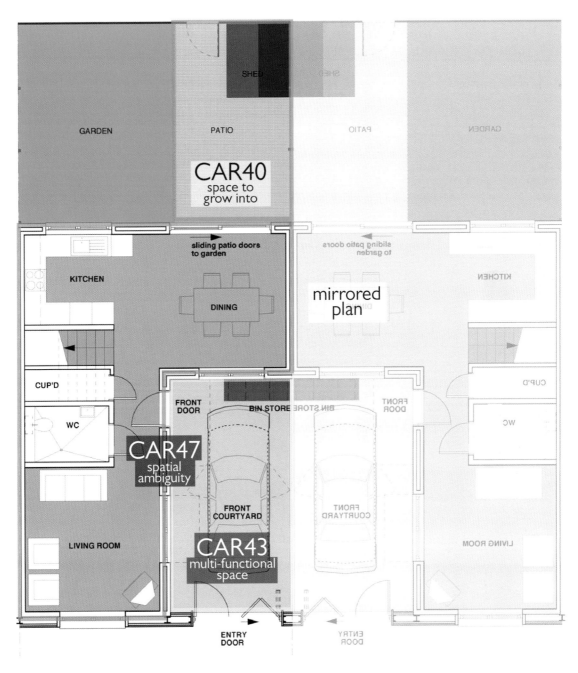

GARDEN

PATIO

PATIO

GARDEN

SHED

SHED

CAR40
space to
grow into

KITCHEN

sliding patio doors
to garden

sliding patio doors
to garden

KITCHEN

DINING

mirrored
plan

CUP'D

CUP'D

WC

WC

FRONT
DOOR

BIN STORE

BIN STORE

FRONT
DOOR

CAR47
spatial
ambiguity

LIVING ROOM

FRONT
COURTYARD

FRONT
COURTYARD

LIVING ROOM

CAR43
multi-functional
space

ENTRY
DOOR

ENTRY
DOOR

▲ Figure 14.28
L-shaped plan
Courtesy FAT Architecture

functional possibilities enhanced with a ground floor height of 2.9m (CAR20, CAR22, CAR29, CAR43). Every space has a window and proportions that allow a variety of furniture layouts (CAR43). After observing that several residents had a computer uncomfortably stuck in a second bedroom or living room, the architect activated the vertical circulation space with a deep bay window on the landing large enough for a desk with nice views (CAR51) and natural light (CAR39) – one resident put a piano in the space. In addition, the residents are given open space at the rear to extend their living environment (e.g. conservatory, CAR40) as the large glazed door provides an easily linkable connection, despite not having a panellised exterior system. Residents also benefit from a garden shed as a 'loose-fit' way to provide bicycle storage.

The design focused on providing the users multiple ways to appropriate the spaces – starting not finishing the residences (CAR42). Planning regulations dictated that every home has a parking space; however, the space can be used as a front garden (CAR43). The space is defined by pairing two L-shaped units as a courtyard and carrying the façade across the front (see Figure 14.28). The L-shape (CAR20) not only creates a 'hidden' courtyard space, but also enables doors and internal walls to be moved around easily, providing flexibility in how the interior and exterior spaces work together (CAR29, CAR43).

Residents were allowed to customise elements of the home including kitchen and bathroom styles along with exterior colour specifications (CAR42; Figure 14.29) and certain DIY elements such as bird and bat boxes (CAR52).

The two-dimensional façade shape embraces 'cookie-cut' artistic shapes rather than straight lines. The intriguing shapes (CAR54) are coupled with

▼ Figure 14.29
Exterior wall colours chosen by residents
Courtesy Len Grant

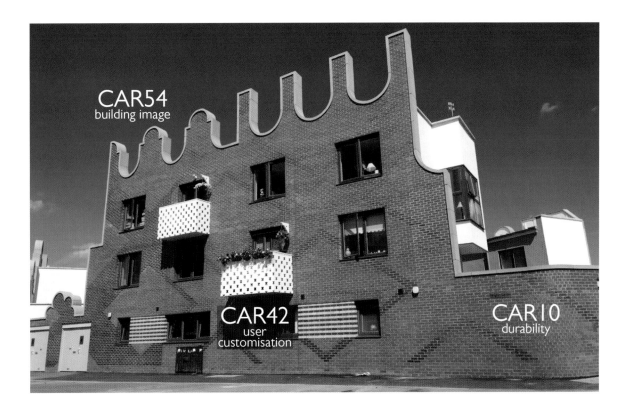

brickwork and balconies embodying clever and distinct patterns (Figure 14.30), but is grounded in the use of a mature, durable material (CAR10, CAR15, CAR16). While the units are social housing, they transcend aesthetic stereotypes, giving the residents a sense of pride and social durability (CON3, CAR54).

▲ Figure 14.30
Street facing façade
Courtesy Paul Adams

A10 The Cube

Building type: mixed use (office, residential, hotel, restaurant, parking, retail)
Adaptability types: versatile, convertible
Location: Birmingham, United Kingdom
Completion date: 2010
Architect: Make Architects
Website: www.makearchitects.com

The Cube is situated prominently as a gateway to Birmingham's canal and city centre with a strong visual presence anchored to a jewellery box design concept linked to the local tradition of jewellery manufacturing (CAR56, Figure 14.31).

The Cube has six vertically stacked uses (CAR44) with transitional floors that can function as the use above or below providing a level of convertibility (Figure 14.32). Each group of floor plates has been tailored to its intended use by varying floor-to-floor heights (3.5–4.5m), floor loadings (4–5kN/m²),

▲ Figure 14.31
The Cube 'standing out' in its
context
Courtesy CREW Photography

fire strategies, lift and service strategies (CAR23). The transitional floors have already proven valuable as the market has shifted (CON18) from 2005 (inception) to 2010 (building opening) – office space was designed for levels 9 to 14, but level 8 became office space and level 4, which was intended for A1/A3 retail, opened as a spa (top and bottom of retail zone shrunk).

The framed structure and servicing strategy creates an open, versatile floor plan that allows floor plates to be subdivided based on tenant needs (CAR20, CAR24). Office levels can be subdivided into quarters (up to four tenants) equipped with individual on-floor plant rooms for greater occupational control. The speculative office space was finished to BCO specifications (CAR42), while the hotel space was left as shell and core – however, the soil vent stacks, which needed to be coordinated with the apartments below, will restrict possible hotel bathroom positions (CAR44).

The residential units are combinable with the use of stud walls – something dictated by the market (original analysis suggested smaller single apartments). From the outset the developers separated tenure for the residential units into two parts to increase unit and building value (CON21, CAR46): the west side as 'investor' (predominantly rental property) accessed via a lobby at level 6 and the east side, 'owner-occupied' accessed from the shared lobby at level 7. The shared lobby with multiple entry points (CAR49) serves several of the upper floors including the hotel, sky bar, restaurant and east residential apartments.

The overall size of the plan was fixed based on the cube concept; thus the space provided for an interior courtyard was used to accommodate

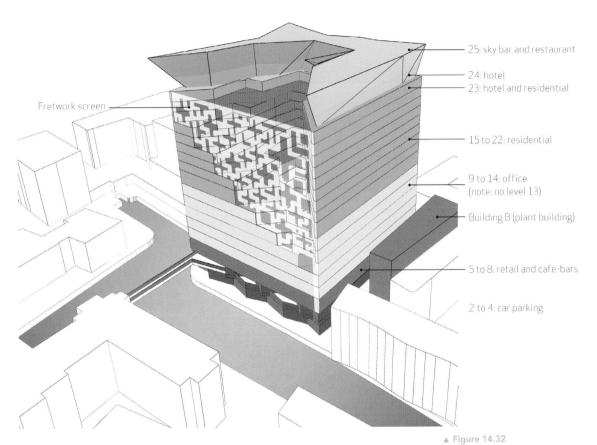

25: sky bar and restaurant
24: hotel
23: hotel and residential

Fretwork screen

15 to 22: residential

9 to 14: office
(note: no level 13)

Building B (plant building)

5 to 8: retail and cafe-bars

2 to 4: car parking

▲ Figure 14.32
Mixture of uses
Courtesy Make Architects

◄ Figure 14.33
Courtyard space
Courtesy David Ryle

programmatic shifts. While the courtyard provides a unique character, a shared public space, visible circulation, good daylighting and views (CAR39, CAR50, CAR53, CAR60), the jagged geometry creates wedge-shaped interior spaces for the residences that seem inefficient, but add a sought-after quirkiness (CAR55; Figure 14.33). Window ledges in the courtyard that face the sky were painted blue and the underside pink and purple (CAR52) determined by the shade of colour's life expectancy. The courtyard also creates a diagonal pedestrian route enhancing the connectivity of the surrounding area linking the street to the towpath, footbridge and the neighbouring mixed-use development (CAR59).

A11 Oxley Woods

Building type: residential
Adaptability types: adjustable, refitable, scalable
Location: Milton Keynes, UK
Completion date: 2008
Architect: Rogers Stirk Harbour and Partners
Website: http://oxleywoods.mk

The residential development of Oxley Woods is part of a wider master plan providing residents with a local high street, new public transport links and a new primary school as adjacent developments are progressed (CAR57). The development provides a variety of housing types and sizes that range from two- to five-bedroom houses, most with gardens, and allows for different forms of tenure including housing association lets, shared ownership and traditional sales to encourage a varied community (CAR28, CAR46). The 145 houses that make up the total development are all slightly different scaled rectangles that adjust to the site and number of bedrooms – the rectangle is generally broken into two slightly offset rectangular volumes splitting the home into two distinct zones (fixed and flexible; CAR30, CAR32; Figure 14.34). The fixed spaces represent a standardised core of bits (CAR16 – staircase, toilet and bathroom), while the flexible spaces are the large open living spaces with no 'fixed' objects (living, dining and bedrooms, CAR20).

The architect worked with an off-site manufacturer to develop a closed timber panel solution capable of adapting to a variety of site configurations (plot sizes, shapes and topography) including shifting the roof orientation and fenestration pattern (CAR16, CAR18; Figure 14.35). The panels have very low infiltration rates (U value = 0.1) and are easily replaced with any material that complies with planning requirements (CON9, CAR54). The project was thus able to deliver a slightly larger volume (for practically no cost) by elongating the panels the length of the trailer bed. The architect used the additional two meters to provide additional storage (CAR21) as the initial occupants suggested there was insufficient storage space (CON14).

The homes have large windows to provide natural daylight (CAR39), but are non-operable to retain a higher thermal performance (CAR12; Figure 14.36).

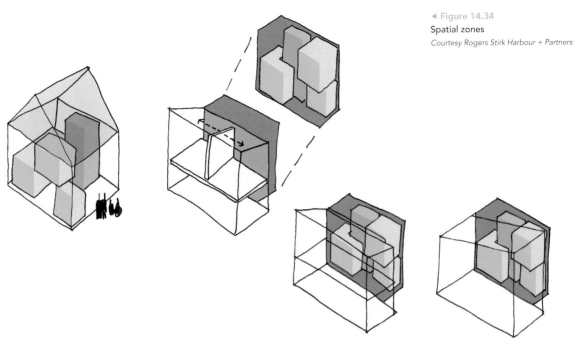

◀ Figure 14.34
Spatial zones
Courtesy Rogers Stirk Harbour + Partners

▲ Figure 14.35
Exterior of homes
Courtesy Katsuhisa Kida

CAR6
configurable
stuff

CAR39
good
daylighting

CAR20
open space

▲ Figure 14.36
Interior view with large windows
Courtesy Katsuhisa Kida

The windows are adjacent to smaller opaque, operable panels that provide natural ventilation. The houses can afford much larger windows than conventional passive houses because the fabric works so well.

The bathrooms and kitchens are standardised across the range of house types including volumetric bathpods. The design has an additional service riser so that the units can hook up easily to alternative energy systems when they become more available (CAR9) including a hot-water loop for CHP (CAR12). The houses incorporate standardised 'Eco-Hats' which package alternative energy technologies into a core off-site unit (CAR18). Various technologies were implemented to reduce heat gains as a method to reduce service demand including high specification lighting, highly efficient glazing assemblies and solar control glazing.

The ground floor is 2.9m in height, while the upper floor takes advantage of the roof space. The houses could add an additional storey by removing the roof panels, adding the additional wall panels and replacing the roof panels – this is aided by the bundling of elements into off-site assembled modules (CAR1, CAR14, CAR19). One or more panels could also be removed to extend into the back garden (CAR40).

The architects designed add-on pieces in a kit-of-parts approach as future extensions but although the planners liked the palette of components, approval was refused on the basis that current policy doesn't cover such a future condition (CON9). Each house has manufacturer drawings that allow the occupant to cut holes in panels (new window) at designated locations to avoid any structural problems. The housing for Oxley Woods came finished, but in a subsequent project the architect completed the housing sufficiently for the owners to receive a mortgage (CON18), but left the spaces raw (CAR41) with a standardised exterior structural panel system that is fire and water proof.

A12 CPC

Building type: office, industrial
Strategy: adjustable, convertible, scalable
Location: Yoqneam, Israel
Completion date: 2009
Architect: Schwartz Besnosoff Architects
Website: www.arch-sb.com

Located in the outskirts of Yokneam in Israel, the simple cube-shaped concrete frame and aluminium and glass panel headquarters for CPC serves as an office and production plant for electronic circuits (CAR44). The building is shaped by formal and informal spaces allowing a variety of activities (CAR28). Its U shape is formed by two rectilinear wings connected by a service core and is filled by an atrium entrance (CAR34; Figure 14.37). The proposed phase II takes advantage of the strategic location of the core for vertical circulation (CAR26, CAR40) and provides production space for CPC or leased start-up companies (CAR46). Initially the new wing will be constructed as shell and core (CAR41), with the gap between the buildings serving as an internal patio (CAR60).

The atrium provides a social space for events and informal meetings, its undulating planes conform to the site topography (Figure 14.38) to create a patio with outdoor furniture, vegetation and a wooden deck (CAR29, CAR43, CAR58, CAR60).

Only the top floor was meant to be hired to other companies, but CPC has rented out the top two floors given the demand for start-up space and moved the dining space from the third floor to the basement (CAR43). The

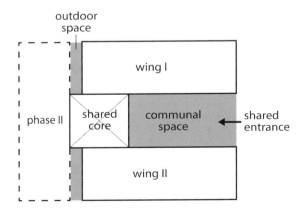

◀ Figure 14.37
Concept plan

▲ Figure 14.38
Atrium space used for dining function (left) and presentation (right)
Courtesy Schwartz Besnosoff Architects

▼ Figure 14.39
Active perimeter of CPC's (A12) atrium space
Courtesy Schwartz Besnosoff Architects

wall separating office spaces and the corridor can change transparency levels to reflect the level of privacy needed by the internal use (CAR6). Walls dividing the open office spaces can be easily shifted, added or removed using a panelled system (CAR1, CAR2). The ceiling and window units are modular which allow for the lighting to be adjusted and windows to be replaced easily (CAR1, CAR16).

The building has been adapted several times since occupation in 2009. For example, with the closing of the production line, the ground floor space with a 6m high ceiling has become a rented gallery. Because of the need for

convertibility between manufacturing and office space, the latter also has 6m storey heights (CAR22). The renting success has led to the owner wanting to construct and occupy phase II releasing the entire phase I to start-up companies (CAR40 and 46).

The design promotes connectivity between perimeter spaces and the central atrium space (Figure 14.39) by encasing the production rooms in glass and wrapping the atrium space with internal circulation connecting the various levels of the building (CAR51).

A13 The King's School Theatre

Building type: school
Strategy: adjustable, versatile
Location: Cheshire, UK
Completion date: 2011
Architect: CGL Architects
Website: www.cgluk.com

The King's School in Chester has occupied the current site since the 1960s and has developed over time as the school's needs have grown and evolved. The architect was asked to provide a master plan that would make better use of the existing facilities and guide future development. In response, the architect proposed a flexible approach to development rather than a single vision including a menu of development opportunities for the short-, medium- and long-term needs but with each forming part of a holistic picture as opposed to the piecemeal approach of the past (CAR56).

The school then approached the architect to review the refurbishment of the theatre hall adjacent to the main entrance. The school desired a versatile space, but the proposed solution complicated access, damaged the spacious qualities of the neighbouring dining hall and was limited to retractable seating. The original 1960's hall had a permanent stage and proscenium arch with plastic stackable chairs that provide a level of adaptability, but are time-consuming to store, which created a significant barrier to alternative uses. In addition, a lightweight retractable partition closed the rear of the hall off from the main school foyer, but provided very poor acoustic separation.

The architect saw more potential in the space than simply providing for drama, and worked diligently with the client to communicate how the space could serve a variety of uses, be better suited for its primary use as a theatre and save them approximately £500,000 in comparison to their original study.

The staff offices, meeting rooms and storage space were strategically located below the existing balcony making best use of the lower single storey height space and forming a stronger acoustical buffer between the theatre and the circulation space of the main foyer (CAR30). Changing rooms and additional storage were placed at the opposite end, at the rear of the stage, allowing the remainder of the space to be unfixed with the installation of a retractable seating system, a retractable curtain system, removable staging, adaptable lighting rigs and movable side wings (CAR2, CAR6, CAR20). The simple design concept placed the fixed spaces as bookends, maximising the open space (26m × 13.5m and 6.7m high) and allowing the remaining 'stuff' inside the theatre to be versatile. The design particularly considered the speed and ease of transforming the space, as they wanted to remove any barriers for change (e.g. the motorised seats can be fully retracted in 10 minutes by a single person). Additional loose chairs are provided for special events (CAR2) and stack on a trolley for storage (CAR21). The full height movable side wings sit flush against the wall, opening up the space, and when fully open form part of the proscenium or set at a midpoint act as sound deflectors for a musical performance (Figure 14.40).

The staging is a modular solution that can quickly expand or be removed (CAR16). A retractable blind system enables quick transformations to full black-out and vice-versa, allowing them to benefit from the large amount of natural light when appropriate (CAR39, CAR43). The school wanted to use dark colours to help to promote a theatrical atmosphere, but the architect convinced the client that lighter colours would support the use of the space for a variety of activities (CAR43, CAR52). Moreover, the architect illustrated to the school that if they increased the level of WC provision they would

▼ Figure 14.40
Configurable seating
Courtesy Jonathan Banks

not have to rely on other facilities within the school to meet public licensing requirements. This allowed the school to hire the theatre and keep the rest of the school closed off (CAR48) reducing costs and management of external hire and increasing its attractiveness. The theatre has been transformed from a rarely used space to a much enjoyed location for school activities, teaching and hired events.

A14 Vodafone Headquarters

Building type: office
Strategy: adjustable, versatile, refitable, convertible, scalable
Location: Newbury, UK
Completion date: 2001
Architect: Fletcher Priest Architects
Website: www.fletcherpriest.com

From the beginning, Vodafone did not want an iconic landmark headquarters (CAR54), but a set of buildings that were functional and comparable to the local market (CON18, CAR23). The complex is comprised of seven buildings currently occupied by a single tenant, linked together by bridges (CAR26), although different tenants could occupy the buildings with each building having its own car parking, access and services (CAR5). The connecting bridges are easily demounted over a weekend (CAR26; Figure 14.41).

The standardised buildings of different lengths cater for different sized organisations within the regional market (CAR43, CAR54). The floor plates are extrusions of a doughnut plan with a central atrium (CAR32). All of the buildings provide good daylight penetration so the general section is 15m, 6m atrium, 15m (total 36m). Each building can be subdivided by floor to operate as doughnuts (single tenant) or as wings (two tenants) (CAR24). Spatial versatility is augmented with raised floors, movable wall solutions, and large projection screens (CAR2, CAR3).

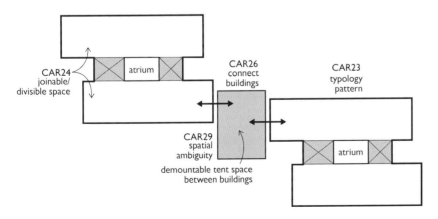

◀ Figure 14.41
Concept plan

A number of tent spaces connect to the buildings with no specific purpose (CAR43). Their use has gone beyond the original intention (corporate presentations, training activities) to include unforeseen activities including marriage ceremonies (CAR45). The spaces are subdivisible (CAR24) and contain a series of movable objects (CAR2) to allow for multiple configurations, e.g. large movable digital screens that are two and three storeys high.

The top of the atrium has an ETFE roof that provides better insulation than glass, a tint to reduce solar gain and is simple and cheap to maintain (CAR12). In addition, the driving decks of the car parks are open grate to allow natural light to penetrate through the structure and to enhance their multifunctionality (CAR43). Large windows provide views of the surrounding countryside (CAR51). Exterior materials of natural terracotta rain-screen cladding and cedar cladding (CAR1) were selected to complement the surrounding natural landscape (Figure 14.42) – the standardised panels are hung from light metal framing (CAR1, CAR16).

A key strategy was to maximise the undulating site to their advantage (CAR58). Thus the buildings are positioned to include the versatility of having a common ground floor following the contours of the site with harmonious simple rectangular plans above (CAR32) that appear organically throughout the site. The building orientation exploits the natural air flow of the small valley (CAR35) – the buildings lie on either side of the lowest point, positioned across

the prevailing wind patterns making them ideal for natural ventilation with the wind hitting the buildings at 90 degrees. The design set out to be entirely naturally ventilated, but resulted in a mixed mode solution due to the difference its inclusion made to the building value (CON17) in comparison to the cost (a result of the client's focus on market trends – CON18).

A15 Kettering Old Persons Unit (KOPU)

Building type: healthcare
Strategy: adjustable, versatile, refitable and scalable
Location: Kettering, UK
Completion date: 2014
Architect: IBI Group, Inc.
Website: www.ibigroup.com

The new unit will be constructed on a very tight site after the first phase of demolition. The floor plan of the single-storey steel frame and cladded solution is divided by a central courtyard that also allows the building to function as two separate buildings (CAR24; Figure 14.43). The scheme is designed to provide two neighbourhoods of living spaces clustered around support and shared spaces (CAR21, CAR47) which form symmetrical halves.

The design includes an internal courtyard, which allows natural light to enter the centre of the building and provides a safe external space for patients (CAR60). The client struggled to understand the benefit of having a space without a defined purpose, but the architect illustrated an array of activities that the courtyard could support – for example allotments, objects to prompt memory, drying laundry, concerts, sensory garden and barbeques. The benefits needed to outweigh the danger of a patient injuring themselves, which forced the architect to clarify the additional value.

▼ Figure 14.43
Sketch of building
Courtesy IBI Group, Inc.

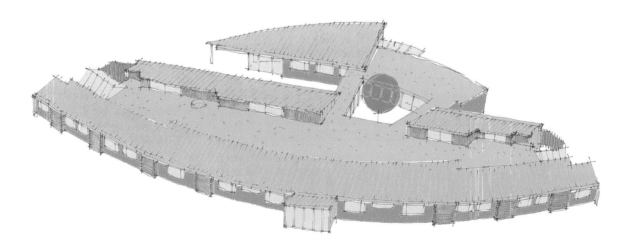

In an effort to activate the corridor space, unique seating areas are provided for occupants not only to rest, but as a destination for their 'wandering' (CAR55). Moreover, the architect is advocating intermediate corridors to add variety to the wandering loop experience – the corridor also functions as an activity space (CAR43). The design team discussed whether doors should be used to close off patient areas or obstacles as a softer, more open barrier (CAR2, CAR29).

There are two standard bedroom sizes (CAR27). The larger room size consists of an assisted bath/shower for patients that need staff more often. The design team investigated placing en-suite bathrooms along the outside wall which would give more versatility for the rooms to change size as the bathrooms are currently located between rooms (Figure 14.44); however, the location worked against several other characteristics including good daylighting (CAR39), visual linkage (CAR51) and minimising the need for services (CAR35). Thus, it was decided to keep the bathrooms between the rooms, which can still be scaled in a single direction along the opposite wall as the bathrooms are paired (CAR24).

Patients can customise their doors with graphics and signage and the rooms have 'monitors' that can display personal images, including those emailed by friends/relatives directly to the screen (CAR42). The height of washbasins can be adjusted for disabled patients and privacy curtains are controlled by the user (CAR42). Several of the furniture choices are collapsible for easy storage and a building management system enables automated control of service elements including lighting levels and room temperature (CAR6).

The window design enhances the multifunctionality of the rooms by allowing for three conditions: 100mm restricted, fully operable and sealed – healthcare patients are restricted to 100mm operability, but the restriction doesn't apply to other occupants, e.g. an administration space. In addition, the windows are triple glazed to provide greater insulation (CAR12) and have blinds integrated

▶ Figure 14.44
Exploration of en-suite bathroom locations

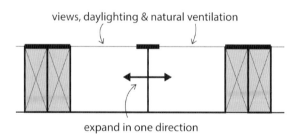

views, daylighting & natural ventilation

expand in one direction

poor views, daylighting, & ventilation

expand in two directions

into the window (CAR37) – the integrated solution goes against the layer principle integrating stuff (blinds) with skin (window). The project considered the use of clipped window details that allow the windows to be replaced easily without affecting the exterior wall, but this was rejected due to its high cost (CON19) and limiting future replacement options as a closed system (CAR15).

The scheme has a generous amount of strategically located random storage so that bulky equipment is nearby. The extra space (CAR21) of the pitched roof has clerestory windows and roof lights with the higher level providing ample space to distribute services (CAR39). The modular services are located outside the building to be accessible from inside and out. Off-site, integrated solutions such as bathroom pods and pre-plumbed washbasins with mirrors, shelf, shaving outlets, taps and pipes were also incorporated (CAR18).

The staff do not have assigned desks and will keep personal items in a locker. With additional staff space needed at night-time the daytime lounge spaces will be used as staff space at night (CAR43). Several social spaces that were very narrow in the brief, were widened to combine their function as larger social spaces; some also include movable partitions to allow for the size to change (CAR2, CAR43).

The scheme has the potential to add an adjacent building upon the demolition of a neighbouring building. In such a case it would mirror the curve (Figure 14.45) avoiding direct views between patient rooms (CAR41). The design would also connect to the existing hospital with a new entrance (CAR26, CAR49).

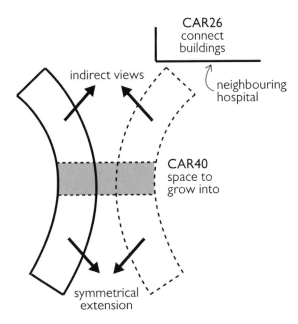

CAR26
connect
buildings

indirect views

neighbouring
hospital

CAR40
space to
grow into

symmetrical
extension

◄ Figure 14.45
Expansion plan

Chapter 15

Designing for adaptability

The competition entries showcase the participants' ideas on adaptability first presented at the AF conference at the Building Centre in London in 2011 to developers, clients and occupiers. Designs had to challenge existing orthodoxies while illustrating a degree of pragmatism regarding implementation. The competition encouraged creative responses to our evolving theory and models. The proposals include design philosophies, design rules, building components, technologies (both existing and emergent) and kit-of-parts solutions.

Table 15.1 maps the six adaptability types against the 10 case studies. Versatile, refitable and convertible were the most consistently implemented.

Table 15.1 Adaptability types mapped against competition entries

		Adjustable	Versatile	Refitable	Convertible	Scalable	Movable
B1	Industrial Democratic Design		X	X	X	X	
B2	An Adaptable Building App	X		X	X		X
B3	An Emporium for Education		X		X	X	
B4	Leicester Waterside		X	X	X	X	X
B5	Adapt and Survive	X	X	X	X	X	
B6	An Approach to Adaptability		X	X	X	X	
B7	Adaptability through Hybridity		X	X	X		
B8	Ad Hoc Urbanism		X	X	X	X	
B9	Adaptable Primary School	X	X	X		X	
B10	Adaptable Apertures		X	X	X		

B1 Industrial Democratic Design (IDD)

Building type: residential, office
Adaptability types: versatile, refitable, convertible and scalable
Designer: Vandkunsten Architects
Website: www.vandkunsten.com

▲ Figure 15.1
Example of 'finished' building

Inspired by the configuration possibilities by brick and timber block buildings of first generation industrialism, Industrial Democratic Design (IDD) is an open system of best-practice rules for the design of 'ordinary' buildings offering a range of everyday purposes (re)approaching an adaptable building culture. IDD has three aims – a better understanding of embodied energy, the use of industrial production and a wider stakeholder influence. The open system supports a variety of structural platforms (e.g. concrete, steel, wood), façades, and exterior applications (e.g. balcony, sun screen, windshield), while providing a set of general composition rules surrounding building depth (e.g. 13–17m), storey height, load-bearing façades, central zones for service and access and modularity (CAR3, CAR4, CAR30, CAR36). The system deploys intermediary elements as a product innovation to separate two or more building layers

◄ Figure 15.2
Transformation scenarios (scalable)

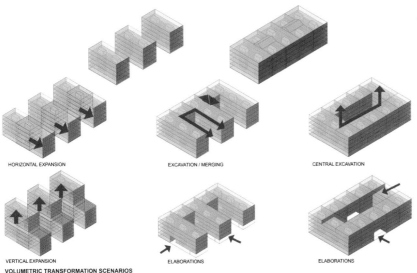

HORIZONTAL EXPANSION

EXCAVATION / MERGING

CENTRAL EXCAVATION

VERTICAL EXPANSION

ELABORATIONS

ELABORATIONS

VOLUMETRIC TRANSFORMATION SCENARIOS

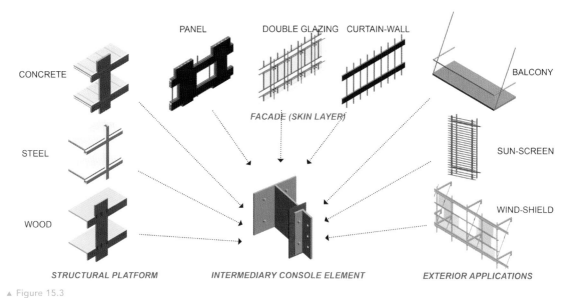

▲ Figure 15.3
Intermediate component between structural system and façade elements (refitable)

▲ Figure 15.4
Convertibility between residential and workplace uses

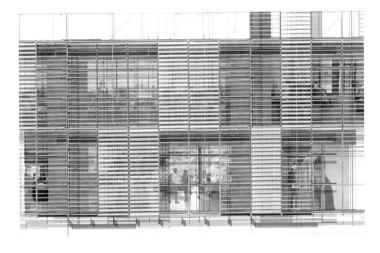

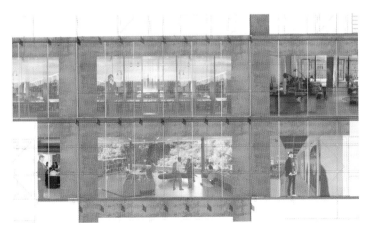

◄ Figure 15.5
Façade configurations based on
use: residential (top), office (middle)
and studio (bottom)

aiding in the reversibility of construction and providing a clearer hierarchy of assembly (CAR1). These are augmented by a set of rules for each building layer (e.g. skin – use of lightweight construction, modularity and subdividing, detachable fixations and preservation of materials). The proposal provides examples of an interesting range of future scenarios in form, use and occupier customisation (CAR42).

B2 An adaptable building app

Building type: office

Adaptability types: adjustable, refitable, convertible and movable
Designer: Robin Partington Architects (RPA)
Website: www.rpalondon.com

The design seeks to unlock the potential of a smart phone app to mediate between user preferences and building conditions. The idea could be applied to any building with devices people already have through Bluetooth technology and consensus software. The smart phone is envisaged to provide a common language that is constantly up to date. Whether it is automatic/high-tech (developed country) or manual/low-tech (developing country), it's not about how you do it, but about communicating the data to the users or the building (via the smart phone). The concept would allow space to be programmable and constantly changing based on user needs

▼ Figure 15.6
Building, user and environment communicate via an app

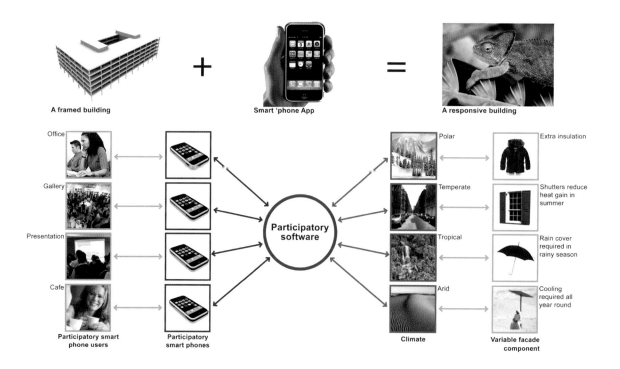

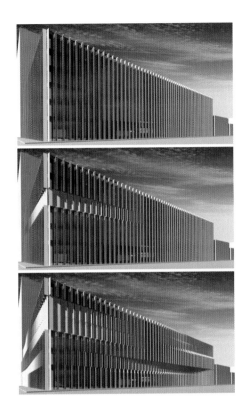

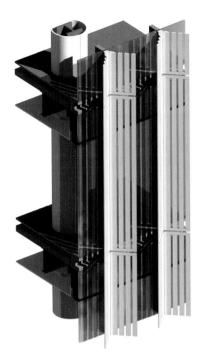

◄ Figure 15.7
Façade mechanism enables a
dynamic façade

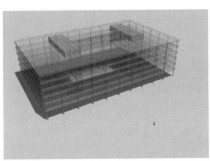

Blank canvas

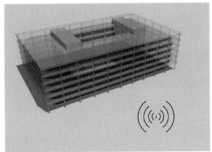

One size fits all

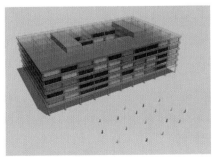

Different user preferences

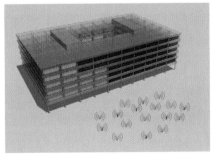

Hybrid system

◄ Figure 15.8
Similar user preferences are
grouped together in the hybrid
system

and the external environment grouping similar conditioned preferences (e.g. warm, cool, quiet, noisy) and activities together, removing the traditional 'one size fits all' building management approach (CAR37, CAR42, CAR43). The example illustrates how an external shading device adapts to inside and outside climate conditions creating a dynamic and always fresh looking façade.

B3 An emporium for education

Building type: higher education
Adaptability types: versatile, convertible, scalable and movable
Designer: Studio Egret West (SEW)
Website: www.egretwest.com

SEW's proposition creates an emporium of urban form for Lewisham College genuinely open to outside trade with a ground floor marketplace and flexible teaching spaces above (CAR44). The scheme has 10 principles: collected (consolidate all the courses into one flexible structure); grand entrance (promote, collect and gather students and the public); emporium (the capacity for the school to 'trade' itself in activity, knowledge and achievement); showcase (vertical window shopping opening the college to the public); proud structure (creative articulation of the materiality of the building); active balance (replacing the corridor with a place for learning); inhabitation (each

▼ Figure 15.9
An adaptable form based on cellular units

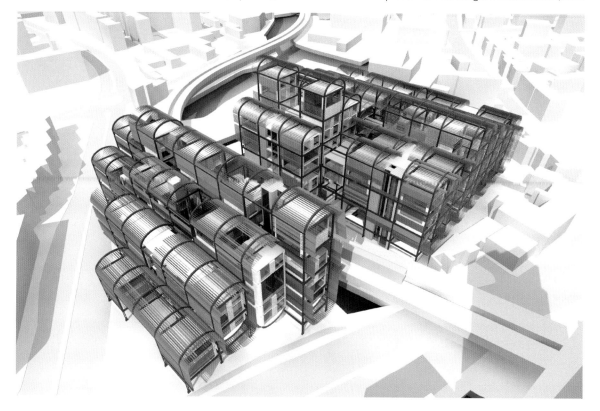

◀ Figure 15.10
Ground floor marketplace

▼ Figure 15.11
Corridors replaced w/ activities

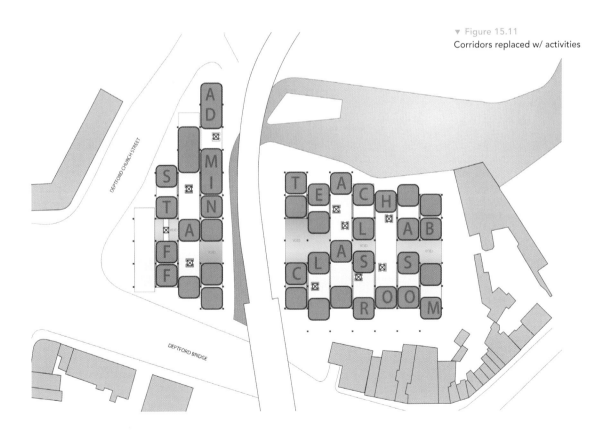

faculty can inhabit the evolving building in their own way); daily to annual flexibility (allow teachers to adapt spaces to their needs); aggregation (the structure can aggregate over time with additional resources); and amenity roof gardens (a green space for ubiquitous activity and faculty- specific means).

B4 Leicester Waterside

Building type: neighbourhood
Adaptability types: versatile, convertible, scalable and movable
Designer: Ash Sakula Architects
Website: http://adaptableneighbourhoods.com/waterside

Leicester Waterside takes a bottom-up approach to adaptability driving incremental change through a variety of small acts led by and empowering the community's immediate and tangible needs for places to live and work. An adaptable neighbourhood is about understanding and supporting rather than suppressing constant and incremental change as a community-driven, urban economy – a thriving ecosystem of small enterprises. The proposal looks to capture small wins at first, raising the profile of the area – new signage to shout about the local businesses, pop-up gardens, events and markets using leftover spaces, and small modifications to buildings, like enlarged openings on the ground floor, to help to liven up the public realm (CAR12, CAR50, CAR54, CAR60). Meanwhile uses (pop-up shops and cafés) animate the street level, artist gardeners green the area, regular events begin to happen daily, weekly, seasonally or annually, flexible licences and varied forms of tenure attract increasing numbers of people creating a cluster of small-scale enterprise and experimentation.

▼ Figure 15.12
Leicester waterside today

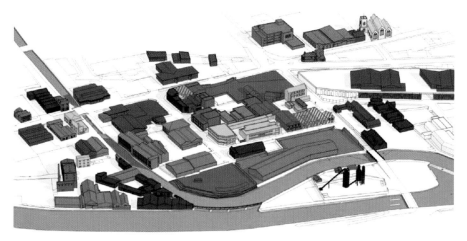

 Industry

Tarmac (Cement Works)

 Offices

Business Base

Action Business Centre (Bright College)

WM ProServ (accountants, IT support)

Leicester Vocal Tech (singing school)

Pat Keeling, John Bird (Model agency)

Stayfree Music (Rehearsal & recording Studios)

The Stockhouse (fashion design)

 Food | Drink

Ship Inn

Huckleberry's Café

Marmåra café

Foresters Arms

 Religion

Jubilee Worship Centre

All Saints Church

 Not in use

 Residential

Landlord of Ship Inn

 Manufacturing

Premier Frames (Conservatory roof specialists)

Nile Trading (underwear manufacturing and wholesale)

J.A. Footwear | UK shoe components (shoe manufacturing and warehouse)

Forward Electronics (electrical engineers)

European Motor Factors (paint panels equipment)

ABL Labels (Printed Fabric Woven and self adhensive Labels)

Central Patterns (Engineers Pattern Makers)

Richard Kew & Albert Thurston (leather belt and brace manufacturers)

Auto Vallet Services

Cahill Plastics Ltd

 Motoring

Leicester Taxis (motor garage)

Hurst Automotive (motor garage)

K.P.J. (Motors Polski Garage)

Go-Renault

CCR (Auto paint specialists)

Bridge Motors (car repairs)

Autocraft (car repairs)

 Wholesale

Eyre & Elliston (Electrical Wholesale distributor)

Travis Perkins (Timber and building supplies)

Decormax (Timber merchants)

Norton Cash & Carry (Toy and sale wholesale)

Samsom's Cash & Carry (confectionary and tobacco wholesale)

R.S.T. International (footwear wholesale)

Kitchen Warehouse (kitchen manufacturers and wholesale)

Igloo (Transport, Logistics and recruitment)

Design Metal (retail solutions)

The space place (self storage)

Autosigns (car sales and accessories)

Office Update (quality new and used office furniture)

Hockey Warehouse (hockey equipment)

 Retail

East Midlands Vans (car wash, sales and café)

Stratstone (car sales)

Kubek Furniture (furniture sales)

Bathroom Centre (bathroom furniture sales)

Gattsbys (furniture warehouse)

West end picture framing (art supplies and photo framing services)

▲ Figure 15.13
Existing building uses

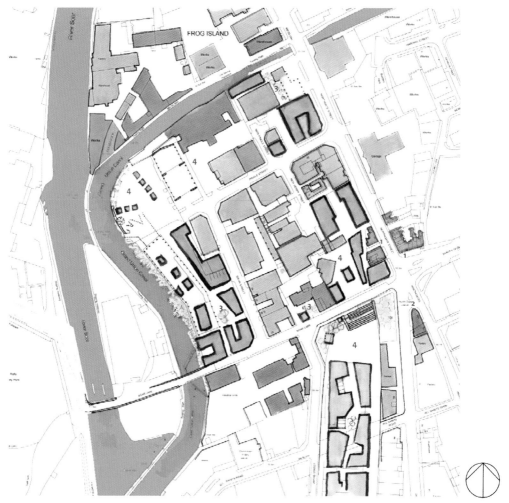

Key

■ Very precious buildings by virtue of their shape, corner position or craftsmanship are 'character champions' and vital to new neighbourhood.

■ Adapt and insulate factories: large spans, useful massing, usable courtyards. They each offer specific clues as to how they can be adapted in the most dramatic or quiet way using the creative energy of agencies such as Transition Leicester.

□ Existing buildings whose frames can support unheated, highly transparent enclosures.

■ Density: new buildings which offer non-dogmatic, zero-carbon floorspace for living, working, learning, creating.

1 Reinstate recently demolished Northgate buildings

2 Protect exquisite corner on axis of Northgate

3 Greening co-designed courtyards to extend useful space of building: micro-climates of character with green walls, sun traps and shady spots on ground and roof

4 Public squares for performance, cooking market use

▲ Figure 15.14
Site analysis

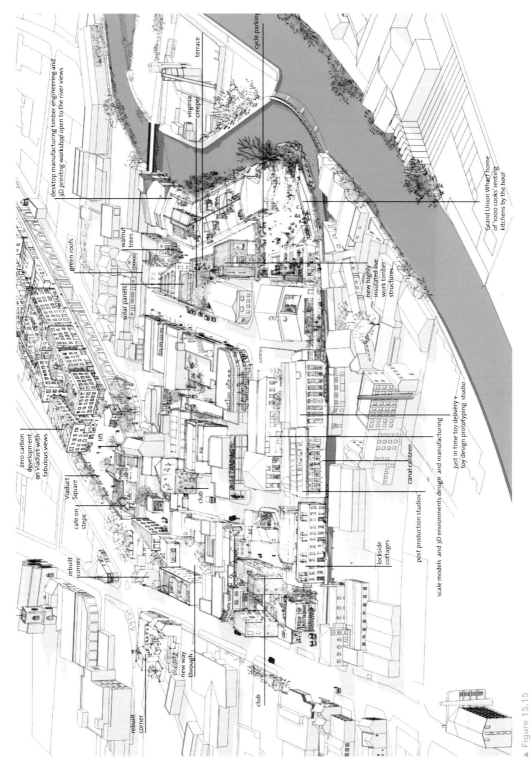

zero carbon development on Viaduct with fabulous views

rebuilt corner

rebuilt corner

new way through

Viaduct Square

cafe on steps

lift

club

club

green roofs

walnut trees

solar panels

desktop manufacturing timber engineering and 3D prinitng workshop open to the river views

virginia creeper

terrace

cycle parking

new highly -insulated-live work timber structures

lockside cottages

post production studios

scale models and 3D enviornments design and manufacturing

canal canteen

just in time toy delivery + toy design prototyping studio

Grand Union Wharf home of '1000 cooks' renting kitchens by the hour

▲ Figure 15.15
Snapshot of the neighbourhood in its continual evolution

Voices of the people 3

"We tried to develop the area ourselves but the council put rockers in the way."

"Leicester is too fragmented. The council's destroyed the city centre with the road system. You need to bind it all together."

John Hurst was all ready to relocate his business. Hurst Automotive, to make way for the new masterplan four years ago. Then it all fell through: 'typical Leicester', according to John.

Hurst Automotive specialises in repairing BMW and Mercedes and is in a good location for clients, close to the city centre and by the main road. But John despairs at the rundown state of the area.

John believes the problem lies in the council being over-ambitious, seeing Leicester as bigger than the little market town that it is.

"In Leicester, empty buildings get burnt down."

John teamed up with his neighbours at Norton and Samsom to put in outline planning to redevelop their sites for housing.

"Samsom's is the important one as it's along the water. But it got turned down because the council want to develop the whole site in one go."

John is resigned to moving his business if the area is to be redeveloped.

"There's only one way the town can expand and it's this way. It's a waiting game fo us."

"The corner site needs to be developed the best it can to generate interest in the area."

Three young mechanics work for John and prefer to eat their lunch inside the garage rather than outside by the river, a few minutes' walk away.

"Leicester is changing. The other night, we were out on Highcross St. by the tapas bar, you wouldn't know you were in Leicester – the sun was out, everyone was happy. So, it is possible."

▲ Figure 15.16

Voices of the people

A
Tell tall tales

Don't plan, narrate. Imagine your neighbourhood through the looking glass, as if anything were possible. Inspirational stories will capture other people's imaginations and become a reality. The ones that don't become part of the area's Imaginary Resources Department.

B
Activate a piece of public space near you regularly

Make one of your imaginings a part of everyone's day, or week, or month.

So: Set up a regular event or activity (bake-sale, bric-a-brac market, donkey rides, story telling camp-outs, shed-building contests, sports-day-reunions) in a street, square, corner, or vacant lot.

And: Try to do this in an unused building in the area. It deepens a place when everyone remembers that before a place is what it is, that we all did life classes there, or it used to be a piano marathon hall for a couple of years...

C
Open up to your neighbours

Either: Socially, organizing community shared interest events where you bring together porcelain lovers with an eye for avant-garde teapot experimentation, or setting up and participating in a community forum online where sub-forums can proliferate and people can type away to their hearts content, and meet up if an idea is catching...

And: Physically opening up your building/home, removing gates, opening up the ground floor, semi-public outdoor spaces, larger windows. Personalize your façade, make your walls tell tales to kids passing by. Talk about yourself through your front garden, your architecture, your hedge.

D
Transform a public corner

Together, commit to transform your favourite public corners and streets. Personalise them so that they embody local passions, needs, idiosyncrasies and pride. Make your local junction a great cathedral, that is grand not through its size but through its joy in communicating… every bench can say something (Jonathan always loved to look at Jane's house from this spot, and still does, and is very much alive thank you very much…) and every plant should whisper.

E
Make and maintain a neighbourhood tale

Put all the stories, experiences and myths of your shared neighbourhood life into an oral saga that will keep living room campfires alight with stories of the streets and characters of the area. You are the hero.

◀ Figure 15.17
Ideas for promoting an adaptable neighbourhood

B5 Adapt and survive

Building type: commercial – office, flats, hotel, retail, restaurant
Adaptability types: adjustable, versatile, refitable, scalable and convertible
Designer: Tec Architecture & 3D Reid Architects
Website: www.tec-architecture.com

Adapt and Survive proposes a form-based design code primarily for commercial urban buildings broken into three distinct areas: planning codes (e.g. space between buildings and overall building height), building control codes (e.g. structural and façade design) and tax incentives (e.g. furniture tax reductions). The design code is contextualised through the adaptive reuse of the Abbey Mill in Bradford upon Avon and a new proposal which is wedged between the two existing structures. The proposal focuses on understanding both physical and social dimensions concerning the long-term adaptability of such buildings like Abbey Mill which has undergone at least five use changes in its 150-year life, which they argue is as much a result of its positive social presence (e.g. people like it, provides a place for social gathering) as its physical characteristics (e.g. tall storey heights, CAR22; deep ground floor, CAR44).

Planning codes

1   Space between buildings and overall building height (max height is 3x the width between neighbouring building):

- allows sufficient daylight into buildings and therefore allows for potential changes of use
- creates spaces which contribute to the public realm and therefore the long-term value of the buildings
- allows space for future expansion

2   Ground floor storey (max width is 5x the height):

- proposed minimum internal height of a double height ground floor would be 5m in order to achieve a mezzanine structure

▲ Figure 15.18
Section through building (in use)

w of existing and new Abbey Mill buildings from river car bridge (south east)

3   Upper storeys (max width is 5x the height):

- suggested depths are in multiples of 1.5m (planning module) and the heights are in modules of 0.15m to assist with standard staircase modules
- a plan depth of over 15m is more likely to require mechanical assistance to ventilation
- net floor space as 'support' space (storage, filing, printing, communications rooms) does not need natural daylight or natural ventilation

Building control codes

4   Design occupancy (structural loading, fire escape, toilet provisions):

- stairs spaced 30m where there is a choice of routes and 18m in one direction will cater for most uses
- the spacing rule fits well with most mechanical and electrical services having a reach of about 30m before needing some form of boost or additional risers
- toilets are designed as demountable fit-out items (not integrated within structural walls)
- use demountable partitioning where possible so that circulation and rooms can be relocated as necessary

5   Structural design:

- use of framed structures with wide column spacing (ideally 7.5 to 9m plus) is preferred in order to maximise long-term flexibility between different uses

6   Façade design:

- at least half the windows serving a floor should have heads located as high as the ceiling in order to maximise daylight penetration, as well as promoting better natural air movement
- there should be a window at least every 3m on main elevations, which would be consistent with minimum likely room widths

B6 An approach to adaptability

Building type: school
Adaptability types: versatile, refitable, convertible and scalable
Designer: Buro Happold
Website: www.burohappold.com

Figures 11.3 and 11.7 are additional visualisations from this scheme.

Buro Happold's proposal for an adaptable primary school focuses on a design approach centred on understanding user behaviours and stakeholder values through surveys, precedent visits, workshops and 'day-in-the-life' scenarios. It foregrounds climate change adaptation as a critical scenario by identifying critical climate parameters, their physical consequences and a plan of action for each correlated with building layers. The adaptable strategies and solutions include options for each layer based on a matrix analysis of variables such as constructability, cost, embodied energy and adaptability. General rules for each use scenario (school, retail, office and residential) are compared by room area, room height, minimum and maximum plan depth, glass area and more (CAR20, CAR22, CAR36). Change scenarios are presented in two forms: minor and major retrofit with two scales – single use or shared use. The feasibility of changes is explored for different transition levels. The approach is a holistic and iterative process that starts early in briefing and carries through to the handover, occupation and subsequent use stages through a variety of tools and protocols.

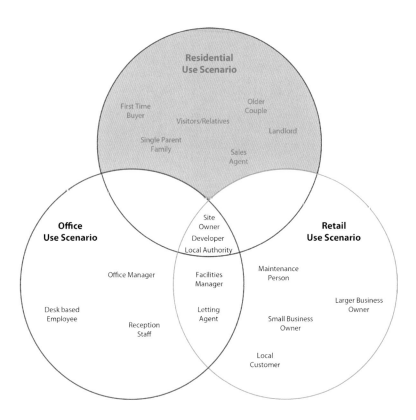

▶ Figure 15.20
Stakeholder analysis for different uses

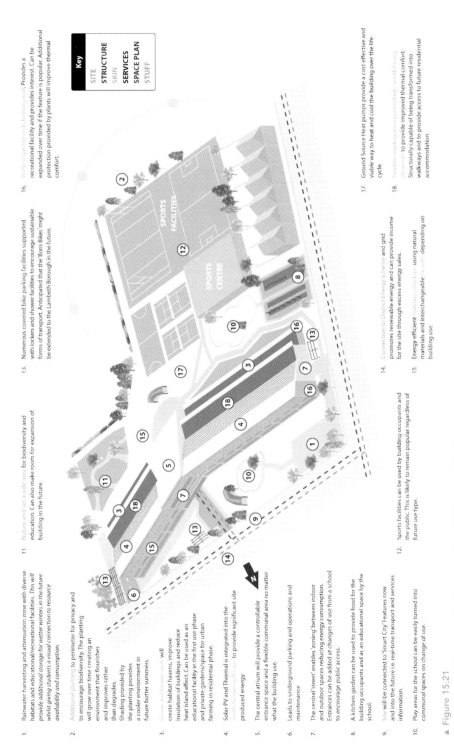

1. Rainwater harvesting and attenuation zone with diverse habitats and educational/recreational facilities. *This will provide additional storage for wetter winters in the future whilst giving students a visual connection to resource availability and consumption.*

2. Additional planting to perimeter for privacy and to encourage biodiversity. The planting will grow over time creating an environment that flourishes and improves rather than degrades. Shading provided by the planting provides a cooler environment in future hotter summers.

3. Green and brown roof will create habitat havens, improve insulation of buildings and reduce heat island effect. Can be used as an educational facility in the first use phase and private gardens/space for urban farming in residential phase.

4. Solar PV and Thermal is integrated into the south facing rooftops to provide significant site produced energy.

5. The central atrium will provide a controllable entrance space and a flexible communal area no matter what the building use.

6. Leads to underground parking and operations and maintenance

7. The central 'street' enables 'zoning' between indoor and outdoor spaces reducing energy consumption. Entrances can be added at changes of use from a school to encourage public access.

8. A kitchen garden can be used to provide food for the building occupants and as an educational space by the school.

9. Site will be connected to 'Smart City' Features now and into the future i.e. real-time transport and services information.

10. Play areas for the school can be easily turned into communal spaces on change of use.

11. Nature and 'set a side' area for biodiversity and education. Can also make room for expansion of building in the future.

12. Sports facilities can be used by building occupants and the public. This is likely to remain popular regardless of future use type.

13. Numerous covered bike parking facilities supported with lockers and shower facilities to encourage sustainable forms of transport. Anticipated that the 'Boris Bikes' might be extended to the Lambeth Borough in the future.

14. Connection to District Energy scheme and grid promotes renewable energy and can provide income for the site through excess energy sales.

15. Energy efficient building envelope using natural materials and interchangeable façade depending on building use.

16. Vertical garden and 'building wall'. Provides a recreational facility and provides interest. Can be expanded over time if the feature is popular. Additional protection provided by plants will improve thermal comfort.

17. Ground Source Heat pumps provide a cost effective and viable way to heat and cool the building over the life cycle.

18. Double glazing incorporated into south facing elements to provide improved thermal comfort. Structurally capable of being transformed into walkways and to provide access to future residential accommodation.

Key

SITE
STRUCTURE
SKIN
SERVICES
SPACE PLAN
STUFF

▲ Figure 15.21

Use analysis of elements on site for now and possible future applications

	1	poor
	2	fair
	3	good
	4	very good

LATERAL RESISTING SYSTEM	Load-Bearing Capacity	Combination with different vertical structural systems	Constructability	Cost	Embodied Energy	Adaptability	Totals
Steel Bracing Elements	3	3	4	3	1	3	17
Steel Moment Frames	4	2	2	2	1	2	13
Concrete Shear Walls	2	4	3	4	2	2	17
Concrete Moment Frame	4	2	2	3	2	1	14
Wood Shear Walls	2	1	3	3	4	1	14
Reinforced Masonry Shear Walls	2	1	2	3	3	2	13

VERTICAL LOAD SYSTEM	Max Span	Strength	Constructability	Cost	Embodied Energy	Adaptability	Totals
Steel Framing	4	4	4	4	1	3	20
Wood Framing	2	2	3	2	4	3	16
In situ Concrete Systems	3	3	3	4	2	1	16
Precast Concrete	3	3	3	3	2	3	17
Rammed Earth Construction	3	1	1	2	4	4	15
Reinforced Masonry	2	2	2	3	3	2	14

INTERNAL SECONDARY FRAMING	Strength	Durability	Constructability	Cost	Embodied Energy	Adaptability	Totals
Lightweight Steel Framing	4	4	4	2	1	3	18
Wood Framing	3	3	3	3	3	3	18
Bamboo Construction	2	3	1	2	2	2	12
Strawbale Construction	2	3	2	2	3	2	14
Rammed Earth Construction	1	3	1	2	4	4	15
Unfired Earth	1	3	2	2	4	3	15
Masonry Walls	3	2	2	3	3	1	14

INTERNAL PARTITIONS	Thermal Performance	Durability	Constructability	Cost	Embodied Energy	Adaptability	Totals
Gypsum Boards	3	3	4	3	3	3	19
Bamboo Plywood	2	3	3	2	2	3	15
Cardboard Panels	3	3	3	1	3	3	16
Hemplime Construction	3	3	3	2	3	2	16

▲ Figure 15.22
Structural system analysis against six design concepts (no solution is perfect)

	Schools (classroom)	Office	Retail	Residential
Room Area	60–90 m²	Column Grid 7.5m, 9m, 12m	Flexible	Flexible
Room Height	3m	3m	3.5m	2.4m
Minimum Plan depth	12–15m	13.5m	15m	8–11m
Maximum Plan depth	21m	21m	45m	15–21m
Glass Area (Ext. Wall)	40%	No specific guidance	Increase for shop fronts	Decrease for privacy
Overheating	a) Not to exceed 28°C for more than 120 hrs. b) The average internal to external temperature difference should not exceed 5°C c) The internal air temperature when the space is occupied should not exceed 32°C	Not to exceed 25°C for more than 5% occupied hrs. Not to exceed 28% for more than 1% occupied hrs.	No specific guidance	Minimise degree hours over 27°C (EST)
Natural Ventilation	8 l/s per person at any occupied time.	12–16L/person	5L/person	Purge rate of 4ach (ADF)
Mechanical Ventilation	Minimum daily average of 5 l/s per person. Capability of achieving a minimum of 8 l/s per person at any occupied time	No specific guidance	No specific guidance	1 bed = 13l/s, 2 = 17 l/s, 3 = 21 l/s, 4 = 25l/s (ADF)
Daylight	>2% to avoid frequent use of electric lighting	2% Average	No specific guidance	Between 2–5% depending on use
Design conditions	Classroom 20°C, Corridor 19°C	Summer 24°C +/– 2°C, Winter 20°C +/– 2°C	18°C–22°C (CIBSE B)	No specific guidance
Occupancy Hours	9–5, 52 weeks a year	9–5, 52 weeks a year	9–5, 52 weeks a year	27/7/365
Surface reflectances	Ceiling, Wall, Floor - 70/50/20	Ceiling, Wall, Floor - 70/50/20	Ceiling, Wall, Floor - 70/50/20	Ceiling, Wall, Floor - 70/50/20
Room Occupancy	29 Adults at 75W (Sensory) 65W (Lat)	29 Adults at 75W (Sensory) 65W (Lat)	Variable	Variable

▲ Figure 15.23
Design parameters across different uses

	Minor Retrofit		Major Retrofit	
	Shared Use	Single Use	Shared Use	Single Use
Optimising Form and Orientation				
Alter building form	○ ○ ○	● ● ○	● ● ○	● ● ○
Alter building orientation	○ ○ ○	○ ○ ○	● ○ ○	● ○ ○
Optimise glazing orientation	○ ○ ○	● ○ ○	● ● ○	● ● ○
Add new openings	● ○ ○	● ○ ○	● ● ●	● ● ●
Improving Envelope Performance				
Replace building frame	○ ○ ○	● ○ ○	● ● ○	● ● ○
Insulate walls	● ● ○	● ● ●	● ● ●	● ● ●
Insulate roof	● ● ○	● ● ●	● ● ●	● ● ●
Insulate floors	● ○ ○	● ○ ○	● ● ○	● ● ○
Upgrade windows	● ● ○	● ● ●	● ● ●	● ● ●
Improve air tightness	● ○ ○	● ● ○	● ● ○	● ● ●
Upgrading building services				
Improvement in heat production	● ○ ○	● ● ○	● ● ●	● ● ●
Optimisation of hot water production	● ○ ○	● ● ○	● ● ●	● ● ●
Solar thermal and photovoltaic energy	● ○ ○	● ● ○	● ● ○	● ● ●
Recovery and use of rainwater	● ○ ○	● ● ○	● ● ●	● ● ●
Drinking water network and facilities	● ● ○	● ● ○	● ● ●	● ● ●

○ ○ ○ not feasible ● ○ ○ not easily feasible ● ● ○ somewhat feasible ● ● ● easily feasible

▲ Figure 15.24
Feasibility of change scenarios

B7 Adaptability through hybridity

Building type: office, student accommodation
Adaptability types: versatile, refitable, convertible
Designer: Alison Brooks Architects (ABA)
Website: www.alisonbrooksarchitects.com

ABA's proposition for a twenty-first century warehouse extracts features from nineteenth-century warehouses (e.g. simple forms, CAR34; robust structures, CAR10) in combination with contemporary office formats, workplace standards and the required modularity of residential buildings to offer a hybrid 'warehouse' typology catering to a range of uses as an economically viable 'new build' scenario. The approach is visualised through their proposal for a large-scale development in Cambridge on a brownfield site. It includes a programme matrix to establish possible uses while a typology matrix explores how the uses can be linked and interchanged within a single building (CAR43). The dynamic elevation is a result of the programmatic and spatial variations in section and plan. Overall, the concept is grounded in a context sensitive design approach towards architecture's materiality to make meaningful connections with the community (e.g. playful use of neighbouring university emblem on façade) promoting the building's longevity (CAR56, CAR58).

▼ Figure 15.25
Renderings of the building throughout the day

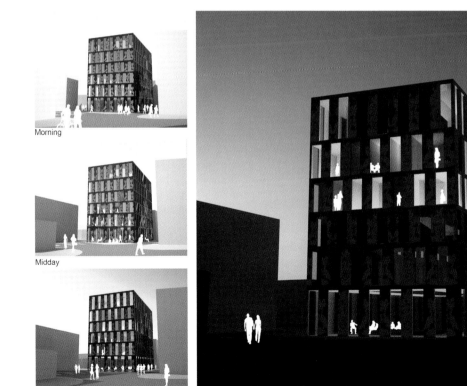

Morning

Midday

Afternoon

Evening

► Figure 15.26
Programme matrix

▼ Figure 15.27
Dynamic elevation and section

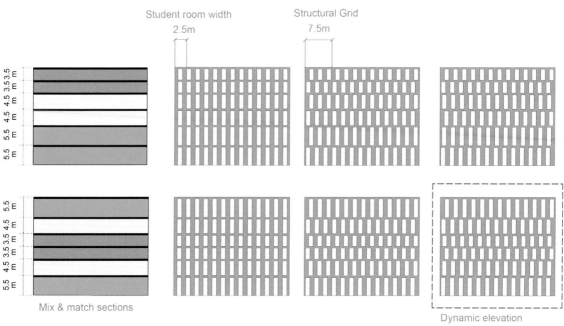

Student room width 2.5m

Structural Grid 7.5m

Mix & match sections

Dynamic elevation

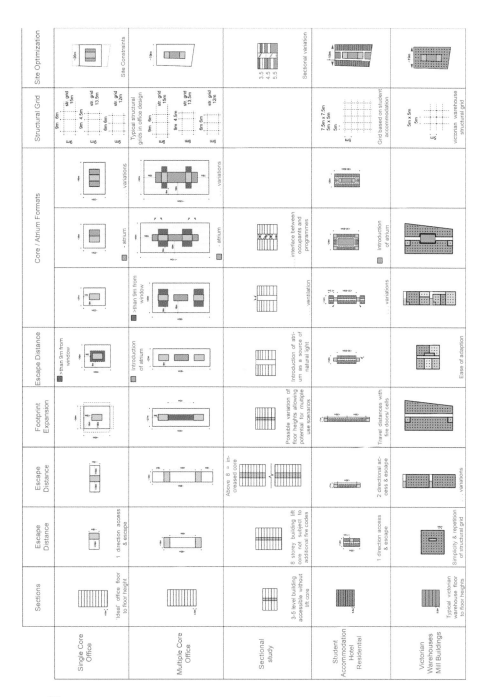

Notional core design allowing for WC's

Notional core design no allowance for WC's

Student accomodation module

▲ Figure 15.28
Typology matrix

B8 Ad hoc urbanism

Building type: system

Adaptability types: refitable, scalable, convertible and movable
Designer: Fashion Architecture Taste (FAT)
Website: http://fashionarchitecturetaste.com

FAT's scheme amplifies the decorative and expressive potential of off-site panel technology through the hybridisation of digital fabrication techniques to offer a structural system with a softer and more informal quality that can add dynamism and visual interest to the city (CAR18, CAR54). The timber panel system (pre-assembled or 'flat packed') can be assembled into any shape, or form complex interlinked volumes (CAR16). There is a range of additional

▶ Figure 15.29
Volumetric units to adapt, extend or enhance any building type

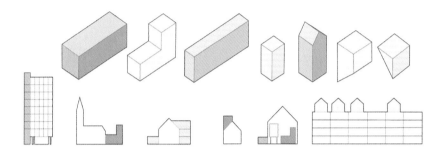

▶ Figure 15.30
Customised building

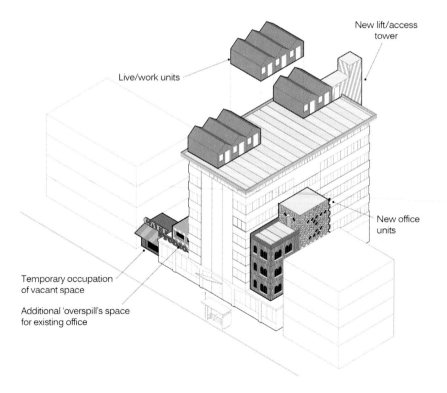

New lift/access tower

Live/work units

New office units

Temporary occupation of vacant space

Additional 'overspill's space for existing office

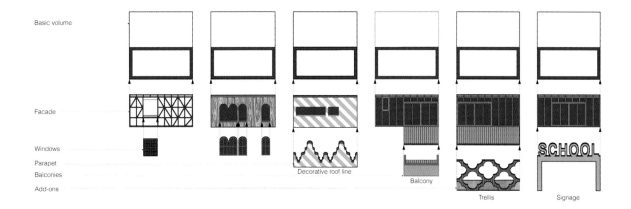

Basic volume

Facade

Windows

Parapet

Balconies

Add-ons

Decorative roof line

Balcony

Trellis

SCHOOL

Signage

elements such as decorative parapets, balconies, bays and window shapes that encourage setbacks, projections and other forms of modelling offering a huge variety of spatial and stylistic expression. The DIY-oriented system promotes the use of dry joints and non-specialist skills allow smaller-scale, local modifications to occur activating areas of unused, vacant and currently inaccessible urban spaces (CAR1, CAR42).

▲ Figure 15.31
Range of stylistic expressions (exterior panel configurations)

B9 Adaptable primary school

Building type: primary school
Adaptability types: adjustable, versatile, refitable and scalable
Designer: Sarah Wigglesworth Architects
Website: www.swarch.co.uk

SWA proposes a series of adaptable school buildings based on a system of solid (cross-laminated) timber units, using the technology to balance standardisation

▼ Figure 15.32
Kits of parts are used to create a variety of structures and spaces

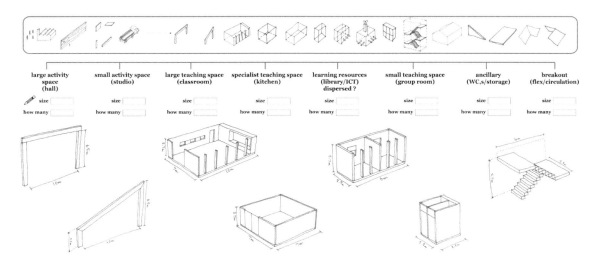

large activity space (hall)	small activity space (studio)	large teaching space (classroom)	specialist teaching space (kitchen)	learning resources (library/ICT) dispersed ?	small teaching space (group room)	ancillary (WC,s/storage)	breakout (flex/circulation)
size	size	size	size	size	size	size	size
how many	how many	how many	how many	how many	how many	how many	how many

▶ Figure 15.33
Timber logic system for
a teaching space

Classroom module

structural elements
sized to allow for
future loading of
potential upper floors

monopitch roof piece
for single storey and
top floors

Plug in connections to
services grid in
classrooms and
corridors

distribution of
services on high level
grid in classrooms

suspended lighting
grid fixed back to
timber soffit

Serviced 'smart wall'
component with built
in storage, sink etc as
required. Factory
assembled with 'plug
in' connections to
ceiling grid and risers
to (future) upper
floors

clerestory glazing in
monopitch single or
top storey classes

integrated storage
within wall + options
for openings

planar wall with factory cut
openings and pre installed
windows and doors

Timber fins support
glazing

Opening in wall infilled
with stud on site or left
open. Allows future
connections to be made

Extendable in standard
increments. Max span 13.5m
(limited by size of lorry)

external cladding and
glazing options.
Installed on site

Open/Flat Site	Urban Site	Existing Site

This is a school for an open site with the potential to expand on all sides of the site. The buildings are arranged around a central hub and the teaching accomodation radiates out like spokes. The school can be expanded by simply adding to the spokes.

This school is located on a constrained urban site, surrounded on all sides, therefore the only way to extend the school is upwards. The roof top spaces of the teaching accomodation can be built upon or could be used as break-out space for the school.

This school constitutes an addition to an existing school. A new performing arts space and associated circulation and services have been added. The new additions are simple to plug into the spaces between the existing school buildings.

Components

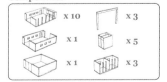

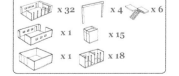

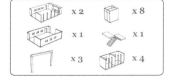

(repetitive elements) with customisation (specific features) in conjunction with brief and site (CAR16, CAR18). The proposal presents a structural system of flat panels (walls, floors, ceilings) that assemble on site to make volumetric units (kit of parts) and an exposed and surface-mounted service distribution system (suspended grid). It also includes the concept of a 'smart wall': a pre-plumbed, pre-wired unit that connects to the grid above and contains a white board, sink and storage as a standard classroom component. The skin of the building can be fitted out and changed easily with a variety of materials (e.g. brick slips, timber clapboard, flat fibre-cement sheet, corrugated fibre cement sheet) (CAR1). The submission is cleverly organised as a design process flowing from macro to micro as a decision-making process to aid a client to understand the applicability of the system to their needs.

B10 Adaptable apertures

Building type: residential, commercial
Adaptability types: versatile, refitable and convertible
Designer: Toh Shimazaki Architects (TSA)
Website: www.t-sa.co.uk

TSA's ethos is rooted in a human-oriented approach to adaptability through narratives in time focused on the inhabitation and experiential qualities of architecture. The proposal is for a brick extension of a staircase at the rear of a Georgian building in Soho, London. It creates a wider circulation path as well as promoting qualities of the converted spaces (commercial and residential; CAR22, CAR43). The building respects the adaptable Georgian structure for its simplicity in overall arrangements, intricacies of details, careful composition of

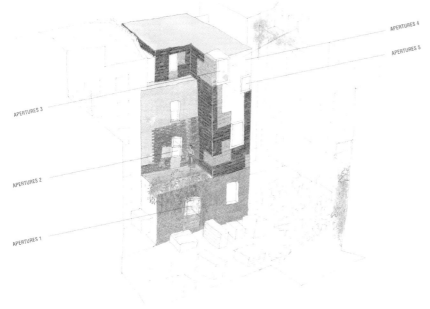

◄ Figure 15.35
Staircase and roof extension to existing fabric (aperture locations)

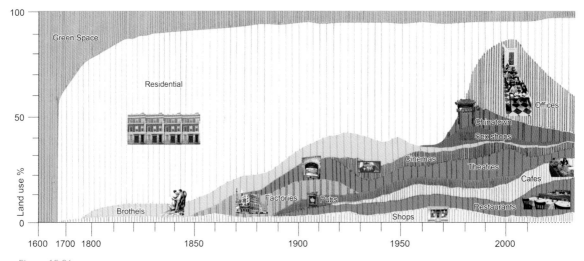

Change of uses in the SOHO area over time

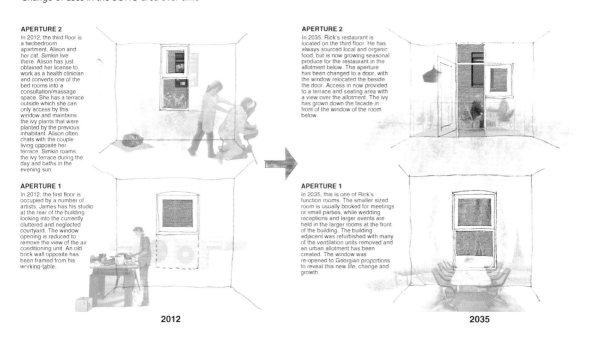

APERTURE 2
In 2012, the third floor is a twobedroom apartment. Alison and her cat, Simkin live there. Alison has just obtained her license to work as a health clinician and converts one of the bed rooms into a consultation/massage space. She has a terrace outside which she can only access by this window and maintains the ivy plants that were planted by the previous inhabitant. Alison often chats with the couple living opposite her terrace. Simkin roams the ivy terrace during the day and baths in the evening sun.

APERTURE 2
In 2035, Rick's restaurant is located on the third floor. He has always sourced local and organic food, but is now growing seasonal produce for the restaurant in the allotment below. The aperture has been changed to a door, with the window relocated to beside the door. Access in now provided to a terrace and seating area with a view over the allotment. The ivy has grown down the facade in front of the window of the room below.

APERTURE 1
In 2012, the first floor is occupied by a number of artists. James has his studio at the rear of the building looking into the currently cluttered and neglected courtyard. The window opening is reduced to remove the view of the air conditioning unit. An old brick wall opposite has been framed from his working-table.

APERTURE 1
In 2035, this is one of Rick's function rooms. The smaller sized room is usually booked for meetings or small parties, while wedding receptions and larger events are held in the larger rooms at the front of the building. The building adjacent was refurbished with many of the ventilation units removed and an urban allotment has been created. The window was re-opened to Georgian proportions to reveal this new life, change and growth.

2012   **2035**

Shifting narratives (today and future)

proportions and hierarchy of spatial organisation. The proposal focuses on the building fabric and the use of the openings as apertures for light, views and air (CAR35, CAR39, CAR51). The apertures shift and change over time to reflect both shifts in the internal functions and the changing physical and cultural surroundings of Soho.

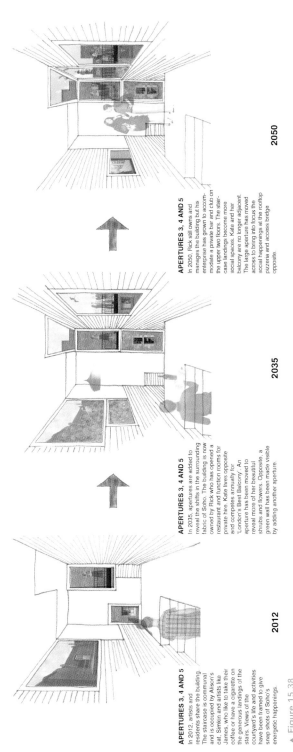

APERTURES 3, 4 AND 5

In 2012, artists and residents share the building The staircase is communal and is occupied by Alison's cat, Simkin and artists like James, who like to take their coffee or have a cigarette on the generous landings of the stairs. Views of the courtyard's life and activities have been framed to give snap shots of Soho's energetic happenings.

2012

APERTURES 3, 4 AND 5

In 2035, apertures are added to reveal the shifts in the surrounding fabric of Soho. The building is now owned by Rick who has opened a restaurant and function rooms for private hire. Kate lives opposite and competes annually for 'London's Best Balcony'. An aperture has been moved to reveal more of her beautiful shrubs and flowers. Opposite, a green wall has been made visible by adding another aperture.

2035

APERTURES 3, 4 AND 5

In 2050, Rick still owns and manages the building but his enterprise has grown to accommodate a private bar and club on the upper two floors. The staircase landings become more social spaces. Kate and her balcony are no longer adjacent. The large aperture has been moved across to bring into focus the social happenings at the rooftop pizzeria and access bridge opposite.

2050

▲ Figure 15.38

Adaptable aperture over time

Chapter 16

Designing for adaptable futures

Adaptation of Venturi and Scott
Brown's 'I am a Monument' graphic

The competition asked architectural students to illustrate how the life of their building will unfold through time – over an hour, day, year, decade or perhaps a century. The submissions had to demonstrate the integration of time in their design proposal, highlighting how it could accommodate change (the six adaptability types).

The following pages highlight a select number of images from a handful of the submissions. Table 16.1 maps the adaptability types across the seven projects. Similar to the practitioner competition, versatile refitable and convertible were most commonly implemented. To view the entries in their entirety (boards and films) along with many of other submissions please visit the Adaptable Futures website (www.adaptablefutures.com).

Table 16.1 Adaptability types implemented by the student projects

		Adjustable	Versatile	Refitable	Convertible	Scalable	Movable
C1	New Addington's Village Green	X	X	X	X	X	X
C2	Adaptable Street		X		X	X	
C3	Factory Home		X		X		
C4	Designing for Sport		X	X	X		
C5	How to Grow a City		X	X	X	X	
C6	Inside and outside the box			X		X	
C7	In Response		X	X	X		

C1 New Addington's Village Green

Building type: public park

Adaptability types: adjustable, versatile, refitable, convertible, scalable and movable
Designer: Jeffrey Adjei
University: University for Creative Arts, Canterbury

Village Green (for the people by the people) in New Addington proposes several ideas about how to construct transient social structures for a high quality public space that evolves with community needs. The proposal embraces Walter Segal's concept of self-build and considers the collaborative process, linking the community with a network of charity and government organisations through a continual building process.

▼ Figure 16.2
Park in action

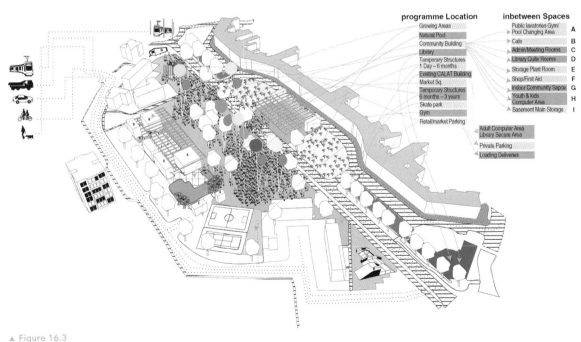

programme Location	inbetween Spaces	
Growing Areas	Public lavatories Gym/ Pool Changing Area	A
Natural Pool	Cafe	B
Community Building	Admin/Meeting Rooms	C
Library	Library Quite Rooms	D
Temporary Structures 1 Day – 6 months	Storage Plant Room	E
Existing CALAT Building	Shop/First Aid	F
Market Sq.	Indoor Community Sapce	G
Temporary Structures 6 months – 3 years	Youth & kids Computer Area	H
Skate park	Basement Main Storage	I
Gym		
Retail/market Parking		

Adult Computer Area
Library Secure Area
Private Parking
Loading Deliveries

▲ Figure 16.3
Distribution of programme throughout site

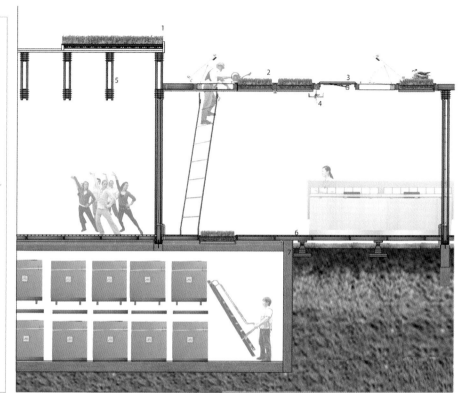

1/50 SECTION

1 GREEN ROOF
 plants
 growing medium
 filter
 drainage layer
 support

2 PLANTS & BIRD NESTING TRAY
 plants
 various planting media
 filter
 excess water collection
 support
 tray: 1,000 x 200 x 1,000mm

3 SELF-FLASHED SKYLIGHT
 insulated glass lens
 wood frame: protective cladding
  mounts directly to the roof deck,
  1,000 x 1,000mm

4 CABLE TRAY/LIGHTING
 H 100mm x 200mm x 3,000mm
  steel basket tray

5 GLULAM TIMBER TRUSS
 main support for green roof

6 FLOORING
 timbering flooring: 50mm
 timber joist
 floor insulation

7 TEMPORARY PLINTH
 FOUNDATION
 heavy gauge steel bracket: 50mm
 precast reinforced stone for
  bearing bracket
 interlocking base to ensure no
  slippage
 load-bearing grid to improve
  drainage around foundation

▲ Figure 16.4
Section of temporary stage

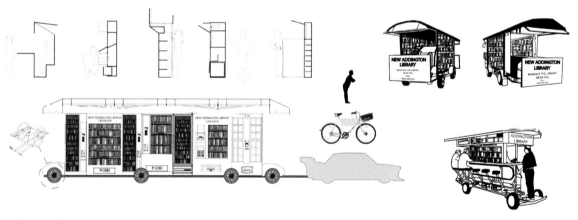

▲ Figure 16.5
Mobile library

C2 Adaptable Street

Building type: urban landscape
Adaptability types: versatile, convertible, scalable
Designer: Maxime Rousseau and Paul Jaquet
University: Université de Montréal/Ecole Nationale Supérieure d'Architecture de
Nantes

Adaptable Street focuses on exploiting (and expanding) the capacity in our major cities to create and adapt spaces at and around street level creating 'thick streets' for a vibrant mix of uses. The entrants explored how the uses and spaces would transform linearly, seasonally and over time.

▼ Figure 16.6
Observation of existing functional separation

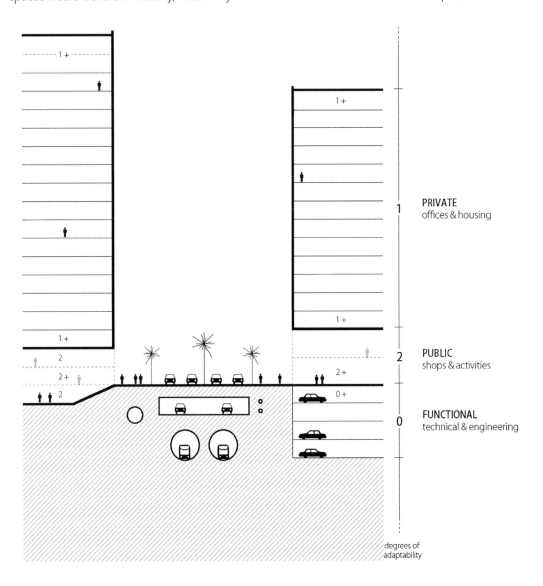

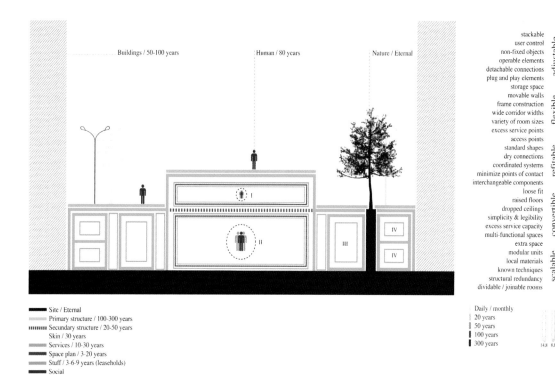

Buildings / 50-100 years   Human / 80 years   Nature / Eternal

stackable
user control
non-fixed objects — adjustable
operable elements
detachable connections
plug and play elements
storage space
movable walls
frame construction — flexible
wide corridor widths
variety of room sizes
excess service points
access points
standard shapes
dry connections — refitable
coordinated systems
minimize points of contact
interchangeable components
loose fit
raised floors
dropped ceilings
simplicity & legibility
excess service capacity — convertible
multi-functional spaces
extra space
modular units
local materials
known techniques — scalable
structural redundancy
dividable / joinable rooms

Site / Eternal
Primary structure / 100-300 years
Secundary structure / 20-50 years
Skin / 30 years
Services / 10-30 years
Space plan / 3-20 years
Stuff / 3-6-9 years (leaseholds)
Social

Daily / monthly
20 years
50 years
100 years
300 years

14,8   8,8   17,6   20,6   38,2

▲ Figure 16.7
Adaptable street concept
illustrating speed and type of
changes

ACTIVITIES (SPORTS, LEISURE, STREET BUSINESS)
CAR PARK
SHOPS
SPORT
CULTURE
OFFICES
HOUSING
SUBWAY

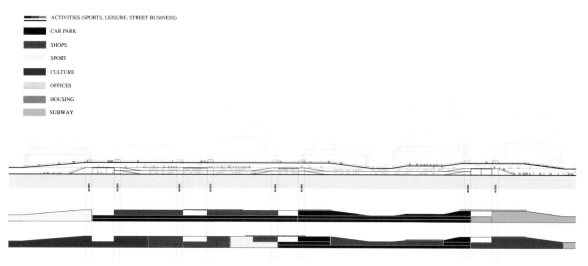

▲ Figure 16.8
Street section illustrating functional redistribution

SECULAR CHANGES OF INTERIOR PROGRAMS

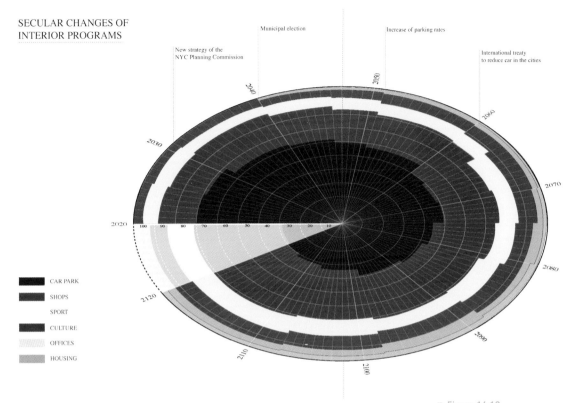

New strategy of the
NYC Planning Commission

Municipal election

Increase of parking rates

International treaty
to reduce car in the cities

■ CAR PARK
■ SHOPS
  SPORT
■ CULTURE
  OFFICES
  HOUSING

▲ Figure 16.9
Functional use shifts over time

▼ Figure 16.10
Rendering of adaptable street
section

C3 Factory Home

Building type: mixed use

Adaptability types: adjustable, versatile and convertible
Designer: John Killock
University: University of Westminster

Factory Home examines reshaping the live/work spatial relationship as part of a third industrial revolution. The proposal organises the building as three distinct zones – living, working and transition – which are blurred through cooperative ownership and the use of flexible live and work modules sliding in and out of the transition zone as needed throughout the day.

1:200 Elevations

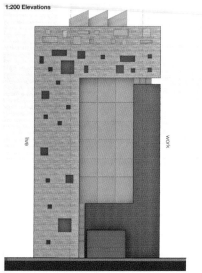

live   work

West Elevation

North Elevation

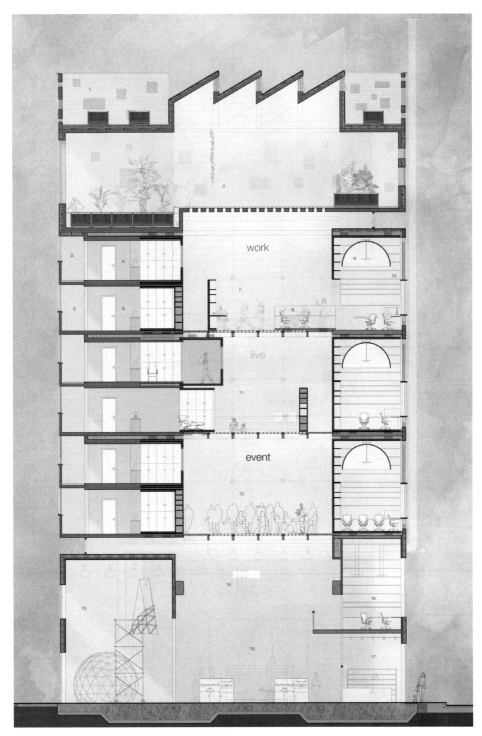

work

live

event

▲ Figure 16.13
Building section

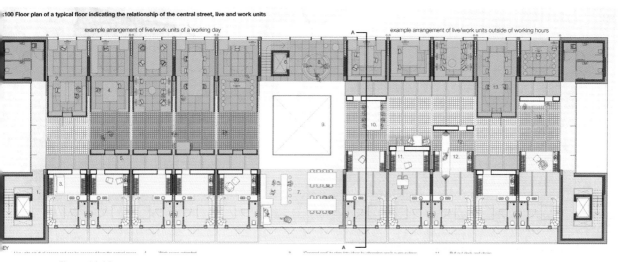

1:100 Floor plan of a typical floor indicating the relationship of the central street, live and work units

example arrangement of live/work units of a working day   example arrangement of live/work units outside of working hours

▲ Figure 16.14
Plan of work (blue) and live (red) dynamic

▲ Figure 16.15
Perspectives of work (above) and live (opposite) dynamic

▲ Figure 16.15
(Continued)

C4 Designing for Sport

Building type: dome
Adaptability types: versatile, refitable and convertible
Designer: David Weir-McCall
University: Robert Gordon University

Designing for Sport looks at the legacy of the buildings constructed for the Commonwealth Games in Glasgow – it proposes an energy-generating dome as a 'permanent' public landmark that adapts to shifting climatic and use conditions underneath (stadium to college to park). The submission proposes several smaller aluminium-framed venues under a single roof (as opposed to one large shared venue).

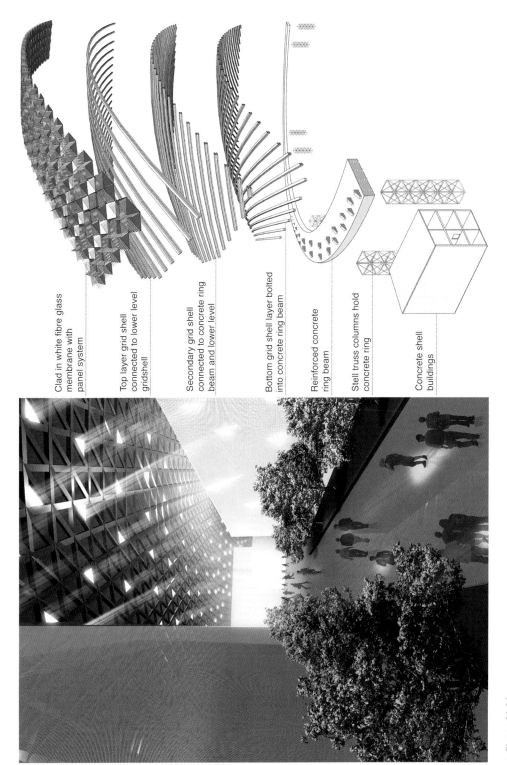

Clad in white fibre glass membrane with panel system

Top layer grid shell connected to lower level gridshell

Secondary grid shell connected to concrete ring beam and lower level

Bottom grid shell layer bolted into concrete ring beam

Reinforced concrete ring beam

Stell truss columns hold concrete ring

Concrete shell buildings

▲ Figure 16.16
Roof structure

PART IV ADAPTABILITY IN PRACTICE

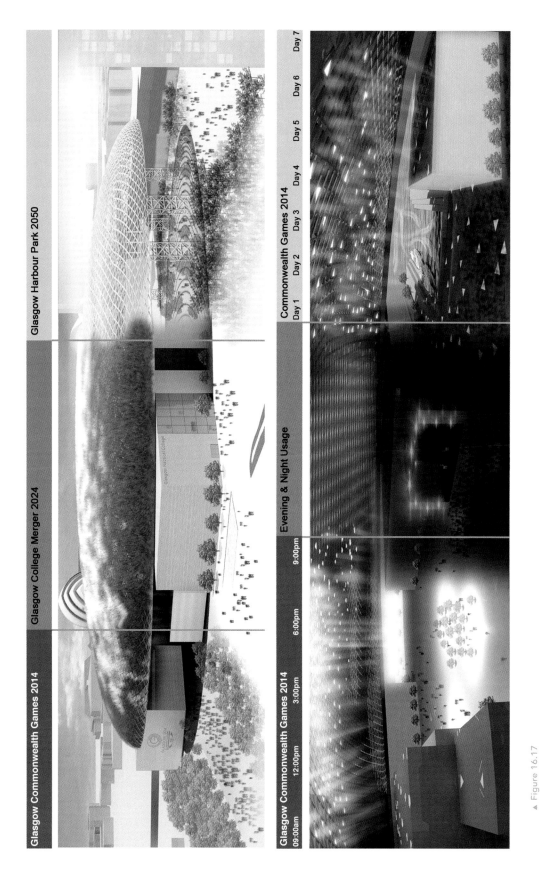

Glasgow Commonwealth Games 2014

Glasgow College Merger 2024

Glasgow Harbour Park 2050

Glasgow Commonwealth Games 2014
09:00am   12:00pm   3:00pm

Evening & Night Usage
6:00pm   9:00pm

Commonwealth Games 2014
Day 1   Day 2   Day 3   Day 4   Day 5   Day 6   Day 7

▲ Figure 16.17
Building transformation over time of the exterior (top) and interior (bottom)

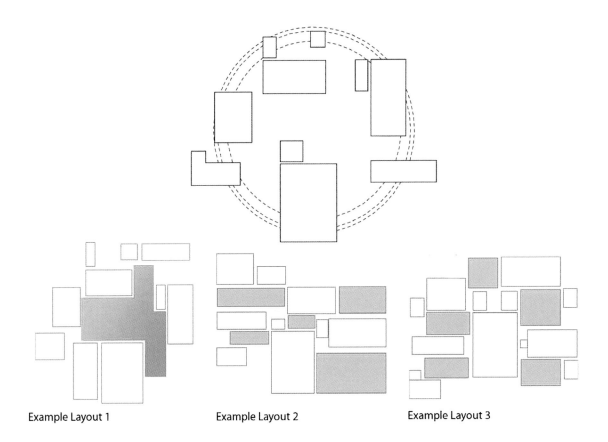

Example Layout 1   Example Layout 2   Example Layout 3

Various spatial configurations
possible under roof structure

C5 How to grow a city

Building type: mixed use
Adaptability types: versatile, refitable, convertible and scalable
Designer: Stanislaw Mlynski
University: University of Technology in Poznan

How to grow a city illustrates a layered module (the crate) which can adapt to lifestyle and activity shifts via self-organisation to regenerate the Gdynia shipyard. It embraces its cultural and social context (proposed form, use and construction) through the implementation of unused objects on site (cranes, rail tracks) and a community workshop. The proposal focuses on three evolving variables over time – age, function and social preferences – offering an appropriate blend of social catalysts for change.

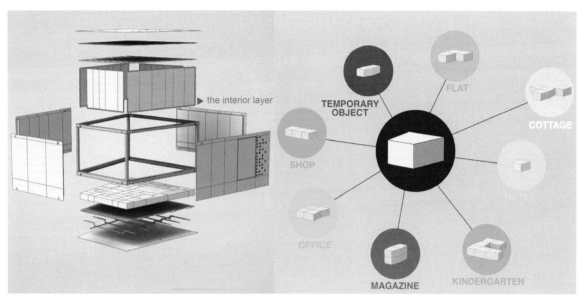

▲ Figure 16.19
Layers and possible functions of designed module

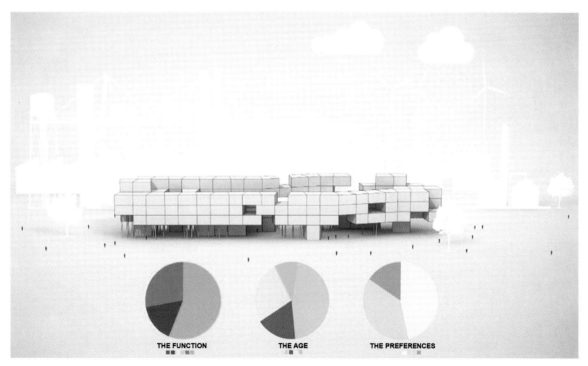

▲ Figure 16.20
Building adapts to shifts in function, age and preference

▲ Figure 16.21
Workshop allowed users to understand and configure modules

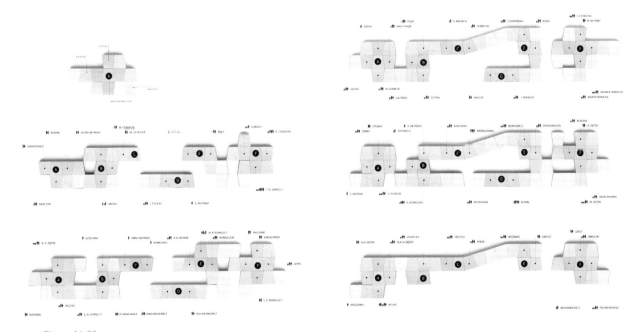

▲ Figure 16.22
Assemblage of modules into different family units and building forms

PART IV ADAPTABILITY IN PRACTICE

C6 Inside and out of the box

Building type: residential
Adaptability types: refitable, scalable
Designer: Megan Jenkin
University: University of Cincinnati

This submission provides a DIY guide (rules) to 'expanding' one's home via the wall as an element of focus, applying sustainable practices for small, incremental changes that are conventionally desirable. The steps are interchangeable, allowing the user to mix and match as needed to transform their home over time. The tall, tight units are designed for single person urban living conditions where 'waste' becomes ubiquitous being reused by the owner or filtered into a larger trade network.

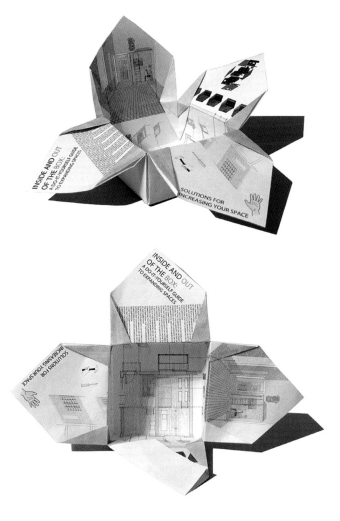

◀ Figure 16.23
Folding box concept

▲ Figure 16.24
Exterior perspective

PART IV ADAPTABILITY IN PRACTICE

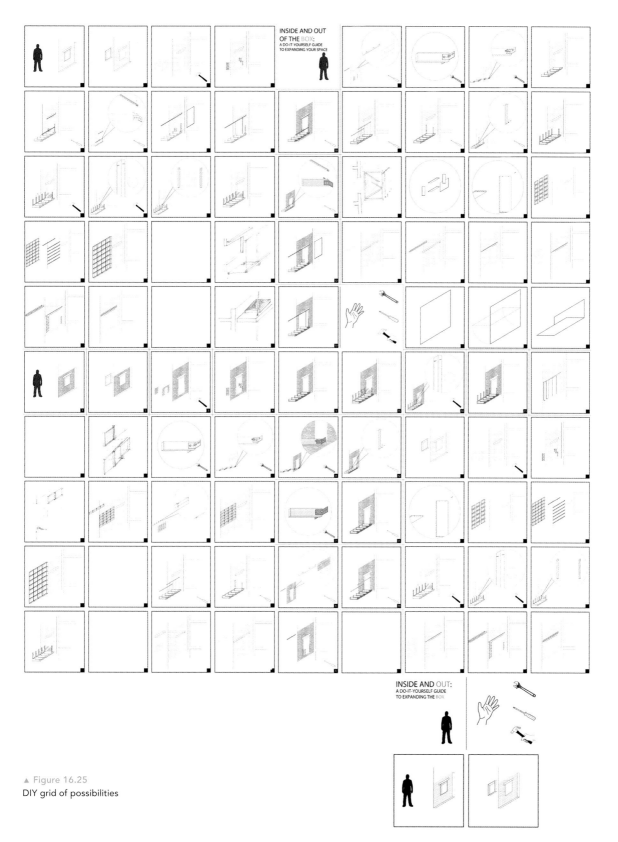

▲ Figure 16.25
DIY grid of possibilities

C7 In response

Building type: residential
Adaptability types: adjustable, versatile, refitable and convertible
Designer: Pete Austin
University: Cal Poly San Luis Obispo

This project challenges architecture to meet the expectations of society with regards to advances in digital technologies. Digital technologies such as smart phones, computers and automated services allow the user to adapt them to a specific setting. Architecture is conventionally designed as a static, non-operable object that doesn't respond and move with its occupants unlike digital tools.

In this scenario, space has no specific purpose; it can be a kitchen, bedroom, yoga studio, bedroom, ping-pong room and so on, or any combination of these rooms at once. Living can be broken down into a set of basic components like TV, chair, food, sleep, etc. Decomposing them into simple components allows for a highly specific combination of parts. Walls are designated with basic living components, e.g. TV wall, drinking wall, sleeping wall and so on. Walls move freely from one side of the unit to the other. Users can build up layers of walls literally, functionally and qualitatively.

▼ Figure 16.26

Each family selects a set of components tailored to their needs

EACH FAMILY SELECTS A SET OF COMPONENTS FOR THEIR UNIT

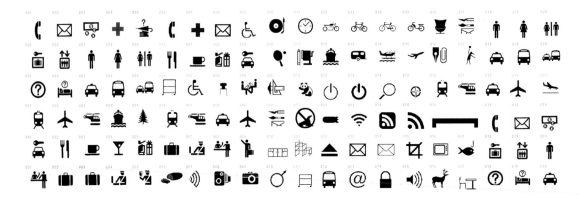

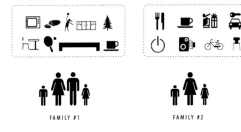

FAMILY #1

FAMILY #2

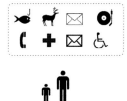

FAMILY #3

FAMILY #4

▲ Figure 16.27
Wall units

FAMILY #3

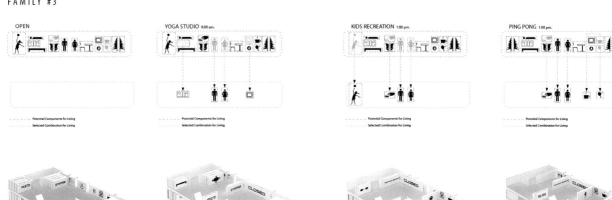

▲ Figure 16.28
Configuration of Family #3's space changes throughout the day

YOGA STUDIO 9:00 a.m.

Interior wall components are organized in a way that suggests child play space with adult socializing. The play wall component is pulled out at the left while a kitchen socializing space is created at the right. This small space is shaped into a unique social setting that otherwise might not be possible. As seen in image at bottom left

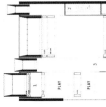

KIDS RECREATION 1:00 pm.

Interior wall components are organized in a way that suggests yoga and exercise with the projection wall moved out on the left, storage wall with mats and equipment moved out on the right. Users can adapt their space to a high specific program that meet a specific need or desire. As seen in the image at top right

PING PONG 1:00 pm.

Like seen previously this single large space can take on specific characteristics based on need or desire. At the left we see a ping pong table pulled out and on the right a micro brew is pulled out. This unique spatial construct is possible by giving the user control over their environment. This is not limited to simple spatial arrangements but can become complex highly specific constructs. As seen in image at top right

▲ Figure 16.29
Floor plan and visualisation of spatial transformation throughout the day

PART IV ADAPTABILITY IN PRACTICE

Part V

CONCLUSIONS

Chapter 17

It's a living thing

It's often the thing that comes for free that is the most memorable because it's the thing that actually extends the ability to manage or use the building in a way that nobody thought they ever would; it offers possibilities.

As others before us have found, setting out a clear, unambiguous definition and position on the adaptability of buildings is a challenging, if not impossible task. Adaptability is a complex phenomenon, characterised by interdependent goals, concepts and the underlying relationships between the many components of a building. It is also part of a broader objective of improving the sustainability of the built environment, and is therefore at times difficult to untwine. However, we believe the notion still has currency, given that it still forms a critical part of the everyday conversations and ambitions of clients, designers and planners. We have argued for the need of a theoretical backbone on which we can hang our definitions and interpretations of adaptability as we wrestled with the (often contradictory) needs of different stakeholders and their varying perspectives on adaptability. Some may regard this approach as overly academic, but we believe all design is rooted in theory and that it should be embraced as a vital way of developing a collective understanding of the world around us. This book has attempted to offer such a theory – much of it with roots in the ideas of those that have gone before us – presented in the form of concepts and models that can become tools to assist the design process.

Appropriately, adaptability itself requires a flexible attitude towards buildings and their social context – viewing the built environment as an open-ended and long-term process. This reflects Friedman's (2002) concept for a master vision that accommodates multiple options as a descriptive design code, rather than a static master plan. We wholeheartedly embrace Jeremy Till's (2009) language of thick time and the need to break down the stranglehold of first-use thinking. We acknowledge that a theory for adaptability cannot encompass everything because adaptability is context specific. However, we hope this book makes a contribution by revealing the finer grains of adaptability and providing a layered set of models that can be adapted to suit individuals and circumstances.

Adaptability is the combination of elements that provide a stable infrastructure that supports the change of infill elements.

17.1 A manifesto for adaptability

We have learned much on our journey and conclude this book by recounting the larger lessons – propositions – that we argue should shape future design for adaptability.

within the complex web of contextual contingences. Adaptability requires that buildings maintain a degree of fluidity to allow changes to be dealt with more easily. This mutability can be facilitated by design concepts that are permeable to time and context; for instance, including a historic narrative engages the human perception of time and associates the design as a new layer of historic reference. Such an approach – indeed mindset – can be bolstered by deploying adaptability design tactics that afford user comprehension, appropriation and appreciation and a quirkiness of character that encourages adaptation.

Proposition 5: Industry's short-termism deters adaptability

The structure and culture of the building industry hinder the inclusion of adaptability to the extent that it remains a marginal concern.

The long view of adaptability is at odds with the increasingly shorter timescales of business and society. This tension is compounded by a lack of awareness among stakeholders, as decisions about adaptability often rest across multiple stakeholders and therefore are a function of competing values and demands.

The way that the construction industry delivers buildings, combined with the role that stakeholders have in the process, often prioritises risk management (construction) over occupational experience (use) – in direct opposition to proposition 4. For some stakeholders, buildings are simply financial assets rather than cultural and social devices. This reflects the two distinctive client groups that were identified in our research: one that is focused on the market value of buildings (merchant developers); and the other focused on a more complicated value judgement involving use, cultural and business benefits. For the former group, the inclusion of adaptability is only about mitigating risk, equating adaptability with money. Furthermore, the long periods of time required to design, construct and occupy a building exacerbates the competing demands of stakeholders. While statutory requirements can force clients to think about adaptability, they can also limit it through prescriptive remedies, tick-box compliance and one-size-fits-all solutions – in conflict with proposition 2.

The fundamental obstacle to the implementation of adaptability is that it often has little immediate quantifiable market value, which in turn is due to the way that buildings are conceived and valued – the focus being on specific (initial) needs rather than multiple uses. For example, adaptability is usually synonymous with floor space flexibility, which means that designing for broader adaptability often occurs covertly. Moreover, the relationship between the often much higher land value and building value can act as an additional deterrent to adapt a building, regardless of the building's capacity to adapt. This situation is reinforced by traditional funding methods (lump-sum funding, split between phases, formulaic and in functional silos) that place an emphasis on initial capital costs and discount downstream costs, particularly the cost of change against the probability of its need. Defining buildings as bands of use types that reflect similar physical characteristics could help to resolve this quandary.

Simply focusing on the initial capital costs of buildings means that adaptability becomes subordinate to more immediate design considerations in an effort to produce the most efficient design solution. For instance, designers described how adaptable tactics often get value-engineered out of a scheme, as the broader benefits of adaptability are not considered and particular tactics are associated with cost increases. Financial decisions must be broadened into value judgements; for example the cost savings of a simple form and plan may be a worthwhile trade-off against the added cost of providing oversized circulation paths.

Figure 17.1 depicts an idealised conceptual view of an industry in which adaptability in buildings is the norm due to an alignment in the interests of the main stakeholder groups. It is based upon the 'circle of blame' (Figure 10.1). The negative feedback is principally broken by a change in attitude of owners and end users in that developers procure buildings that are more adaptable because they attract higher prices from investors, who in turn find that they are more attractive to a wider range of occupiers and end users because they are easier to adapt to their specific requirements. This 'virtuous circle' is reinforced by a series of other influences: valuers factor the benefits of adaptability into their appraisals and industry bodies encourage their members to think about adaptability when procuring, designing or constructing buildings. Similarly local authority planners encourage clients and developers to construct more adaptable buildings, and banks lend to investors and developers at more favourable interest rates because adaptable buildings are seen as less risky investments. Underlying all of these relationships is a higher education system that instils in architects, engineers, planners and members of other professional disciplines the importance of 'valuing the future' (Heal, 2000; Pearce et al., 2004).

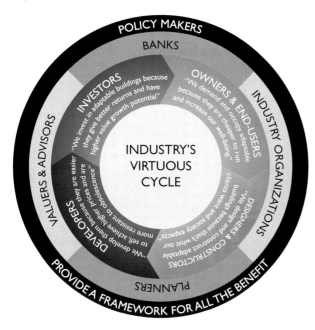

◀ Figure 17.1
Virtuous cycle for adaptability

Glossary

Adaptability   Capacity of a building to accommodate effectively the evolving demands of its users and environment, thus maximising value through life.

Adaptability type   Classification of a particular change objective which relates to a subset of approaches and methods under the umbrella of adaptability.

    adjustable change of task/user
    convertible change of use
    movable change of location
    refitable change of performance
    scalable change of size
    versatile change of space

Benefits & barriers   Application of the general variables that either enable (benefit) or hinder (barrier) the deployment and/or implementation of adaptability strategies and tactics.

Briefing question   Prompts for clarifying client/user needs.

Building   Complex product constructed from parts and components (a set of systems) with varying service lives that change at different rates demanding strategies to mitigate against the cost and time of accommodating change.

Building characteristics   Prominent feature pertaining to a building and/or its constituent parts.

Building layers   Nominal categorisations that describe a building at a given scale that allow for the stratification (decomposition) of a building as a way of gaining further insight into how it will change over time.

Change scenario   Narrative for how a building could change; provides a measure for envisaging and testing adaptability strategies.

Component relationships   How components relate to each other either structurally, spatially or through service flows (e.g. visualised through product structures).

Components   Group of parts that can be identified as a constituent of a system.

Contextual contingency   Project contingencies or parameters that are not specifically defined by the physical and spatial building (design parameters).

Critical Adaptability Parameters (CAPs)   Subset of design parameters that have a high importance towards adaptability. Parameters will have varying levels of importance based on the type of adaptability considered.

Decomposition   Categorisation of building elements into discrete labels that can enable a better understanding of a building by investigating the relationships between the different categories (levels, layers or subsystems).

Design guideline   General rules that help designers make decisions on the design parameters and structure, but are not absolute and can be adjusted based on the specific context.

Design parameters   Different units or decisions that make up a building; e.g. height, width, material, colour. Parameters can be ranges (continuous variables, e.g. storey height) or options (nominal variables, e.g. partition system).

Design resource   Source or tool used as a means to accomplish designing for adaptability.

Criteria for defining something as a layer:

1 can be defined at a similar abstraction scale with other layers;

2 has a different role;

3 has a relationship that 'interacts' with other layers;

4 has an approximate life cycle; and

5 change in one affects change in another.

Design strategy   Overarching approach towards a way of doing things (methodology) that can be defined through a set of characteristics (e.g. modularity, convertible) and methods – i.e. provides a way of thinking.

Design tactic   Specific method to achieve a goal/approach (strategy) – i.e. provides a way of doing.

Evaluation tool   Evaluates a design or an existing building's capacity to adapt through numerical techniques.

Function   The way a building is being used at a particular point in time (a use classification).

Interaction   Dependency between two elements.

Module   Group of 'functionally' or 'structurally' independent components.

Service flow   Transferring a material element which services the inhabitability/function of a building (e.g. water, energy, air, data).

Services   Components which supply and transport physical flows – energy, water, communications, elevators.

Site   Legal boundary in which a building sits.

Social   Humans in and around a building that interact with and play a role in the life of a building.

Space   Physical void inside, between and outside the physical bits. Spatial characteristics include size, proportion, height, depth, etc.

Space plan   Components which enclose the spaces users inhabit.

Spatial flow   Transferring a spatial constraint through the physical relationship of two elements (e.g. adjacency, proximity, boundary).

Spatial relationships   How two spaces relate to each other through access, proximity or separation (e.g. visualised through bubble diagrams).

Stakeholders   People engaged in the building development process who influence how buildings are designed and constructed (Olander, 2007).

Structural flow   Transferring a physical load, either vertically or horizontally/directly or indirectly (e.g. gravitational, lateral).

Structure   Components which support the primary transferring of vertical loads and horizontal bracing.

Stuff   Components/objects which reside inside the space users inhabit.

Surroundings   Larger physical context on which a building sits, outside of its specific lot boundaries, comprising both man-made objects and natural geographic conditions.

References

3D Reid (2005) 'Multispace: adaptable building design concept', unpublished report, Reid Architecture, London.

Abley, I. and Schwinge, J. (2006) 'Architecture with Legs', in I. Abley and J. Schwinge (eds), *Manmade Modular Megastructures*. New York: Wiley.

Alberti, L. B. (1988) *On the Art of Building in Ten Books*. Trans. N. Leach, J. Rykwert and R. Tavenor. Cambridge, MA: MIT Press.

Alexander, C. (1964) *Notes on the Synthesis of Form*. Cambridge, MA: Harvard University Press.

Alison, J., Brayer, M-A., Migayrou, F., & Spiller, N. (Eds.) (2006) *Future City: Experiment and Utopia in Architecture*. Thames & Hudson, London.

Altas, N. and Ozsoy, A. (1998) 'Spatial Adaptability and Flexibility as Parameters of User Satisfaction for Quality Housing', *Building and Environment*, 33(5): 311–23.

Ant Farm (1971) *Inflatocookbook*. Sausalito, CA: Rip Off Press.

Arge, K. (2005) 'Adaptable Office Buildings: Theory and Practice', *Facilities*, 23(3/4): 119.

Austin, S., Baldwin, A., Li, B. and Waskett, P. (2000) 'Analytical Design Planning Technique (Adept): A Dependency Structure Matrix Tool to Schedule the Building Design Process', *Construction Management & Economics*, 18(2): 173–82.

Baldwin, C. Y. and Clark, K. B. (2000) *Design Rules: The Power of Modularity vol. 1*. Cambridge, MA: MIT Press.

Baldwin, J. (1997) *BuckyWorks: Buckminster Fuller's Ideas for Today*. New York: Wiley.

Ballantyne, A. (2002) *Architecture: A Very Short Introduction*. Oxford: Oxford University Press.

Blakstad, S. H. (2001) *A Strategic Approach to Adaptability in Office Buildings*. Norwegian University of Science and Technology.

Blyth, A. and Worthington, J. (2001) *Managing the Brief for Better Design*. London: Spon.

Bogner, W. (1942) 'The New House 194X: 4. Prefabrication', *Architectural Forum*, 77: 78.

Bottom, C., McGreal, S. and Heaney, G. (1998) 'The Suitability of Premises for Business Use: An Evaluation of Supply/Demand Variations', *Property Management*, 16(3): 134–44.

Boyd, D. and Jankovic, L. (1992) 'The Limits of Intelligent Office Refurbishment', *Property Management*, 11(2): 102–13.

Brand, S. (1994) *How Buildings Learn: What Happens After They're Built*. New York: Penguin.

Browning, T. R. (2001). 'Applying the Design Structure Matrix to System Decomposition and Integration Problems: A Review and New Directions'. *IEEE Transactions on Engineering Management*, 48(3): 292–305.

Bryson, J. R. (1997) 'Obsolescence and the Process of Creative Reconstruction', *Urban Studies*, 34(9): 1439–58.

Carthey, J., Chow, V., Jung, Y. M. and Mills, S. (2011). 'Flexibility: Beyond the Buzzword – Practical Findings from a Systematic Literature Review', *Health Environments Research & Design Journal*, 4(4): 89–108.

Christensen, J. (2008) *Big Box Reuse*. Cambridge, MA: MIT Press.

Collins, G. and Collins, C. C. (1965) *Camillo Sitte and the Birth of Modern City Planning*. New York: Random House.

Colquhoun, A. (1981) *Collected Essays in Architectural Criticism*. Cambridge, MA: MIT Press.

Cowee, N. and Schwehr, P. (2009) 'Are our buildings "fit" to resist incommensurable evolution?', conference, Changing Roles – New Roles, New Challenges, Noordwijk aan Zee, the Netherlands, 5–9 October, pp. 375–86, available at: www.changingroles09.nl

Davies, C. (1988). *High Tech Architecture*. London: Thames & Hudson.

Davison, N., Gibb, A., Austin, S., Goodier, C. and Warner, P. (2006) 'The multispace adaptable building concept and its extension into mass customisation', Adaptables2006, TU/e, conference, On Adaptable Building Structures, Eindhoven, the Netherlands, 3–5 July.

de Neufville R., Lee Y. S. and Scholtes S. (2008) 'Flexibility in hospital infrastructure design', IEEE Conference on Infrastructure Systems, Rotterdam, 10–12 November.

Dent, R. (1972). *Principles of Pneumatic Architecture*. New York: Wiley.

Derbyshire, A. (2004) 'Architecture, science and feedback', conference, Closing the Loop. Windsor, UK.

Douglas, J. (2006) *Building Adaptation* (2nd edn). London: Elsevier.

Duffy, F. (1990). 'Measuring Building Performance', *Facilities*, 8(5): 17.

Duffy, F. and Henney, A. (1989) *The Changing City*. London: Bullstrode, p. 61 [capital cost over time diagram broken into the three layers].

Durmisevic, E. (2006). 'Transformable building structures: Design for disassembly as a way to introduce sustainable engineering to building design & construction', TU Delft, Ph.D. dissertation.

Eckert, C., Clarkson, P. J. and Zanker, W. (2004) 'Change and Customisation in Complex Engineering Domains', *Research in Engineering Design*, 15(1): 1–21.

Ehrenkrantz, E. (1989). *Architectural Systems: A Needs, Resources, and Design Approach*. Texas: McGraw-Hill.

Eppinger, S. and Browning, T. (2012) *Design Structure Matrix Methods and Applications*. Cambridge, MA: MIT Press.

Fernandez, J. (2003). Design for Change: Part 1: Diversified Lifetimes', *Architecture Research Quarterly*, 7(2): 169–82.

Finch, E. (2009) 'Flexibility as a Design Aspiration: The Facilities Management Perspective', *Ambiente Construido*, 9(2): 7.

Fletcher, B. (1946) [1896]. *A History of Architecture on the Comparative Method*. London: Batsford.

Francis, S., Glanville, R., Noble, A. and Scher, P. (1999) *50 Years of Ideas in Health Care Buildings*. London: Nuffield Trust.

Friedman, A. (2002a) *Planning the New Suburbia: Flexibility by Design*. Vancouver: UBC Press.

Friedman, A., (2002b) *The Adaptable House: Designing Homes for Change*. New York: McGraw-Hill.

Gann, D. and Barlow, J. (1996) 'Flexibility in Building Use: The Technical Feasibility of Converting Redundant Offices into Flats', *Construction Management and Economics*, 14(55): 55–66.

Gelis, J. (2000) 'Adaptable workplaces', Facilities Net website, August. http://www.facilitiesnet.com/designconstruction/article/Adaptable-Workplaces-Facilities-Management-Design-Construction-Feature–1603. Accessed: December 2009.

Geraedts, R. (2006) 'Upgrading the adaptability of buildings', Adaptables2006, TU/e, conference, On Adaptable Building Structures, Eindhoven, the Netherlands, 3–5 July, p. 33.

Geraedts, R. (2011) 'Success and Failure in Flexible Building', *Open House International*, 36(1): 54–62.

Geraedts, R. and Cuperus, Y. (2011) 'Timeless flexible building: matching demand and supply in flexible housing', conference, Architecture in the Fourth Dimension, Boston, USA, November 2011.

Geraedts, R. and de Vrij, N. (2004) 'Transformation meter revisited: three new evaluation instruments for matching the market supply of vacant office buildings and the market demand for new homes', 10th annual conference of CIB 104 Open Building Implementation, 20–22 September, Paris, France.

Gold, C. and Martin, A. (1999) *Refurbishment of Concrete Buildings: Decision to Refurbish (GN 7/99)*. London: BSRIA.

Gorgolewski, M. (2005) 'Understanding how buildings evolve', conference, 2005 World Sustainable Building, 27–29 September, p. 2811.

Graham, P. (2005) *Design for Adaptability: An Introduction to the Principles and Basic Strategies*. Australia: Royal Australian Institute of Architects, GEN66.

Grinnell, R., Schmidt III, R. and Austin, S. (2012) 'Classifying components based on change propagation potential', 14th International Dependency and Structure Modelling Conference, DSM'12, Kyoto, Japan, 13–14 September.

Groak, S. (1992) *The Idea of Building* (1st edn). London: Spon.

Guy, B. and Ciarimboli, N. (2008) *DfD: Design for Disassembly in the Built Environment: A Guide to Closed-Loop Design and Building*. Seattle: Hamer Center for Community Design.

Habraken, N. J. (1998) *The Structure of Ordinary: Form and Control in the Built Environment*. Cambridge: MIT Press.

Harper, D. (2001) *Online Etymology Dictionary*. www.etymonline.com

Harrison, A. (1992) 'The Intelligent Building in Europe', *Facilities*, 10(8): 14–19.

Hartenberger, U. (2008) *Breaking the Vicious Circle of Blame: Making the Business Case for Sustainable Buildings, Findings in Built and Rural Environments*. London: RISC.

Hashemian, M. (2005) 'Design for Adaptability', Ph.D. thesis, University of Saskatchewan Department of Mechanical and Manufacturing Engineering.

Heal, G. (2000) *Valuing the Future: Economic Theory and Sustainability*. New York: Columbia University Press.

Hertzberger, H. (2005) *Lessons for Students in Architecture*. Rotterdam: 010 Publishers.

Hill, D. (2006) 'Architecture and interaction design via adaptation and hackability', City of Sound website, 23 May. http://www.cityofsound.com/blog/2006/05/architecture_an.html. Accessed: October 2010.

Hollis, Edward. 2009. *The Secret Lives of Buildings*. London: Portobello Books.

Horning, J. (2009) *Simple Shelters: Tents, Tipis, Yurts, Domes and Other Ancient Homes*. Glastonbury: Wooden Books.

Iselin, D. and Lemer, A. (eds) (1993) *Fourth Dimension in Building: Strategies for Avoiding Obsolescence*. Washington, DC: National Academy Press.

Israelsson, N., and Hansson, B. (2009) 'Factors Influencing Flexibility in Buildings', *Structural Survey*, 27(2): 138.

Jencks, C. (1973) *Modern Movements in Architecture*. Harmondsworth: Penguin.

Julta, R. S. (1993) 'Notes on the Synthesis of Form to a Pattern Language', *Design Methods: Theories, Research, Education and Practice*, 27(4).

Kendall, S. (2009) 'Integrated design solutions: what does this mean from an open building perspective?', paper presented at Changing Roles; New Roles, New Challenges, Noordwijk aan Zee.

Kendall, S. and Teicher, J. (2000) *Residential Open Building* (1st edn). London: Taylor & Francis.

Kincaid, D. (2000) 'Adaptability Potentials for Buildings and Infrastructure in Sustainable Cities', *Facilities*, 18(3/4):

Kincaid, D. (2002) *Adapting Buildings for Changing Uses: Guidelines for Change of Use Refurbishment*. London: Spon.

Kronenburg, R. (2007) *Flexible: Architecture that Responds to Change*. London: Laurence King.

Lambot, I. (ed.) (1989) *Norman Foster, Foster Associates: Building and Projects Vol. 2* (1971–8). Hong Kong: Watermark.

Langston, C., Wong, F., Hui, E. and Shen, L. (2008). 'Strategic Assessment of Building Adaptive Reuse Opportunities in Hong Kong', *Building and Environment*, 43: 1709.

Larssen, A. and Bjorberg, S. (2004) 'User needs/demands (functionality) and adaptability of buildings – a model and a tool for evaluation of buildings', Facilities Management and Maintenance Conference: Human Elements in Facilities Management, 3 June, Hong Kong.

Laugier, M. A. (2009 [1756]) *An Essay on Architecture*, trans. W. Hermann. Los Angeles: Hennessey & Ingalls.

Lawson, B. (2005) *How Designers Think* (4th edn). Amsterdam: Elsevier.

Leaman, A. and Bordass, B. (2004) 'Flexibility and Adaptability', in S. Macmillan (ed.), *Designing Better Buildings*. London: Spon, pp. 145–56.

Leaman, A., Bordass, B. and Cassels, S. (1998) 'Flexibility and adaptability in buildings: The "killer" variables', Technical University of Delft, Department of Real Estate and Project Management, the Netherlands, 7–8 October.

Leatherbarrow, D. (2008) *Architecture Orientated Otherwise*. New York: Princeton Architectural Press.

Lerup, L. (1977). *Building the Unfinished: Architecture and Human Action*. Beverly Hills: Sage.

Leupen, B. (2005) 'Towards Time Based Architecture', in B. Leupen, R. Heijine and J. V. Zwol (eds), *Time-based Architecture*. Rotterdam: 010 Publishers.

Leupen, B. (2006) *Frame and Generic Space*. Rotterdam: 010 Publishers.

Lifschutz, A. (2003) 'Rewind and Repeat'. *Building Design*, 4 April, p. 9.

Lin, Z. (2010). *Kenzo Tange and the Metabolist Movement*. Oxford: Routledge.

Lynch, K. (1958) 'Environmental Adaptability', *Journal of the American Planning Association*, 16(1): 16–24.

Maccreanor, G. (1998) 'Adaptability', *A+T*, 12: 40–5.

Maslow, A. H. (1962). *Towards a Psychology of Being*. Princeton, New Jersey, D. Van Nostrand Company.

May, P. (2003) 'Performance-Based Regulation and Regulatory Regimes: The Saga of Leaky Buildings', *Law & Policy*, 4(25): 381–401.

Mellor, D. (1974) 'Hertzberger: The Central Beheer Office Complex, Appeldoorn', *Architectural Design*, February, 108.

Merritt, F. S. (1979). *Building Engineering and Systems Design*. New York: Chapman & Hall.

Mills, G. R. W. and Austin, S. A. (2014) 'Making Sense of Stakeholder Values Emergence', *Engineering Project Organization Journal*, 4(2–3): 65–88, doi: 10.1080/21573727.2014.940895

Minami, K. (2010) 'The new Japanese housing policy and research and development to promote the longer life of housing', paper presented at the 16th International Open and Sustainable Buildings Conference, Bilbao, Spain. 17–19 May.

Mostafavi, M. and Leatherbarrow, D. (1993) *On Weathering: The Life of Buildings in Time*. Cambridge, MA: MIT Press.

Moudon, A. V. 1986. *Built for Change: Neighborhood Architecture in San Francisco*. Cambridge, MA: MIT Press.

Olander, S. (2007) 'Stakeholder impact analysis in construction project management', *Construction Management and Economics* 25(3): 277–287.

Olsson, N. and Hansen, G. (2010) 'Identification of Critical Factors Affecting Flexibility in Hospital Construction Projects Health Environments', *Research & Design Journal*, 3(2): 30–47.

Pawley, M. (2007) 'The Time House of 1968', in D. Jenkins (ed.), *The Strange Death of Architectural Criticism*. London: Black Dog.

Pearce, D., Groom, B., Hepburn, C. and Koundouri, P. (2004) 'Valuing the Future: Recent Advances in Social Discounting', *World Economics*, 4(2): 121–41.

Pimmler, T. and Eppinger, S. (1994) 'Integration analysis of product decompositions', ASME 6th Design Theory and Methodology Conference, Minneapolis, MN, pp. 343–51.

Pinder, J., Schmidt III, R. and Saker, J. (2013) 'Stakeholder Perspectives on Developing More Adaptable Buildings', *Construction Management and Economics*, 31(5): 440–59.

Priemus, H. (1968). *Wonen. Kreativiteit en aanpassing*. Delft, Technische Hogeschool Delft.

Quatremere de Quincy, A. C. (1788). *Architecture. Encyclopedia methodique*. Tome III. Paris.

Rabeneck, A., Sheppard, D. and Town, P. (1973) 'Housing Flexibility?', *Architectural Design*, 8: 698–727.

Rabeneck, A., Sheppard, D. and Town, P. (1974) 'Housing Flexibility/Adaptability?', *Architectural Design*, 74(2): 76.

Random House *Dictionary.com Unabridged*. Random House, Inc. http://dictionary.reference.com/browse/adapt

Rogers, R. (1991). *The Artist and the Scientist in Bridging the Gap*. New York: Van Nostrand Reinhold, p. 146.

Rush, R. D. (1986) *The Building Systems Integration Handbook*. New York: Wiley.

Russell, P. and Moffatt, S. (2001) *Assessing Buildings for Adaptability*. IEA Annex 31 Energy Related Environmental Impact of Buildings Report.

Rybczynski, W. (2001) *The Look of Architecture*. Oxford: Oxford University Press.

Schmidt III, R., Austin, S. and Brown, D. (2009) 'Designing adaptable buildings', 11th International Design Structure Matrix Conference, DSM'09. Greenville, SC, 12–13 October.

Schmidt III, R., Deamer, J. and Austin, S. (2011). 'Understanding adaptability through layer dependencies', International Conference on Engineering Design, ICED11, Copenhagen, Denmark, 15–18 August.

Schneider, T. and Till, J. (2007) *Flexible Housing* (1st edn). Oxford: Elsevier.

Schulze, F. (1985) *Mies van der Rohe: A Critical Biography*. London: University of Chicago Press.

Sennett, R. (2008). *The Craftsman*. New Haven, CT: Yale University Press.

Sharman, D. and Yassine, A. (2004) 'Characterising Modular Architecture', *Systems Engineering*, 7(1): 35–60.

Sharp, D. (2005). 'Kenzo Tange (1913–2005)', *Architectural Review*, May, p 36.

Slaughter, E. S. (2001) 'Design Strategies to Increase Building Flexibility', *Building Research & Information*, 29(3): 208–17.

Spuybroek, L. (2005) 'The Structure of Vagueness', in B. Kolarevic and A. Malkawi (eds), *Performative Architecture – Beyond Instrumentality*. Oxford: Routledge.

Steward, D. (1981) *Systems Analysis and Management: Structure, Strategy, and Design*. Princeton, NJ: Petrocelli.

Takenaka Corporation (2005) 'Sustainable Architecture – New Office Experiment: Takenaka Corporation Tokyo Main Office', *Shinkenchiku* (special issue) (May).

Thomson, D. S., Austin, S. A., Devine-Wright, H. and Mills, G. R. (2003) 'Managing Value and Quality in Design', *Building Research and Information*, 31(5): 334–45.

Till, J. (2009) *Architecture Depends*. Cambridge, MA: MIT Press.

Tschumi, B. (1996) *Architecture and Disjunction*. Cambridge, MA: MIT Press.

Tsukamoto, Y. and Kaijima. M. (2010) *Behaviorology*. New York: Rizzoli.

Utida, Yositka (1983) 'Century Housing System – A Systems Approach to Component Coordination', *Micro IF 3211*, (4): 41.

Utida, Yositika (2002) *The Construction and Culture of Architecture Today: A View from Japan*. Tokyo: Ichigaya.

Venturi, R. and Scott Brown, D. (2004) *Architecture as Signs and Systems*. Cambridge, MA: Belknap Press.

Vibæk, K. (2011) 'System structures in architecture', Ph.D. thesis, Royal Danish Academy of Fine Arts, School of Architecture, Design and Conservation.

Viollet-le-Duc, E. 2010 [1876] *The Habitations of Man in All Ages*. Charleston, SC: Nabu Press.

Watkin, D. (2000) *History of Western Architecture* (4th edn). London: Laurence King.

Weston, R. (2011) *100 Ideas that Changed Architecture*. London: Laurence King.

Wotton, H. (1903). *The Elements of Architecture*. Springfield: Bassette.

Index

Page numbers followed by 'f' refer to figures and followed by 't' refer to tables.

Key to theory labels (see pages 41–2): A, B, C case studies; AT adaptability type; CAR building characteristic; CON contextual contingency; DR design resource; DS design strategy; L layer; M model.

human-centric vs. building-centric
  adaptability 54
hybridity, adaptability through 241–3

I

IBI Group, Inc. 194–7, 197–200, 217–19
IFD (Industrial Flexible and
  Demountable) 33–4, 34f, 70f
impact analysis 78–82, 79–80t, 81f;
  implications of 82–3
inclusive design 44
increase interactivity (DS10) 105
industrial building: CPC 211–13
Industrial Democratic Design (IDD) case
  study (B1) 220–4
Industrial Flexible and Demountable
  (IFD) 33–4, 34f, 70f
industrialised architecture 22–5, 23f,
  24f
industry standards (CON10) 104, 123,
  130; case studies 192, 194
inflatable architecture 27, 27f
Inside and out of the box case study
  (C6) 265
Integrated Project Deliveries (IPDs) 62,
  67
intelligent buildings 27–8, 28f
IPDs (Integrated Project Deliveries) 62,
  67
Islington Square case study (A9) 202–5
isolatable (CAR48) 100, 104; case studies
  179, 186, 193, 215

J

Japanese traditional houses 12–13, 13f
Jaquet, Paul 253–6
Jencks, C. 15, 16, 16f, 25, 27, 30, 38
Jonga concept 175, 175f
Jenkin, Megan 265
joinable/divisible space (CAR24) 97, 99,
  100, 104, 121, 130, 137, 159; case
  studies 180, 186, 197, 198, 199f, 200,
  206, 215, 216, 217, 217f, 218

K

Kahn, Louis 20, 21f
Kentish Town Health Centre case study
  (A1) 174–81
Kettering Old Persons Unit (KOPU) case
  study (A15) 217–19
Killock, John 256–9

Kincaid, D. 139, 152
kinetic architecture 25–8, 26f, 27f, 28f
King's School Theatre case study (A13)
  213–15
Kodan Experimental Housing Project
  system 34
Kurokawa, Kisho 26–7, 26f

L

L-shaped plans 202–4, 202f, 203f
laboratories: Bio Innovation Centre
  197–200; Flexilab 70, 71f; Richard
  Medical Laboratories at UPENN 20,
  21f
Larssen, A. 151, 152f
layers, building 36–7, 55–67; adaptability
  types, stakeholders and 155–6, 155f;
  Cellophane House clustering analysis
  60–7, 61f, 63–6f; definitions 55;
  design tactics for 58t; diagram 37f;
  distribution of relationships between
  57, 57t; influence of change on 55–8;
  model (M4) 56f; pathways meta-model
  centred on 162f; relationship of CARS
  to 108, 109–10t; understanding
  dependency 58–60 *see also individual
  layers*
Le Corbusier 20, 20f, 23
leasing policies 130
legibility and simplicity 96–7, 97f, 167
Leicester Waterside case study (B4) 149f,
  228–34
levels of specificity 51–3
lexicon of theoretical elements 41–2f
libraries: Cedar Rapids Public Library
  187–90; change scenarios 144;
  mobile 252f; PS340 Manhattan 192,
  193f; Queens Central Library 106,
  107f
Lifetime Homes 44, 95, 120, 123
lighting at night: Cedar Rapids Public
  Library 189, 190f; Southwark Street
  183, 184f
linking meta-model (M14) 155–6, 155f
listed buildings 122
location *see* good location (CAR57)
long life (DS3) 94–6
Loomeo 62, 65f
loose fit 18–20, 167, 171; design
  strategy (DS5) 97–8; vs. tight fit
  51–3